Camilla
THE KING'S MISTRESS

Camilla
THE KING'S MISTRESS

A Love Story

CAROLINE GRAHAM

CB
CONTEMPORARY
BOOKS

CHICAGO

Library of Congress Cataloging-in-Publication Data

Graham, Caroline, 1931–
Camilla : the king's mistress : a love story / Caroline Graham.
p. cm.
ISBN 0-8092-3407-6
1. Charles, Prince of Wales, 1948- —Relations with women.
2. Great Britain—Princes and princesses—Biography. 3. Bowles,
Camilla Parker. I. Title.
DA591.A33G72 1994
941.085′092—dc20

[B]

94-24235
CIP

Published simultaneously in Great Britain
by Blake Publishing Ltd, London, England

Copyright © 1994 by Caroline Graham
Published by Contemporary Books, Inc.
Two Prudential Plaza, Chicago, Illinois 60601-6790
Manufactured in the United States of America
International Standard Book Number: 0-8092-3407-6
10   9   8   7   6   5   4   3   2   1

ACKNOWLEDGEMENTS

For obvious reasons, some of the most pivotal people involved in the research and content of this book cannot be named. As with any project about the royal family, many sources quoted in this book spoke only if assured of anonymity. There is a golden rule within the British aristocracy that to discuss the royals is at the very least 'bad form'; at worst, tantamount to treason. Yet when I began approaching those within Camilla's closest circle for assistance with this book, they proved surprisingly helpful. Some simply wished to set the record straight. Other seemed grateful for the opportunity to paint a truer portrait of a remarkable woman they *know*, yet who has received so much harsh and unfair criticism in the past. To those who were brave enough to tell the truth, I am deeply indebted.

A heartfelt thanks to my editor, Stuart Higgins, for so generously opening up his contacts book and for his tremendous support, help, guidance and friendship. Without him, this book would never have been written.

I am also grateful to previously published royal authors whose works have proved invaluable. Where possible, I have tried to credit them in this book. If, by chance, I have missed any credits through oversight, my apologies.

Many thanks to my publisher John Blake and to his brilliant executives Sadie Mayne and Rosie Ries for all their hard work and words of encouragement.

Thanks also to Jon, for support above and beyond the call of duty.

Finally, special thanks to my friend Kelvin MacKenzie – for being as brilliant as he always said he was!

Caroline Graham
New York, August 1994

'. . . I have found it impossible to carry the heavy burden of responsibility and to discharge my duties as King as I would wish to do without the help and support of the woman I love . . .'

King Edward VIII, Abdication Speech, December 1936

'Your great achievement is to love me . . .'

Prince Charles to Camilla Parker Bowles, December 1989

For Mutti

Contents

INTRODUCTION

It was one of the most astonishing confessions in history. Prince Charles, the future King of England, cleared his throat and stared directly into the television camera. 'Did you try to be faithful and honourable to your wife when you took on the vow of marriage?' he was asked.

'Yes, absolutely,' Charles replied.

'And you were?' asked the interviewer.

'Yes,' replied the man who would be king.

Then, after a dramatic pause, he added: ' . . . until it became irretrievably broken down, after us both having tried.'

For the first time in history, a member of the British royal family had confessed to being an adulterer. It was a staggering admission. For in that one brief sentence, Prince Charles had confirmed years of rumour and speculation.

On 29 June 1994, in front of 12.7 million of his future subjects and millions more around the world, Prince Charles guaranteed his place in the history books as the only future king who confessed to the entire world he cheated on his wife.

It was a remarkable postscript to one of the most remarkable love stories of all time.

In that one brief sentence Prince Charles guaranteed his name would forever be inextricably linked through the centuries with that of 'the other woman'.

From that moment on, Camilla Parker Bowles would be forever known as 'The King's Mistress'.

The fairy-tale marriage of the Prince and Princess of Wales was barely three years old when Prince Henry Charles Albert David Windsor was born on 15 September 1984.

As the proud new parents presented the child who would be known as Prince Harry on the steps of St Mary's Hospital Paddington the following day, the country rejoiced. The nation already had an heir – Prince William – but now the world's most glamorous and photographed couple had produced 'a spare'.

Telegrams flooded in from around the world. Prince Charles beamed: 'I've nearly got a full polo team now. It is a great moment. Now I want to get home for a drink.'

What no-one realized as Charles and Diana played Happy Families that day was that their marriage was already over in all but name.

Not long after the beaming Prince showed off his youngest son, he was making love to the only woman he had ever loved: Camilla Parker Bowles.

His marriage to Princess Diana had degenerated into a farce. The couple slept in separate beds, they led separate lives. If their paths did happen to cross, bitter slanging matches would erupt. The marriage was at the point where, when Diana walked into a room, Prince Charles would walk out.

The birthday of Prince Harry was the day the dream finally died. Prince Charles, trapped in the loneliness of a sexless, loveless marriage, telephoned his old love Camilla Parker Bowles that same afternoon. The couple arranged to meet at the Prince's home at Highgrove later that week. One of the greatest love stories in history was about to resume.

The love between the Prince and Camilla had first blossomed fourteen years earlier on a rain-swept polo field. From the moment he first set eyes on her, the Prince declared Camilla was 'the one'. But she rejected his proposal of marriage twice.

Instead, on that overcast September day in 1984, he found himself married to a woman whom he did not understand, whom he did not love and whom he liked even less.

His mind was made up: he would resume his affair with Camilla, for, as he was later to say: 'She is the only woman I have ever loved. I have never loved anyone the way I love Camilla.'

Charles's decision would rock the monarchy to its very foundations. When the full, devastating details of the affair became public in the shattering 'Camillagate' tapes and later in Charles's own dramatic televised confession of adultery, it became clear to the world that Camilla was the only true, great love of Prince Charles's life.

But what was it about this woman with flyaway hair, now middle-aged, which captivated the Prince so much that it destroyed his marriage to a woman considered the greatest beauty of her day; which led him to lay not only his own future, but the very future of the monarchy itself on the line?

'It is quite simple,' says one close confidante of Camilla. 'Prince Charles could not live with Camilla, but he could not live without her either.

'She captivates him. They are like two peas in a pod. When all the scandal has died down, their love affair will be remembered as one of the great romances of all time. They are a couple who, but for a quirky twist of nature, would have lived out their lives in obscure bliss, happy in each other's company.

'As it is, their names have been splashed over the front pages, the intimate details of their affair have become public knowledge.

'It is comparable only to a Shakespearian tragedy. The man who will be king happened to fall helplessly and madly in love with a woman who can never be his queen.

'And yet, to this day, they love each other. And they always will.

'Their love has stood the test of time, it has overcome every obstacle which has been put in its way. It is a love which will never die. But it is a love which will never be allowed to live. That is the greatest tragedy of all.'

Camilla Parker Bowles is a woman who, but for one chance meeting with a prince, would have lived her life in total obscurity, yet her name has become synonymous with one of the great love stories – and scandals – of the twentieth century.

Prince Charles himself told her: 'Your great achievement is to love me . . . '

It is a story more passionate and extraordinary than any Hollywood scriptwriter could dream up, for it is a *real* story about *real* people – and a love affair which refused, against all the odds, to die.

Camilla Parker Bowles is a woman who knows what it is to enjoy the heights of passion – and the depths of despair. But, above all, 'The King's Mistress' is a survivor.

This is her remarkable story.

First Love

It all began, quite inconspicuously, at seven o'clock on a perfect English morning, 17 July 1947.

Inside a primrose-coloured maternity room in the private wing of King's College Hospital, London, as the first rays of morning sunlight glinted through the window, a child was welcomed into the world. It had all the hallmarks of a blue-blooded birth. A simple bunch of wild country flowers sat on the table. The congratulations cards carried gold-embossed messages from the finest addresses in Mayfair, Park Lane and the Home Counties.

As the child's mother, the Honourable Rosalind Shand, rested in her bed, she could never have imagined just what life held in store for the beautiful baby girl, her face framed by a mop of golden curls, who lay in her arms that July morning.

Nothing seemed more certain on Camilla Rosemary Shand's birthday than her future. Like the members of the generations before her, she would be educated in the ways of nobility, groomed in the joys of huntin' and fishin' – and then she would land herself a rich husband.

Yet fate had other plans: within forty years, Camilla would become one of the most notorious women in history.

As Camilla Parker Bowles, she would scandalize a nation by having an affair with the future King of England, take centre stage as the most famous marriage of its day crumbled – and bring the monarchy to its knees.

Camilla was a child born with not just one silver spoon in her mouth – she had a whole canteen of silver cutlery. Her credentials for being a society lady were impeccable, her breeding awe-inspiring.

Her mother, the Honourable Rosalind, was the daughter of the fourth Lord Ashcombe, whose forefather, Thomas Cubitt, founded the powerful Cubitt construction company, which built the bulk of Mayfair and Belgravia.

Her father, Bruce Shand, was the partner in a Mayfair wine merchants and had been a major in the 12th Royal Lancers. Twice decorated with the Military Cross for bravery in the Second World War, he spent two years as a German prisoner of war. He was a Master of Fox Hounds and once held the position of Vice Lord Lieutenant of East Sussex.

They were, as one of Camilla's closest friends says, 'the most suitable people. They were not titled, but they were as close to the aristocracy as they could be without having a title of their own. To be blunt, Camilla's parents were "the right sort". In the landed upper classes, Camilla certainly came from fine stock.'

Perhaps the most quirky twist of fate was that Camilla's maternal great-grandmother, Alice Keppel, had been the long-time mistress of Prince Charles's great-great-grandfather Edward VII in the 1870s.

More than a century separates the lives of Alice Keppel and Camilla Parker Bowles. Wars and revolutions have come and gone. Men have explored the outer reaches of space and walked on the moon.

But in the high-society world into which Alice and Camilla were born, little has changed.

Camilla's notorious link with the royals is something she

was not only proud of, but something in which she would positively revel.

One friend says: 'Camilla would often go on endlessly about Alice. She would sit on her mother's knee and beg Rosalind to tell her all about her famous ancestor.

'Camilla never tired about hearing about Alice. While most children are content to be entertained with fairy tales, Camilla would beg her mother to "tell me about granny Alice" again and again and again.

'Camilla's eyes would light up as her mother spoke in her soft tones about Alice, the scarlet woman who was Edward VII's secret lover.

'Her favourite anecdote was the family story of Alice's famous saying: "My job is to curtsy first . . . and then jump into bed." Camilla would smile every time she heard that line.

'Camilla was captivated. She wanted to know how Alice walked and talked. She begged to see crinkled old photographs of Alice.'

Another schoolchum says: 'From the moment Camilla arrived at school, she would regale us with stories about Alice. She told us how Alice would go to Biarritz in Switzerland every year with the King. Camilla would say: 'Down there, Alice was as much the Queen of England as the real one.'

'She was particularly fond of telling the story that when King Edward VII was dying, Alice's position as his mistress was so widely acknowledged that the King's wife, Queen Alexandra, sent for Alice Keppel to join her at the King's bedside as he passed away.

'Camilla was always saying: "My great-grandmother was practically royal, you know. She may not have been Queen, but she had the ear of the King. That made her jolly powerful."'

In her child's mind, Camilla could have had no idea how prophetic those words would be.

Indeed, on the very first occasion when flirtatious Camilla met the young Prince Charles in 1970, she uttered the immortal line: 'My great-grandmother was your great-great-grandfather's mistress. How about it?'

Camilla's early years were traditional and happy. She was raised at The Laines, a five-bedroomed Tudor country home in Plumpton, Sussex – the perfect upbringing for a girl of her class and social bearing, in a sprawling home full of dogs, love and laughter.

Camilla remembers her childhood with fondness. She told a friend only recently: 'If people think I am strong, then it is all thanks to my family. I had so much love and security growing up, I never doubted my family would be there for me in times of crisis. Whatever happened, I knew I was wanted and loved. To give that to a child is the greatest gift of all. I had the best start one could wish for. As I have matured, I have realized the solid foundation I had as a child gave me the stability to face any upset. And there have been a few upsets along the way.'

Two years after Camilla's birth, the family was joined by another daughter, Annabel. Eighteen months later, a brother, Mark, was born. A dashing man with a shock of blond hair, he was to be the adventurer of the family; a man who would pursue a life of exploration, earning his living writing brilliant accounts of his travels around the world.

The family all rode and hunted. Camilla's father would open the grounds of his house once a year for a Conservative Party fête.

A former neighbour says: 'They were classic gentry. They had nannies and held croquet parties on the lawn in the summer. It was pretty idyllic, really. They were a highly respectable family. Camilla would always be impeccably dressed on Sundays when the whole family would go to church. During the rest of the week, she was a tomboy. While the other girls were happy to sit and read and play with their dolls, Camilla was always the one who sided with the boys. She had a rough-cropped short bob hairstyle and, with her muddy face and grazed knees, she could easily have passed for a young boy. She was always shimmying up trees. She was a fine athlete. She had a stocky, powerful figure and was quite fearless.

'Camilla was always as brave as a lion. If there was a tree-climbing contest between the local children, Camilla would be the one to scale the highest bough.

'When the children swam in the local stream during hot summer days, Camilla would be the one leading the way. She was always supremely confident in her own abilities. If her brother Mark could do something, Camilla wanted to do it too – or do it better.

'She was fearless. She was born with a self-confidence rare in women of her generation.'

With her long, golden curls, pert nose and translucent 'English Rose' complexion, Camilla was judged to be a 'pretty' if not stunning-looking young girl, but it was her character which set her apart from the other well-bred young 'gels'.

At five years old, she was sent to her first school, Dumbrells in the village of Ditching, three miles from the family home. The school cost the princely sum of £10 a year and was populated by the daughters of the local gentry.

Spartan and tough, Dumbrells was run along lines similar to those of Gordonstoun, the rigid Scottish boarding school where Prince Charles spent his formative years.

But while Charles was a sensitive child who loathed the rough and tumble of his school, Camilla positively blossomed at Dumbrells.

In the winter, she would be driven to school by her mother, but in the summer, Camilla would happily walk the three miles to and from school, accompanied only by the family nanny. She excelled at hockey, a game played in the winter months, and in 'stoolball', a traditional Sussex game similar to cricket, in the summer.

A fellow pupil recalls how the classrooms were unheated during even the most bitter winter's day: 'We would dress up in thick socks and boots and wear about seven layers of jumpers, coats and scarves to stay warm in the classroom. If you took off your gloves to remove the lid of a pen, your fingers would turn blue. It was bitter in there.

'A school inspector came one day and was dumbstruck. He never knew such a place could exist. The school was so harsh that I used to say if you could survive Dumbrells, you could survive anything. It was like something from a different century. It was a classic upper-class school. The most important thing was to learn how to suffer and endure in silence.

'We would have games lessons on a Wednesday afternoon. The showers were freezing cold. If you dared complain, you would be punished. It was all about teaching the children to survive. It was tough on discipline. From the age of five, children would be punished with a lash of the cane to the bare buttocks for any misdemeanour.

'Camilla was a good pupil, quick-witted and bright. My only memory of her getting into trouble was for being a real chatterbox. She was a bundle of energy who found it hard to be quiet, even for a few moments. She was always getting told off for talking.

'But she had such strength of character, nothing would upset her. That's what I remember most about her – she never allowed anything to get her down.

'Once, she was caned for talking in class. She must have been about six or seven years old. She came back into the classroom and when she sat down you could tell she was wincing in pain. But she did not hang her head in shame and she absolutely refused to cry. The tears were in her eyes and her bottom lip was quivering. But she bit her lip and sat there with her back straight and her face full ahead, looking at the teacher defiantly. She was a tough one, that Camilla, a real tough cookie.'

The Shands had a home in London and when Camilla was ten years old, she was sent to the fashionable Queen's Gate School for young ladies in South Kensington. It was a school proud of its unofficial function of 'providing wives for half the Foreign Office and most of the nobility'.

Lynn Ripley, a classmate, said in one interview: 'We called her "Milla", that was her nickname. She was a Sloane Ranger before Sloane Rangers were invented.

'She was looked up to by the other girls. She had an inner strength. There was no question that she might do badly, with or without A levels. That didn't matter. She would live the life she wanted – that's what she exuded.

'She wasn't a beautiful girl, but she had a certain aura. What she lacked in looks, she made up for in confidence. She had the same hairstyle then as she does today.

'She was always a hoity-toity little madam. I used to wear way-out clothes, but Milla was always in twinsets, tweed suits and pearls. We didn't get on very well because she was into hunting and shooting. We used to have mammoth rows about that because I was totally against it. But she had a magnetism and a confidence I envied like anything.

'She was one of those people who know what they want and know that they will be a success in life. She was only fifteen and a half years old, but I knew even then that the world was going to hear a lot more of Milla Shand.'

Another friend said: 'Camilla fitted in beautifully with the school. She was smart, but not outstanding; she was keen at sport, but not overly so. Milla was always going to do "the right thing" with her life. She was never brash or rude. She was no pushover, but she wasn't a rebel either. She was just a good, solid, dependable type, lots of fun and popular.'

Actress Lynn Redgrave, who was in the year above Camilla, hated the school. She said: 'I remember the place with nothing but disdain. I was the only girl who had a working mother. My mother was an actress. The idea was for us to leave as marriageable young ladies. The girls didn't think they had to learn much because all they had in mind was going to parties. Being a debutante and landing a rich husband was top of the agenda. There would be endless classes teaching us to be good wives and mothers. I was the odd one out because I wanted to have a career – and a career on the stage at that. My dreams were made fun of. Camilla, on the other hand, revelled in the whole concept of the school. She wanted to have fun, but she also wanted to marry well because that would be the best fun of all in her mind.'

As author Penelope Fitzgerald, who gave Camilla French lessons, told top royal author Nigel Dempster in his 1993 best-selling book *Behind Palace Doors*: 'Queen's Gate was changing slightly by the time Milla got there. It had been a place where girls were taught how to write cheques and play bridge. Slowly, it was trying to bring itself into the twentieth century.

'Our girls were so beautiful. Many of them came from old country families where in each generation the man would have married a beautiful young wife. So, of course, many of our girls were quite lovely to look at. Those who were less lovely were allowed to wear a little make-up in a discreet fashion.'

Camilla was one of the girls allowed to wear a little make-up.

Neighbours in Sussex recall that both Camilla and her brother Mark took to the opposite sex early on.

One says: 'They were down-to-earth, wholesomely sexual. She didn't have film-star good looks, but she was one of the first girls to start taking an interest in boys. She was always far more interested in men than she was in women.

'Mark, of course, was devastatingly handsome. He could have had any girl he wanted. He and Camilla were extremely close. She watched over him, and he protected her. They were brother and sister, but it was an extremely close relationship. They were true friends, they would protect one another.'

Carolyn Benson, who was at school with Camilla and remains one of her closest friends to this day, says: 'Camilla was funny and bright; boys loved her. Even when she was too young for them to have a sexual interest in her, Camilla always had lots of boy friends. She could talk to boys about things which interested them. She was never a girl's girl. She was always a boy's girl.

'She wasn't particularly clothes-conscious; nothing's changed there. But she always exuded a sexy confidence over men. She was quite a flirt, she liked men. She still does. Camilla was always the one who made friends with boys first. She was able to talk to them then.'

After school, Camilla spent six months at finishing schools in Switzerland and Paris before returning to London for her grand entry into society.

Her time abroad helped broaden Camilla's horizons.

One girl who knew her well said: 'When Camilla came back from Europe, she was even more confident. She had learned French and knew how to cook. But more than anything, she had adopted the European attitude towards sex. She was still a virgin at this stage, but she would talk quite openly about how she kissed the son of one of her mother's friends. She said it was "quite deliciously wonderful". There was a new gleam in her eye. She had clearly discovered sex. When she went off to finishing school she was still rather pudgy and plump. When she returned to London she'd got rid of her puppy fat. Her cheekbones were more prominent. She was quite the young lady about town, with the added sophistication of having spent the summer abroad. She was quite grown up. Camilla never had any hang-ups about the opposite sex. While most of us would giggle and get nervous around boys, Camilla was always confident and secure around them. And that made her very attractive to the chaps. She always had plenty of suitors.'

In 1965, like the rest of her classmates, Camilla became a debutante and threw herself into 'The Season'.

A fellow debutante says: 'Camilla was never going to be Deb of the Year, but she was determined to have the best fun she could. Her parents didn't have the fabulous wealth of some of the other girls. In fact, several of Camilla's dresses were off-the-peg numbers, not designer gowns like those of some of the wealthier girls. But Camilla carried herself with such aplomb.

'Even as a teenager, she could walk into a room and you felt her presence there. She was no beauty, she did not have a perfect figure, she did not have a title or even particularly great connections. But she had something. She oozed confidence and sensuality. She always held her head high. She had a great sense of humour. She was a very sexy girl. She never spent much time on her hair or her nails. That's one of the things I remember about Camilla, she never painted her nails. They were always rather stubbly and bitten and dirty. Her hair was always unkempt and she had these rosy cheeks from being out in the sun so much. She was a natural-looking girl. If I had to use one word to describe Camilla, it would have to be "earthy".

'But she filled a room when she entered it. Camilla was, quite simply, fascinating. She was born with raw sex appeal.'

'The Season' was a four-month period between the end of March and July when the most socially desirable girls would enjoy endless rounds of parties, dinners, dances and 'top' social functions like Royal Ascot and Henley – in the hope of meeting equally socially acceptable men to marry.

Camilla's 'Season' opened on 25 March 1965, with a cocktail party thrown by her mother at 30 Pavilion Road, Knightsbridge. A partygoer recalls: 'Camilla's London home was not big enough or grand enough to hold a coming-out party at. Pavilion Road was a place you hired if you didn't have a sufficiently grand London address. It was a fairly raucous affair. Most of the coming-out cocktail parties were rather stiff and dull. But Camilla's was fun. She wore a lovely white dress and was the life and soul of the party. Everyone had such fun, the cocktails stretched on until eleven at night. Everyone got tipsy and Camilla was at the centre of it, throwing her head back telling bawdy jokes. She must have danced and flirted with every man in the room. But she was not a girl the other girls felt threatened by. She wasn't pretty enough for one thing. No, Camilla was fun, and that's what everyone loved about her.

'From that moment on, she was one of the stars of the Season. If you wanted a party to go with a swing, you invited Camilla. With Camilla around, you could guarantee the evening would never be dull.'

Two days after her coming-out bash, Camilla went to bed with her first lover.

She told one of her girl friends: 'I may as well find out what all the fuss is about. Who knows, I might enjoy it.'

The friend says: 'It was the Swinging Sixties and she wanted to play a part in it all. She didn't actually proposition the chap in question, but she gave him the very clear signal that if he would like to enjoy her favours, she wasn't going to put up a fight.'

Princess Diana, later her rival in love, was just four years old the night Camilla finally became a woman. Prince Charles, the man Camilla was to captivate for a quarter of a century, was still a fresh-faced virgin schoolboy in his last year at Gordonstoun.

Camilla's first love was Kevin Burke. She was eighteen, he a year older. An Old Etonian, Kevin was the son of aviation pioneer Sir Aubrey Burke, the chairman of Hawker Siddeley.

He recalls: 'She was terrific fun, enormously popular, and although she wasn't a classic beauty she was attractive and sexy. She was never tongue-tied or shy and she always had something amusing to say.

'She was always mentioning Alice Keppel. It was constantly on her mind. It was almost like a talisman, something she wanted to equal, if not better.

'Every night we went to two or three cocktail parties and then a dance. All you needed was enough petrol for the car and to pay for your cleaning and the rest was provided. It was the best time and I had the best partner you could wish for. Camilla was always at the centre of things. She was never bad-tempered. She knew how to have fun. I remained with Camilla all that year.

'I suppose we were in love . . . as much in love as anyone can be at that age . . . Then she ditched me.'

Camilla had met her future husband, Andrew Parker Bowles.

At this time, Camilla was sharing a two-bedroomed, ground-floor flat at No. 1 Stack House in Ebury Street, Chelsea with Virginia Carrington, daughter of Mrs Thatcher's onetime Foreign Secretary Lord Carrington. Camilla was working part-time as a secretary.

A girlfriend who visited Camilla's home said: 'It was typically Camilla. Her bedroom looked like a bomb had hit it. Virginia was fairly tidy and organized and Camilla drove her nuts, in the nicest possible way. Virginia once said to me: "You know, Camilla has this inability to hang anything up on a hanger. And she has an aversion to cleaning fluids of any description. You should see the state of the bathroom when she's been in it!"

'But she was so sweet, it was impossible to be angry with her. She was like a big, boisterous puppy.'

An army friend of Andrew Parker Bowles recalls the first time Camilla met the man she would end up marrying. 'Andrew was a dashing man about town. He was an officer in the Blues and Royals, much more sophisticated than the men she'd known and, of course, very, very handsome.

'She was besotted. I remember the first time she saw him. He walked into the room at one of the endless parties and Camilla nudged me and asked me who he was. I told her his name was Andrew and he was terribly eligible. She said: "Introduce me to him now."

'We walked across and Camilla started talking to him. They were inseparable for the rest of the evening. They left to go off for dinner with each other later that night. She touched his arm as they left the party. I remember thinking she was rather too plain for Andrew, not his type at all. He was so handsome, he had his pick of the most gorgeous girls in London. But he appeared enchanted by Camilla.

'She intrigued him. She wasn't as stunning as his other girlfriends but she had a certain earthiness which he found charming. Camilla could always match his bawdy jokes one for one. It was clear there was something special there from the start.'

Andrew also had the right connections to make him a suitable beau for Camilla. His father, Derek Parker Bowles, was a close friend of the Queen Mother – she was a frequent guest at Donnington House, the Parker Bowleses' family home on a 1,000-acre shooting estate near Newbury in Berkshire.

A Household Cavalry officer, Andrew Parker Bowles was a ladies' man and, according to friends, he and Camilla embarked on 'a very hot affair indeed' in 1967. According to another lady who had enjoyed the advances of Andrew, 'his greatest gift to women was the knowledge that sexuality was healthy – something to be explored. That openness about sex was his gift to Camilla. She was very innocent when they met, but they spent many, many nights together. He schooled her in the ways of the world.'

Lady Caroline Percy, another of the 'in crowd', says: 'Andrew behaved abominably to Camilla, but she was desperate to marry him. They saw each other on and off for three years, but he was always messing around with other women. Camilla was too smart not to know the truth, of course. She tolerated it for a while, then she got fed up.'

But Andrew's bachelor pad in Portobello Road in Notting Hill was where Camilla spent most of her time. A friend says: 'You would go around there on a Saturday morning and Andrew would be up and about cooking breakfast and making coffee. Around eleven, Camilla would stagger downstairs, looking bleary-eyed and a little dishevelled. She would walk around wearing one of his big shirts. She was very open about their relationship, which was unusual for ladies of her class even in the sixties. She would sit on Andrew's knee and tease his hair. Very often, they would disappear upstairs together in the middle of the afternoon and one would hear giggles and moans coming from the bedroom. They clearly had a very lusty, healthy life together.

'But Andrew found it impossible to be faithful. When Camilla wasn't there, he'd pick up some leggy Sloane Ranger type at a party and bring her home. Camilla knew Andrew had a roving eye.

'One morning she turned up unexpectedly. Andrew opened the door dressed just in his underpants. For once he totally lost his cool. Camilla asked to be allowed in and Andrew started fumbling around for excuses.

'Camilla was livid. She said to him: "Who the hell have you got in there? Which tart was it last night?"

'Andrew went very red-cheeked, but Camilla refused to back down. She wasn't the type to burst into tears and run away. She pretty much pushed the door down and barged in. As she walked into his bedroom there was a pretty girl scurrying out of the bathroom, hastily fastening her bra and trying to pull her dress over her head at the same time.

'Camilla just looked at her, then looked at Andrew, then looked back at the girl and said to Andrew: "Rather plain, old man. Couldn't you do better than that? What's wrong with you? Happy to have someone else's shop-soiled goods, are you?"

'Then she turned on her heel and walked out, leaving the other girl in tears.

'That was when Camilla decided that if she couldn't beat him, she would join him. But being such a competitive soul, Camilla decided to go for a big catch. In the back of her mind, I think she wanted to find someone who would make Andrew green with jealousy. She looked around for a while and then she found the biggest catch of all . . .'

The Prince is Smitten

The meeting which was to change the course of history took place on a typical English summer's day. The rain lashed down and gusting winds whipped across the polo fields at Windsor Great Park.

Prince Charles, his hair slicked down by rain, was standing beside one of his beloved polo ponies, stroking the animal's damp mane. Suddenly, a lone figure dressed in green wellington boots, brown corduroy trousers and a dripping wet green Barbour jacket appeared by his side.

'That's a fine animal, Sir', said the woman.

Turning around, Charles found himself looking at the woman who was to dominate his life for the next quarter of a century.

With a relaxed smile, she said: 'My name is Camilla Shand. Very pleased to meet you.'

It was a simple sentence, but it began an affair that was to span more than a quarter of a century; an affair which was to lead Charles to tell a close friend: 'You know, Camilla is simply my best friend in the whole wide world.'

An onlooker who witnessed that very first exchange of words in June 1970 recalls: 'Camilla looked pretty awful that day, we all did. It was chucking it down and most people were feeling pretty dejected because the match was postponed due to the rain.

'Camilla saw the Prince standing alone on the other side of the field. Cool as you like, she walked across and started talking to him. To be honest, no-one thought it surprising or strange. She was part of the inner circle. She'd been at social functions with the royal family before. We all had powerful and influential friends. Most of our families had connections with the royals. There was nothing peculiar about Camilla going over to talk to the Prince.'

Charles was just twenty-two years old, fresh from Cambridge University. Camilla was twenty-three, and already wise in the ways of the world. The couple chatted animatedly for more than an hour.

The Argentinian polo player Luis Basualdo, who played for the same team as the Prince at the time, says: 'If he wasn't precisely a virgin, he was certainly still wet behind the ears. For the Prince, real life began with Camilla.'

Charles was, at this time, an unhappy and troubled young man. A childhood starved of affection and an upbringing in a harsh boarding school he hated had left him lonely and aloof.

But Camilla was a breath of fresh air.

Another friend recalls: 'Charles was smitten with Camilla from that very first day. When she started talking to him, she wasn't affected in the slightest. I think she was the first girl who'd spoken to Charles directly. You have to remember he'd met very few girls before. He'd only met the suitable girls who had been invited to the Palace. Any other girls he met at university were awed by his stature.

'But Camilla was fearless. She knew she was his equal. She spoke to him quite naturally. And he found that refreshing.

'He could talk to Camilla then, as he does now, in an open way he can't talk to anyone else. He feels safe with Camilla.

'She was, and is, frankly not the most pristine of women. You're not sure whether they're today's knickers she's got on. I don't think she ever went to the hairdresser.

'But he loved her from the start. She wasn't intimidated by him. She was his equal. She still is. Even on that first day, Camilla had him throwing his head back in laughter. She always had a dry wit, a great turn of phrase. She was a girl who could make a joke about anything. She never had a cruel sense of humour, it was either a dry observation about something totally absurd or it was making a joke at her own expense. That wit is what first attracted Charles to her. They say the couple that laughs together stays together. I believe that is very true in the case of Camilla and Charles. Even in his darkest depths of depression, Camilla could always make him laugh; see the lighter side of life. That's what made her special back then, that's what made her special through the years.'

The pair shared a love of 'The Goon Show'. It was back then in 1970 that Charles christened Camilla 'Gladys', his favourite character from a Spike Milligan sketch, and she dubbed him 'Fred', a favourite 'Goon Show' name. They would use these names at the end of the regular love notes they began sending to each other, but they were nicknames which were to come back to haunt them both in the turbulent years to come.

Back in the heady summer of 1970, Charles and Camilla were simply young – and in love. Within a matter of weeks they were inseparable.

A friend remembers: 'Camilla offered something he'd never had before. She was worldly-wise and fun. He could let down his guard in front of her. When she was around, there was a lightness in him that had been missing in his life for a very long time.

'She became his ideal, his prototype woman.

'From her point of view, Prince Charles was perfect. She didn't set out to fall in love with him, that happened later. No, when they met, she was still hurt from the way she had been treated by Andrew Parker Bowles. Camilla was madly in love with Andrew but she knew he wasn't being faithful to her. She'd pretty much given up any hope that Andrew would marry her.

'She genuinely liked Prince Charles, but he didn't set her pulse racing. What he did do was create a perfect way of getting even with Andrew. Within a few weeks, the whole of London was buzzing with talk about the Prince and his new lady.

'It was only a matter of time before Andrew heard about Camilla's growing relationship with Charles. And she knew it.'

Camilla was soon spotted regularly by her Prince's side at top London nightclubs like Annabels.

The relationship stunned London society.

One of Camilla's friends of the time says: 'People were amazed by how quickly the relationship blossomed. At first, everyone just smiled inwardly that Camilla had taken up with the rather naïve and innocent Charles. But within a few short months it became clear they were closely involved and very attached to one another. There was a genuine love and friendship there. It was clear to anyone who saw them together.

'Camilla was very discreet about her friendship with the Prince. If one mentioned or teased her about it she would giggle. She would never give anything away. She was always terribly discreet, even back then.

'It was a different time back then. There was no press keeping an eye on the royals, but no-one said a word outside the immediate circle of friends. Why should we? Camilla was one of us. There was no reason to cause a scandal.

'Anyway, they were both single and free to enjoy their romance without hurting anyone.

'When one saw them together, it was clear they were having a physical relationship. I remember one night at Annabels. The Prince rarely drank at that time and almost never danced. But that night he let his hair down. He was drinking champagne and Camilla kept dragging him on to the floor. At one stage, he put his hand around her waist and then allowed it to slip down on to her bottom. It was an extraordinarily intimate thing for him to do in public with a girlfriend.

'But Camilla was clearly very special to him. When you looked at them talking together, his eyes would light up and he was relaxed. They were always laughing in each other's company.

'It was extraordinary to see Prince Charles, at that age, so intimately involved with a real woman like Camilla. One just knew they were having a great time in bed together.'

Indeed, Camilla's sexual hold over Prince Charles is something widely discussed by their closest circle of friends even today.

One pal who has known Camilla for twenty-five years says: 'It's widely known that Camilla is great in the bedroom. She's a woman who knows what she wants and who is an expert in satisfying a man. She's supposed to be mind-bogglingly good at it. If you talk to any of her old boyfriends, that's one of the things they remember most. Back in the sixties, it was unusual for a girl to be so forward in the bedroom. And it was certainly unusual for a girl of Camilla's class to be so adventurous and uninhibited.

'To a young Charles, she must have been a real eye-opener. He was very inexperienced when they met. She was the first woman he had a long-term sexual relationship with. That early sexual relationship has given them an intimacy through the years that no-one can take away. They say you never forget your first love – well, Charles never did.

'But it was always more than sex with Charles and Camilla. It was intimacy. They just bonded. It was like you were talking to one person when, in fact, there were two people there. They just clicked. They shared the same interests, both were very out-doorsy types and sporty and they laughed at the same things. They made a lovely couple.'

As well as his own deep feelings for Camilla, there was another very important reason why Charles felt so relaxed and comfortable with her: his closest ally, his uncle Lord

Louis Mountbatten, gave the burgeoning friendship his seal of approval.

Mountbatten's former private secretary John Barratt said: 'Charles was always closer to Mountbatten than he was to his own father. Charles and Prince Philip always had a difficult relationship. But Lord Mountbatten took Charles under his wing. He always spent time with Charles, both as a boy and a young man. Charles considered him a father figure.

'When Uncle Dickie approved of Camilla, that was the final seal of approval as far as Charles was concerned.'

Mountbatten had a master scheme. His granddaughter, Lady Amanda Knatchbull, would make a perfect bride for the future king. But she was only fourteen years old at the time Charles began dating Camilla. Mountbatten knew Charles needed female company until Amanda could assume her place at Charles's side.

Barratt said: 'Mountbatten knew Camilla would make a perfect mistress for Charles until Amanda was of marriageable age. So he gave the blossoming love affair his full blessing. He encouraged Charles to sow his wild oats while he could. He advised his nephew not to marry until he was thirty. He told Charles that Camilla was "excellent" mistress material.'

Mountbatten invited the young lovers to spend weekends at his magnificent Broadlands estate in Hampshire. He told his loyal manservant: 'Charles needs some privacy. From now on, he can come here for a bit of privacy and not even his own family need know.'

To keep up appearances, Camilla was always given the Portico Room, the same room where the Queen and Prince Philip had consummated their marriage on their honeymoon in 1950.

Charles was assigned the Lady Louis Suite next door. The two rooms had an inner oak door connecting them. That door was discreetly left unlocked.

Barratt recalled: 'Of course everyone knew Charles and Camilla were sleeping together, but things like that were never discussed, they were just expected to happen and no-one batted an eyelid.

'Staff members would go into their suites in the morning and it was obvious only one bed had been slept in. But there was nothing shocking about it. Charles and Camilla were both young and single. Everyone above and below stairs adored Camilla.

'She is someone who is equally charming to everyone. She's not a snob. I remember meeting her on many, many occasions and she always had a cheery smile and a friendly word. She was completely unpretentious. She was sleeping with the future King of England, but she never once tried to pull rank. She was just a tremendously nice, down-to-earth girl who was in love.

'Mountbatten greatly admired Camilla. She was witty, intelligent and very funny. She had this racy sense of humour which appealed to both Charles and his uncle. They both loved her dearly. She had lived, she'd had worldly experiences. Mountbatten loved her character and her strength. He knew Camilla was "the right sort".

'During their weekends at Broadlands, Charles and Camilla were inseparable. They were like any couple in love – holding hands, laughing and joking together. They would go fishing together, go out riding or simply go for long walks around the estate.

'I have never seen him so relaxed with a woman. She made him feel special – the same way her great-grandmother Alice Keppel had made Edward VII feel when she was his mistress.

'Lord Mountbatten once told me how much Camilla resembled Alice. He said the physical likeness and her mannerisms were "extraordinarily" close. He gave a silent nod as if to say that those qualities in Alice had obviously been passed on down. Secretly, he was also rather pleased that Charles was involved in a sexual relationship with Camilla. He thought it was healthy and good for him.'

Throughout 1971, Charles and Camilla were 'an item'. He regularly visited her parents' home in Sussex at weekends, always discreetly and anonymously.

According to a friend of the family, Charles and Camilla's father Major Bruce Shand 'got on famously'. The friend said: 'Bruce Shand was everything Charles admired in a man. He was a decorated war hero, a pillar of the local community. But he wasn't stuffy in the slightest. He was a raconteur who immediately accepted Charles as part of the family. Those weekends with the Shands down in Sussex became veryprecious to Charles. It gave him the chance to experience a normal, happy, intimate family group. He was truly happy in their company. And, of course, he was with the woman he loved.

'Camilla and Charles would often be seen walking the local lanes on a Sunday before lunch. They would stroll along, talking and laughing the whole time. No-one paid Charles much attention. They just looked like any other young couple enjoying each other's company.'

But despite her obvious love for Charles, Camilla was still secretly nursing a broken heart over Andrew Parker Bowles.

Andrew had been sent to Germany with his regiment. At the time Camilla was embroiled in her affair with Charles, she sadly told a friend: 'I love Charles very much, but I simply cannot forget Andrew. I often wonder where he is and what he is doing. I think of him all the time. Is it possible to love two men at the same time?'

Despite Mountbatten's full seal of approval for her affair with Charles, Camilla knew she would never marry her Prince.

Carolyn Benson, who knew them both well, says: 'He was younger, simply a nice boy – Camilla was conscious of her select status but she never wanted to be Queen. He would more than likely have married her – but that's not what she wanted.'

Another friend said: 'Camilla would laugh if the subject of marriage was even mentioned. She had grown up around the royal family, she knew what becoming the Princess of Wales would entail. And she didn't like the idea one bit. Camilla wanted a quiet life. She was always destined to marry well and have a family. Becoming Queen wasn't something she ever wanted.'

In September 1971, Charles enrolled at Dartmouth Naval College, part of the 'master plan' to prepare him for kingship. It would mean long periods away at sea.

He and Camilla bade farewell to each other in his private rooms at Buckingham Palace. A friend of Camilla's said: 'There were tears on both sides, but mostly from Charles. Camilla was the one who had to comfort him. He had been excited about the prospect of going to sea, but when the time came, he was mortified at leaving Camilla. He was more in love with her than she was with him. It was the first great love of his life. And as time has shown, Camilla was *the* great love of his life.

'Charles knew he had to do his duty and go to sea, and he knew he had to give up Camilla, the woman he loved. What he did not realize was that this would not be the first time in his life he would have to give up Camilla in the name of duty to the Crown and the country.'

While Charles was at Dartmouth, the couple wrote to each other on an almost daily basis. A friend says: 'Charles would write these long, passionate letters telling Camilla how much he missed her. She would write back, telling him it was only a matter of time before they would see each other again. His letters were terribly sweet and naïve. Camilla never parted with any of them. She still treasures them to this day.'

In October 1971, Andrew Parker Bowles returned from abroad and quickly re-established contact with Camilla.

A friend says: 'When Andrew came back home he was flattered to discover his Camilla had been having her own fling with the Prince. After all, they were all part of the same social circle and, to be frank, within that social circle, having one's girlfriend bonking the Prince of Wales gave Andrew a certain elevated status.

'He was rather proud of her achievement. It was also a manly challenge to him. He knew Camilla was still in love with him; it was like waving a red rag at a bull. Andrew was hugely competitive. He got a secret kick out of Camilla sleeping with the Prince, but he was determined to win her back.'

Andrew's younger brother Simon says: 'He was flattered that Camilla had caught the Prince's eye. Basically, Andrew and Camilla had known each other for years and it was always Camilla who made the running to marry Andrew.'

As Charles and Camilla drifted apart, Andrew re-entered Camilla's life. A friend says: 'When Andrew came back from Germany he was even more dashing and desirable than when he went away. Camilla was still nursing a deep love for him. The fact that he'd cheated on her numerous times only appealed to her competitive nature. She still wanted him – but now she was determined that if Andrew wanted her, he would have to do the decent thing and marry her.

'She played a delicate juggling game. She continued to write to Charles and saw him during his weekends off from training at Dartmouth, but during the week, she would go out with Andrew.

'Camilla was never certain about her feelings for Charles. She loved him deeply, but she knew early on that she did not want to marry him. At that stage, she loved him but she wasn't in love with him. Camilla is a deeply private woman; the idea of living her life in the public eye did not appeal to her one bit. She used to laugh off the idea of her marrying Charles by throwing her head back and saying: "Why on earth would I want to live my life in a fishbowl? No thank you very much!".'

But Charles was determined to make one last-ditch attempt at happiness.

One one of his visits home, in January 1972, Charles invited Camilla to spend the weekend with him at Broadlands.

John Barratt said: 'Camilla was perfect for Charles. Many of us had expected the proposal for months. It took took place in his bedroom at Broadlands. Charles clasped her hand and whispered: "Will you marry me?" Camilla told Charles that she loved him, but could not marry him.'

Devastated, Charles sought advice from Lord Mountbatten. He was shocked when his nephew confessed he had proposed – and relieved that Camilla had given the 'right' answer.

Barratt said: 'Charles always turned to Mountbatten for advice on affairs of the heart. But when Charles told him about the proposal, Mountbatten's first advice was that he should talk to his family. Mountbatten told Charles it was impossible for him to marry Camilla. As a future king, he had to take a virgin bride – and Camilla was not a virgin.'

Barratt added: 'At first Charles had been obsessed about marrying a virgin. He was a great fan of the novelist Barbara Cartland, who was to become his step-grandmother when he married Diana. He based himself on her romantic heroes. Every time he came to Broadlands, his bags would be packed full of her books.

'Prince Philip thought he should be macho and militaristic, but Charles had different ideas about being a man. He was a romantic.

'But he forgot all about marrying a virgin when he met Camilla. He liked the fact she had slept with other men. That was a trait he inherited from Mountbatten, who liked experienced, usually married women. Camilla had experience.

'But the royal family insisted Charles should marry a virgin. They were worried about a scandal breaking if he took a girl like Camilla as his queen. They feared a girl like Camilla might have skeletons in her cupboard which would embarrass the family if she were placed on such a pedestal.

'Charles was told that Camilla could still remain his mistress – but he would have to keep looking around for a more suitable bride.'

Shocked by the intensity of his young nephew's feelings for Camilla, Lord Mountbatten encouraged Charles to sow his wild oats. He told him: 'Go out and sow them while you may. Be a moving target as far as girls are concerned. For goodness sakes, you are in the most enviable position in Britain – you can fuck any girl you want!'

Charles took his uncle's advice to heart. He embarked on a string of affairs with hand-picked girls from the upper classes.

He enjoyed flings with Georgina Russell, the daughter of Britain's ambassador to Spain; Lady Jane Wellesley, daughter of the eighth Duke of Wellington; Jane Ward, the assistant manager at the Guards Polo Club and heiress Sabrina Guinness.

As one woman who enjoyed a brief fling with Charles in the mid-seventies says: 'Who would turn down the invitation for an intimate dinner with the Prince of Wales at Buckingham Palace? My dear, the very thought is enough to make most girls go weak at the knees. I knew several girls who went there and who ended staying the night. But they all agreed Charles wasn't the best lover in the world. He was rather naïve, the sort who liked to get on top and get the job done, preferably with the lights out. Nevertheless, there was a certain honour in being laid by the Prince of Wales; it was like becoming a member of a rather exclusive club.'

In February 1973, Charles set sail for the West Indies on a six-month stint at sea aboard his ship HMS *Minerva*.

His affair with Camilla had been brought to an abrupt end. But although his heart was broken, the name of Camilla Shand and the extent of the future king's love for her was unknown to all but their most intimate circle of friends.

One says: 'It's ironic that Charles and Camilla had this torrid affair and no-one in the press even knew her name. How that would all change as the years went on . . .'

Just four weeks after Charles set sail, Camilla announced her engagement to Andrew Parker Bowles in the society column of *The Times*.

According to a shipmate, Charles reacted by locking himself in his cabin – emerging three hours later with red-rimmed eyes to join his fellow officers for dinner.

A Dream Wedding

It was the society wedding of the year. On 4 July 1973, Camilla Rosemary Shand, resplendent in an antique lace gown with diamonds in her hair, walked down the aisle as a new bride. As the bells of the Guards Chapel rang out in celebration, the Queen Mother, sitting in the front row, smiled at the happy couple. Next to her, Princess Anne nodded her head in approval.

The guest list at the glittering reception at the St James Club afterwards read like the Who's Who of the British aristocracy.

Princess Margaret raised a glass of chilled champagne to toast the newly-weds. Lord Fermoy, Earl Alexander of Tunis, Lady Jane Wellesley and Lord Charles Spencer Churchill were all there. The Duke of Marlborough's niece, Mary Muir, was chief bridesmaid. One of the pageboys was Maurice Roache, now Lord Fermoy and Princess Diana's first cousin.

Camilla looked stunning in a £2,000 dress designed by the Queen's dressmaker Belville Sassoon; a ten-foot-long white veil flowed down from her upswept hair.

As Mr and Mrs Parker Bowles left in a vintage Rolls-Royce for their new home, the magnificent Tudor mansion,

Bolehyde Manor in Wiltshire, everyone agreed it had, indeed, been a perfect day. But there was one conspicuous absentee, Prince Charles, the blushing bride's former lover. He was 3,000 miles away at sea.

One guest says: 'Charles's absence was mentioned, but only in the most hushed of tones and well out of earshot of the newly-weds. Everyone thought it rather odd he was not there. He sent a telegram and used the excuse that he was aboard ship. But no-one bought it. He is the Prince of Wales, for goodness' sakes; had he wanted to be there, it could easily have been arranged. It would have been no problem for him to have disembarked and taken a Queen's Flight home.

'But everyone knew the real reason. He simply could not face watching Camilla walk down the aisle. He was truly cut up when he heard she was marrying Andrew.

'He refused to discuss Camilla for at least six weeks after her engagement was announced. He really took it badly. He locked himself away in his cabin and rarely came out. For the first time in his life, he'd lost out on something – and that was the woman he loved. For years, he would go on about how he should have grabbed the chance and nabbed Camilla when she was available.

'That was always Charles's problem. He is a ditherer. He simply cannot make up his mind on anything. He's become better as he's grown older, but back then he was terrified of upsetting his family, of doing anything to upset the status quo. He desperately wanted to marry Camilla, but he was afraid it would cause a scandal. His family adored her, but she had been around the block a few times, so to speak. Even his grandmother, the Queen Mother, told him: "Camilla's a lovely girl, darling, but she's not marriage material."

'Back in the early seventies, Charles was still expected to take a virgin bride. It's not like today when Prince Edward can live with a girl before marriage to test the waters. Charles is the future king, he is expected to do things by the rule book. And everyone wanted and expected a fairy-tale princess. Camilla was many things, but she was no fairy-tale princess. Everyone in the circle knew she'd been sexually active for years.

'Charles regretted going against his gut right from the start. As soon as he heard he had lost Camilla to another, he wanted her more than ever. He realized then he should have married her. As the years went on, that belief became even more firmly ingrained in his mind.

'His love for her never died. It just sat there deep inside of him, slowly eating him up. Once she married Andrew, his honour prevented him from pursuing her. At least during the first years of her marriage, it did.'

Camilla quickly settled into married life. But from the onset, the Parker Bowleses did not enjoy a conventional marriage.

After a brief honeymoon in Cap d'Ail in the south of France, Andrew, by now promoted to the rank of major, returned to his regiment in London, travelling down to the barracks from Wiltshire on Sunday night and returning the following Friday. Camilla was happy staying at Bolehyde near Chippenham.

A fellow officer's wife recalls: 'Camilla never liked the bitchy world of life among the officers' wives. She would make an appearance at certain dinners and functions, but only when she absolutely had to. When she did appear, she never dressed up. Her clothes were always more Top Shop or Oxfam than *haute couture*. When you met Camilla, she always looked like she'd been dragged through a hedge.

'She much preferred to remain at home. She spent the first few months of the marriage sorting out Bolehyde. It was a magnificent, very comfortable home. Camilla never fretted much for modern design. Bolehyde was kitted out in furniture they'd acquired from both sides of the family. It was "shabby-grand" if there is such a thing.

'The place had a few ugly antiques and the carpet looked like it had seen better days. But Camilla loved that house. She was in her element in the country. She was much happier at home surrounded by her dogs, working in the garden in her smelliest clothes. She's always been a country girl at heart.

'The extraordinary thing was that she refused to talk about Charles. Everyone knew they had been friends, but if his name ever came up, Camilla would quickly change the subject. Her eyes would cloud over and she would look away. It was clear she still nursed deep feelings for him.'

By December 1973, Charles decided to break the ice with his old friend and again started writing her long letters.

A friend says: 'He decided that if he could not have her as a lover and a wife then he would at least have her as a friend and confidante. Charles always trusted her more than anyone else in his life. He had confided his innermost thoughts to her. She could read him like a book.

'Camilla never judges Charles. She can be firm with him, but her judgements are always fair and most of the time she's spot on. He knows she is totally selfless. She will always give him the best advice she can. She's not out to score any points off him. She simply knows and understands the man behind the mask. And Charles knows that. When things bothered him, he always wrote or called Camilla. She was the one person who would always tell him the truth.'

It may seem astonishing to those outside aristocratic circles, but Andrew Parker Bowles fully accepted his wife's continuing friendship with the Prince.

A friend says: 'Not only did Andrew accept it, he positively encouraged it. He knew all about Camilla's affair with Charles and it didn't bother him one jot if she wished to continue her special friendship after her marriage. He knew Camilla would never leave him. He knew his marriage was solid.

'When Andrew and Camilla married, Andrew did not give up a single one of his friends. Most of them were mutual friends of he and his wife anyway, so why should he force his new wife to break ties with her friend? And anyway, what harm could come of having a pal as influential and powerful as the future king?

'Andrew and Charles got on well. They are very different types. Andrew is outgoing and racy while Charles is more deep-thinking and rather stuffy in Andrew's eyes. But both share a love of horses and country life. They both have this deep-rooted sense of duty. And, of course, they both love Camilla.'

On 18 December 1974, Camilla gave birth to her first child, a son, christened Thomas Henry Charles.

She asked Charles to be the boy's godfather and he willingly agreed. When Tom was christened in the same Guards Chapel at Wellington Barracks where Andrew and Camilla had exchanged their wedding vows, Charles looked on, smiling as he apparently shared the couple's joy.

But inside, he was devastated.

A former naval officer who served with the Prince on HMS *Minerva* said: 'Seeing Tom finally brought home to him that Camilla had a family and a life of her own. He spent several years after that totally lost and bewildered. You know, it was extraordinary, he kept a photograph of Camilla on the mantel in his cabin. It struck us all as extremely peculiar that he would keep a picture of another man's wife on display.'

Four years later, Camilla's daughter Laura Rose was born.

The following year, on 27 August 1979, Lord Louis Mountbatten was killed by the IRA. The tragedy sent Charles running back to Camilla. Indeed, Prince Charles made a second marriage proposal to Camilla just days after Lord Louis was murdered.

A friend of Camilla's says: 'Camilla was the one he turned to to get him through those darkest days shortly after Dickie Mountbatten was murdered. Camilla hardly left his side. The loss of his uncle left Charles devastated. He was at a loss to know what to do. His grief was so overwhelming, he sank into a deep despair.

'Mountbatten was a father-figure to the Prince. Charles and his own father had never enjoyed a close relationship. Philip thought Charles was too romantic, too weak – and Charles thought his father too tough and regimented. They never did anything together. Charles never had enough affection from his own father. But Mountbatten plugged the gap. He was Charles's friend, father, older brother, confidant, adviser. When he died in such a tragic and horrifying way, the Prince was heartbroken. He once said it felt as if the IRA had killed a piece of him too.

'Camilla was the one who pulled him through. She helped him prepare to face the world for the funeral, she was the one who comforted him when he broke down weeping. She was the only one who could console him.

'Charles proposed again to Camilla that summer. He wanted her to leave her husband and marry him. Camilla again turned him down. It was Camilla who pointed out that the scandal would be disastrous for Charles and the monarchy. She knew the country would never accept him marrying a divorcee and that he would be forced to renounce the throne. Camilla rejected him outright. She stressed to him that she would always be there for him, but they could never marry. It was Camilla all the way through who was encouraging him to find a suitable wife.

With no chance of winning Camilla's hand, Charles consoled himself by throwing himself into a series of spectacularly unsuccessful love affairs.

Stephen Barry, his former equerry who was later to die of AIDS, said: 'He seemed reluctant to fall in love again so, quite frankly, he treated a lot of the girls like shit.

'There was no shortage of prospective bedmates, of course, and Charles threw himself into the task of sowing as many wild oats as he could.

'The girls would be invited over for supper, but it was expected that they would spend the night. In the morning, a car would take them back home. The prince never wanted the girls to stay, he never really wanted to give too much of himself. He was using women and he knew it.

'I was always finding ladies' underwear beneath his four-poster bed. I would discreetly send the panties to be laundered and would then return them by messenger to their rightful owners wrapped in brown paper.'

One of Charles's girlfriends at the time was Lady Sarah Spencer, the elder sister of Princess Diana.

Flame-haired Sarah was a fiery girl with a strong personality. She was later to tell her friends that her relationship with Charles was 'a disaster'.

Sarah's affair with the Prince ended when she told a reporter: 'I will not marry the Prince of Wales. I do not love him. I couldn't marry anyone I didn't love if he was a dustbinman or the future King of England.'

Her impertinence at speaking so frankly to the press shocked Charles. He instantly ended their friendship.

Luis Basualdo, the rakish Argentinian polo player who played on the same team as Charles, told royal author Nigel Dempster how he introduced Charles to another lover, the beautiful Venezuelan socialite Cristabel Barria-Borgia, at a ball when Sarah Spencer was the Prince's official escort.

Basualdo told Dempster: 'Charles danced with Cristabel for hours and Sarah wasn't very happy.'

Later, Charles insisted on driving Cristabel home to London in his Aston Martin. She sat in the front passenger seat beside him; Sarah and his detective were scrunched together in the back seat.

A few days later, Charles met Cristabel at a private party. He asked Basualdo to lend him his car.

Basualdo told Dempster: 'He said Cristabel was feeling tired. The next morning she told me that as they were getting into bed, she asked the Prince: "What shall I call you – Sir or Charles?"

'And as he started making love to her, he replied: "Call me Arthur." '

Sarah Spencer, struggling with anorexia, quickly disappeared off the scene. 'Too flighty', according to the Prince.

He then took up with Anna Wallace, a rich, very attractive daughter of a Scottish landowner. Anna, nicknamed 'Whiplash' because of her prowess on the hunting field and in the bedroom, had a blazing row with Charles at a polo ball at the home of Lord Vestey in 1980. His official guest, she stood bored and glowing with rage as Charles danced the night away – with Camilla Parker Bowles. Anna ended up borrowing her host's BMW and driving off at speed into the night.

The following morning, Charles telephoned Anna. As he offered his apologies, she listened to him for a full five minutes before hanging up.

'He asked for it. I'd never been so embarrassed in my life,' Anna later told friends. Within six weeks she had married Johnny Hesketh, the younger brother of Lord Hesketh.

Anna, like all of Charles's 'inner circle', was now certain that Charles's obsession with his great love had never died.

A friend who was there that night says: 'It became painfully clear as the night went on that Charles only had eyes for Camilla. The second he saw her, his eyes lit up and he went across to talk to her. Then they danced closed together all night. It was obvious to anyone with two brain cells to rub together that he was still madly in love with her.'

Another member of the inner circle says: 'He would call her constantly, he would ask her advice. They weren't sleeping together during this time, but they remained firm friends. They were always bumping into each other at polo matches and other social functions. The love never died between them, it was merely put on hold. It was like they were both waiting for the time to be right so they could resume their affair.'

That time came at the end of 1980 when Andrew Parker Bowles, now holding the the rank of lieutenant-colonel, travelled to Rhodesia to work closely with Christopher Soames, the newly-appointed Governor as the country made the bumpy transition from Rhodesia to Zimbabwe.

Camilla chose to stay at home with her children. At the time, she told a friend: 'I have no desire to uproot my family and go all that way. I much prefer to stay at home. It's better for the children and it's better for me. Andrew can do his thing; I'll do mine.'

At the same time, Charles was in the process of buying his

country estate at Highgrove, Gloucestershire, the former home of Prime Minister Harold Macmillan's son Maurice – just a fifteen-minute drive away from Camilla's home Bolehyde Manor. In fact, Camilla had helped Charles choose Highgrove. The pair had spoken at length about finding 'the right place' for the future king to reside. Highgrove was 'perfect'.

Gossips soon began commenting on how often the Prince's gleaming Aston Martin Volante was seen parked outside the Parker Bowleses' home – often arriving on a Friday evening and remaining in the same spot until Sunday afternoon.

A source close to Camilla says: 'It was Charles who made all the running. Camilla was married, but her husband was on the other side of the world, so Charles felt he had an "in".

'He missed the intimacy he had shared with Camilla for too long. It started off innocently enough. But within a short period of time, they were sleeping together again.

'This time, it was an even safer and more secure relationship for Charles. Camilla was married; there was no chance at all – if there had ever been one in the first place – that she would want to marry him. She had turned him down twice.

'They spent a hell of a lot of time together while Andrew was in Rhodesia. Everyone knew. Charles wasn't that discreet. He would telephone Camilla the whole time. He was so smitten, he would call her from the car as he left London to drive down to the country and would stay on the phone talking to her all the way right up until he drew up at her front door. It was an open secret that Camilla and Charles were "on" again.

Indeed, at the end of 1980, Camilla was the cause of a minor royal 'scandal'. She was staying at Balmoral as a guest of the Prince when she suddenly went down with a bad dose of the mumps. She immediately went home to Wiltshire but the Prince, unmarried and childless, was subjected to a rigorous battery of medical tests.

A courtier says: 'At the time it was a real crisis. Everyone knows mumps can affect a man's fertility and the idea of the Prince becoming barren before he married and produced an heir was intolerable. Even the Queen was alarmed. Luckily, he passed all the tests with flying colours. But everyone was seriously worried, for we all knew the extent of Charles's intimacy with Camilla.'

Meanwhile, Andrew Parker Bowles was enjoying a few new friendships of his own.

In Rhodesia he had met Charlotte Hambro, the beautiful daughter of his boss, Lord Soames. She was estranged from her husband, Richard Hambro and, according to pals, the couple became close in Harare.

According to one close friend: 'Charlotte was crazy about Andrew and he was very keen about her. But he kept messing her about. He simply wouldn't make the decision to leave his wife and commit to Charlotte, so in the end it went nowhere.'

A few months later Charlotte met and married the Yorkshire landowner Earl Peel. Andrew then began a relationship with a blonde photographer. This friendship led to a 'very embarrassing' moment, according to a friend of the photographer's.

Prince Charles was due in Rhodesia in April 1980 to preside over the independence ceremonies, but just two weeks before Charles's arrival, Andrew Parker Bowles made headlines of his own.

The *Daily Telegraph* reported that, in anticipation of the Prince's coming, Parker Bowles decided to 'test-drive' a buffalo. He attempted to rise the beast bareback – a feat which was to be copied by Charles if the experiment was successful in order to give the media a dramatic photo opportunity. Unfortunately, on the first 'test-drive', Andrew was thrown from the rampaging beast and badly gored – an accident which required him to have sixteen stitches put in his leg and groin.

Gallantly, Andrew rose to the occasion, telling reporters: 'It was damn near the end of a dynasty.'

Upon his arrival in Rhodesia, Prince Charles was invited to dine at Government House with Lord and Lady Soames, Andrew Parker Bowles and his photographer friend. But three days before the dinner, Camilla phoned from England and said she would be arriving in Rhodesia the following day.

A staff member inside Government House said: 'The table settings had to be hastily rearranged. The gossip mill was working overtime. No-one knew if Mrs Parker Bowles was coming to see her husband or Prince Charles. As it was, the whole evening passed without mishap. The Prince and Mr and Mrs Parker Bowles all sat there and seemed to have a splendid time together. It was as if their friendship overrode any other underlying feelings. It was a quite extraordinary scene to anyone who knew what was going on. But at that level of society, musical beds is a common pastime. They didn't think it was at all strange.'

Andrew Parker Bowles has often been portrayed as the spurned husband, loyally 'laying down his wife' for the sake of King, country and duty.

In fact, he is a devastatingly handsome man, and certainly no wimp. Even during his courtship of Camilla, he had a torrid affair with Princess Anne.

A Catholic, educated at Ampleforth College, Andrew had his own impressive pedigree. His father, Derek Parker Bowles, was a close friend of the Queen Mother and she was a frequent visitor to Donnington Castle House, the Parker Bowleses' family estate near Newbury in Berkshire. He is related to the Earls of Derby and Cadogan and the Duke of Marlborough. He was a pageboy at the 1953 Coronation of the Queen.

From an early age, Andrew was used to mixing with the royal family. A close family member says: 'Andrew was brought up around the royals. He treated the Queen and the Queen Mother with respect, but they were part of his extended family. He knew Charles, Andrew and Anne from the time they were all kids together. They'd meet at friends' birthday parties and at horsy events with their parents. He knew them all very well; you must never underestimate Andrew's position.

'He knew the Prince of Wales long before Camilla came along. He and Charles were riding to hounds together from the age of sixteen or seventeen.'

Andrew first began dating Princess Anne in 1965. A close friend of his says: 'They shared a love of horses; Andrew was a fine amateur jump jockey. He went out with Anne for about a year. Just a few months before his wedding, when he knew Camilla was sleeping with Charles, he went with Anne to the Ascot races. He was her guest in the royal box. He was always one of her favourite boyfriends. Anne had plenty of boyfriends before she married Mark Phillips. But Andrew was special. Of course, Andrew being a Catholic meant they could never marry. Anne would have had to renounce her claim to the throne. Anne wasn't particularly bothered about the claim to the throne, it was highly unlikely even back then that she would ever be in a position to succeed. But her marrying a Catholic would have been a real problem for the Queen in terms of the constitutional issues it would raise and the waves of negative publicity it would inevitably create.

'Anyway, the affair finally burned itself out.

'When her marriage to Mark Phillips hit the rocks, Andrew was the one she turned to to help her pick up the pieces. They started going out for dinner together and Anne would visit Andrew in London while Camilla stayed in the country. Only when Tim Laurence came along did the relationship cool. But Anne and Andrew are still great friends to this day.'

A friend said: 'Andrew always loved a challenge. He has a certain type he has always gone for. He prefers them blonde, rich and preferably titled. He messed around on Camilla right up to their wedding.

'He's not a cuckolded husband. He just enjoys having an open marriage. If he is not with Camilla, he knows exactly who she is with. So that gives him the freedom to pursue his own dalliances. There's nothing surprising in that among the upper classes. It's been going on for centuries. A long as they stick to sleeping around within their own circle, it's acceptable. What causes gossip, talk and scandal is when people have affairs beneath them. That is considered very bad form indeed.'

John Barratt, Lord Mountbatten's former aide, said: 'Camilla and Andrew carried on being invited for shooting weekends at Broadlands even after the death of Mountbatten. It was an extraordinary arrangement. Camilla would arrive with her husband but would spend all her time with the Prince. Everyone knew what was going on, but Andrew Parker Bowles accepted it, so far be it for any of us to judge.

'The Prince would arrive alone and he would telephone Camilla. They would go out for long walks together in the grounds, just like they did before she married. Then, in the evening, Camilla and her husband would leave together and Charles would go upstairs a few minutes later. Camilla would then bypass her own bedroom and go into the Prince's. Nothing was ever said. The next morning, there they would all be at breakfast – Camilla, the Prince and Andrew.

'I often wondered how Andrew coped with it, knowing his wife was sleeping with another man while they were all under the same roof together.'

How Andrew coped was to carry on leading his own active social life.

Indeed, in June 1993, Andrew was photographed leaving the London home of Camilla's best friend Carolyn Benson in the small hours of the morning. Both Andrew and Carolyn strongly denied that anything improper had taken place.

A friend of Camilla's says: 'Camilla saw the pictures. She was back home in Wiltshire. But what could she say? The marriage has been an open one for years. The sight of Andrew leaving Carolyn's house in the wee hours would have sent any other wife into spasms of jealousy. But not Camilla. She knows and understands her husband's needs. She is a woman who knows men better than anyone I've ever met.

'Their marriage may be bizarre, but it's solid. If they were going to break up, they would have done it years ago. The fact is, Andrew has known about Camilla's affair with Charles from the start. Camilla has known about all of his peccadillos. The only one she was slightly concerned about was Charlotte Hambro. They appeared to be getting very close at one stage. But she was hardly in a position to complain.

'It's an arrangement they have followed for years. Both Andrew and Camilla are perfectly happy with it. If the world does not understand, they do not care. To them, it is perfectly normal. The freedom of their marriage does not diminish the love they have for one another.'

Back in the summer of 1980, Camilla was still happily involved in her 'discreet' affair with Charles. But she, like the rest of the inner royal circle, knew pressure was mounting for him to take a bride. As in the past, it was to Camilla that Charles turned to ask advice about a prospective wife.

A friend says: 'Camilla always gave Charles advice on his girlfriends. She thought Anna Wallace a little too flighty. Camilla knew how easily Charles fell in love. She would draw up mental scorecards in her head to give his girlfriends marks out of ten. She looked at them all with detached realism, rather than any romantic notions.

'Camilla always told Charles he should find himself a younger woman, one who hadn't had time to develop too many of her own opinions. Her favourite saying was that Charles should find himself a wife who "wouldn't be too much bother".

'Camilla knew the way the royal family worked. And she understood that, at thirty-two years old, Charles was running short of potential suitors. I remember her saying: "How can it be so difficult to find a virgin from the right background? Surely, there must be one virgin out there?" '

Camilla was also increasingly concerned by conversations she was having with staff close to Charles. Privately, many courtiers confided in her that they feared Charles was becoming a little too similar to his great-uncle, Edward VIII, the late Duke of Windsor.

Edward, like Charles, dithered for years about taking a bride. When he did fall in love it was with Wallis Simpson, an

American divorcee who prompted the biggest constitutional crisis of the twentieth century when Edward abdicated to marry 'the woman I love.'

The spectre of Camilla haunted those within royal circles. They could not afford another scandal. And the last thing Camilla wanted was to become embroiled in the headlines. She preferred her affair to remain quiet and discreet.

In fact, it was Camilla who finally came up with the ideal solution. One night, Camilla and Charles were discussing the growing pressure for him to marry. Camilla told Charles he should look more closely at young Diana Spencer, saying to him: 'She could be perfect for what you are looking for . . .'

Shy Di

Lady Diana Spencer was, indeed, 'quite perfect' for Prince Charles, according to everyone. Everyone, that is, apart from the worried Prince himself.

From the moment her name was first pushed into the frame as a serious potential bride for him, in the summer of 1980, he expressed his 'gravest reservations'.

The couple had first met on a muddy field at Althorp, the Spencer family's magnificent 1,000-acre estate in Northamptonshire in November 1977.

Diana was just sixteen years old at the time, with mousy blonde hair and puppy fat. She was on a weekend break from West Heath boarding school in Kent and the pair did not exchange a single word.

Painfully shy, Diana watched her future husband walking forlornly across the ploughed field. As she later recalled: 'My only thought was, "What a sad man." He had such a forlorn expression. I felt quite sorry for him.'

At the time, Charles was having an on-off fling with Diana's older and infinitely more glamorous sister Sarah.

Diana said: 'I kept out of the way. Sarah was enthusiastic

in her attentions to the Prince. All I remember about that weekend was that I was the podgy one. I wore no make-up, I was the unsmart lady. But I made a lot of noise and he seemed to like that.'

During an interview shortly after their engagement, Charles said: 'I remember her as a lot of fun. She was very jolly and amusing.'

In November 1978, the Queen Mother, already keeping a wily eye out for potential brides for her grandson, suggested Charles invite the young Diana to his thirtieth birthday party at Buckingham Palace. It was the finest party in London that season.

As shy Di sat at her table, watching the assembled heads of state from around Europe and the *crème de la crème* of British aristocracy, she hardly noticed the older woman with the tousled blonde hair who sat at a neighbouring table. Ironically, Diana had caught her first glimpse of Camilla Parker Bowles, the woman she would grow to despise and whom she would one day accuse of destroying her marriage.

That night, Camilla was escorted by her husband. Their second child, daughter Laura Rose, had been born the previous spring.

A friend of Diana's said: 'Diana was just thrilled to be invited. It was like Cinderella had finally been invited to the ball. It never even remotely entered her head that Charles might be interested in her and, indeed, he ignored her totally. She just sat there and watched what was going on around her. She wasn't asked to dance all night. Not once, not by anyone.'

As the Prince's favourite pop group the Three Degrees entertained guests, Charles ignored the blushing Diana – and danced the night away with Camilla. It was a chilling foretaste of what fate held in store for Diana – a life destined to be spent sitting on the sidelines while the Prince devoted his attentions to Camilla.

The Queen Mother was instrumental, with her good friend Lady Ruth Fermoy, Diana's grandmother, in promoting

Diana's charms to the Prince. 'She is so sweet, so terribly quiet, so very innocent', she would tell her favourite grandson a few days later.

'Yes, but she is so *young*,' said an uninterested Charles.

'But she would be perfect for you,' replied the Queen Mother.

Diana Spencer indeed had the perfect credentials as a future queen.

She was born the Honourable Diana Frances Spencer on 1 July 1961 in Park House on the Queen's Sandringham estate.

Growing up at Althorp she was surrounded by beauty and grandeur but, as her brother Charles would later reveal to Andrew Morton in his devastating book *Diana: Her True Story*, she was a lonely and troubled young girl.

Her unhappiness began when she was just seven years old: her father Johnnie, the eighth Earl Spencer, split from her mother Frances. Diana was deeply affected by the split. Her father sank into a deep depression and locked himself away for weeks on end in his bedroom, refusing to speak to anyone, including his own children.

Diana was later to tell a friend: 'It was the worst time ever. It made me decide that when I married, it would be for ever. I would never, ever get divorced.'

A member of staff at the Althorp estate said: 'It was a bleak and lonely time for Diana. She was so young and vulnerable and the split left her devastated. She adored her mother, but her mother was the one who moved out. Diana felt torn between her two parents. On one occasion, she had to attend a wedding. He father bought her a lovely new blue dress to wear. Her mother bought her a frilly green dress. Diana was in agony for days, knowing that she would offend one of her parents whichever dress she decided to wear. She was having to make decisions like that at a tender age. And it profoundly affected her.

'Her schoolwork suffered. Diana always had a brain, but she found it hard to concentrate on school when there were so many other issues to think about. In later life, that manifested itself in her belief that she was stupid. She was always putting herself down by making comments like "Brain the size of a pea, that's what I've got" and "I'm as thick as a plank of wood". In fact, she was a very bright child. She just wasn't academic.

'But right from an early age, she was perfect in social situations. She was, by nature, shy and retiring. But she could make people open up to her in a way no-one else could. When one watches her now talking to the elderly and AIDS patients, she has a flawless charm. It is a gift she was born with. As a child, she developed that motherly, nurturing side at school. Diana was always the one who comforted other girls when they were down or miserable. She knew what it felt like to feel alone, abandoned and afraid. And it was in her gut instinct to help other people going through those same, sad emotions. Her charms exceed anything you could learn from a book.'

When Diana's father remarried, to Raine, the former Countess of Dartmouth and the daughter of the romantic novelist Barbara Cartland, Diana was thrown into even deeper turmoil. She was sixteen years old when her father married his new wife quietly at Caxton Hall register office in July 1977.

She loathed her stepmother from the start. After Raine arrived at Althorp, Diana wrote a not so cryptic entry in her childhood diary: 'Raine stops play.'

According to family friends, Diana and her brother Charles were relentless in their hatred of their stepmother.

But Diana did enjoy her time at West Heath School. A schoolfriend remembers: 'She took to boarding school like a duck to water. She was one of the few girls who never cried on the first day at school. Diana would be the one who cried as the time approached to go home at the end of term. School was a welcome relief for Diana from the turmoil of her home life. She was a very sweet child, she was always a bit of a mother hen with the younger girls. But she also had a will of iron. Diana always knew what she wanted. She wasn't academic, but she had a wise head on those young shoulders. If she was determined to do something, she usually would.'

After leaving school with no qualifications, she spent six months at finishing school in Switzerland. When she returned home, her younger brother Charles, now the ninth Earl Spencer, remembers: 'She had developed high cheekbones and a new-found confidence. The ugly duckling was beginning to blossom into a swan.'

In September 1978, Diana had a premonition. She was staying at the home of an old schoolfriend, Caroline Harbord-Hammond, the daughter of Lord Suffield. A fellow guest asked about her father's health and Diana replied: 'I feel he is going to drop down in some way. If he dies, he will die immediately or otherwise he will survive.'

The following morning, the phone rang. Earl Spencer had collapsed with a massive cerebral haemorrhage in the courtyard of Althorp. Diana immediately threw her things into a bag and rushed to her father's side at Northampton General Hospital.

For days, Diana and her brother and sisters waited at the hospital. It was during this period that the bitter feud with stepmother Raine plummeted to new depths. Raine tried to stop the children visiting their critically ill father, who hovered between life and death for three months in a coma. She even instructed the nurses to prevent the children entering his private room. Diana was later to tell friends that, on several occasions, she and her sister Sarah would have vicious shouting matches with Raine in the hospital corridor.

In 1979, Diana moved to London and was given a three-bedroomed flat at No. 60 Coleherne Court, Pimlico, as a coming-of-age present from her father. The flat cost £50,000. She immediately landed a job at the Young England kindergarten. She made extra money for a while working as a weekend 'char lady' for her sister Sarah who lived nearby.

A friend says: 'Diana wasn't embarrassed to do the washing up, dusting and hoovering. In fact, she was never happier than when she was cleaning Sarah's place. She was simply young, naïve and happy to be living in London. She never really had a care in the world in those days. Diana was never a girl who lived the high life. She would spend free times going to dinner parties at the homes of her Sloane Ranger friends or making up the numbers at bridge. She had no thought for the future. She loved children and she just naturally assumed that, when the time was right, she'd find a suitable chap who would have a nice place in the country and life would take its natural course. Diana knew nothing about sex or men. She would flirt with a few of the chaps, but she never had a serious boyfriend, to anyone's knowledge. I would be surprised if Diana had ever even kissed a boy at that stage. She was always aloof, somehow detached from the rest of the crowd. She was fun-loving, but underneath, she never gave too much away. She was just plodding along in her own little world. She was a girl who always knew that, somehow, her future would be mapped out for her.'

By the summer of 1980, the search for a bride for Charles had become frenetic.

Most importantly for Charles, the two women he trusted more than anyone in the entire world, his grandmother and his mistress, were both putting forward the same name as a prospective bride – Diana Spencer.

The Queen Mother invited him to lunch at Clarence House in May 1980. She said: 'Don't dismiss Diana Spencer. She may be a shy little ugly duckling now, but she could be turned into a beautiful swan. She is unspoilt, Charles. Trust me; I know she will be good for you.'

Charles responded by maintaining a discreet silence.

His former valet Stephen Barry said: 'The Prince was pretty firm about the fact that Diana was a young girl and he was a man of the world. He could not see how on earth any relationship could possibly work out. And, of course, time proved his initial feelings were correct.

'But he knew the pressure was on for him to find a bride. He let out a huge sigh one day and said: "You know, if I had my way, I would happily stay single. But it's always duty, duty,

duty. My only fear is that in my position, divorce is out of the question. If only one could live with a girl beforehand to test the waters. But I can't even do that." '

Two weeks later, Charles spent the weekend with Camilla in Wiltshire. Her husband remained in London 'on business'.

At this time, the Parker Bowleses, by all accounts, had reached an amicable agreement in their marriage. When they were together, they enjoyed a happy and fulfilling partnership, both devoted to their young family. But when apart, they both pursued their 'outside' interests, no questions asked, no recriminations later.

Camilla said: 'I have spoken to several people about Diana and they all concur she is a sweet young thing. She does not have a great mind, but she is kind and caring and good with children. She could be moulded into something good. And she is from the right stock.'

Finally, Charles's resolve began to weaken. What harm could possibly come of meeting this girl his mistress so thoroughly approved of? After all, if it didn't work out, he would still have the loving arms of the woman he adored to escape to.

He told Camilla he would agree to meet Diana again.

The meeting was arranged for early July 1980 at a party at the Sussex home of Prince Philip's polo-playing friend Commander Robert de Pass.

A fellow guest recalls: 'On the Saturday, we returned from polo at Cowdray Park and Diana was talking to HRH. She was sitting on a bale of hay; he was towering above her. She was wearing one of those stripy blouses and a pair of dungarees. It flashed through a few people's minds that perhaps Diana would be a good match for HRH – but we all dismissed it as too implausible. Charles was a man of the world, he'd been sexually involved with Camilla for years. He still was. The idea that this shy little wallflower might interest him in the slightest was absurd. She was a little girl. He was a man. He was used to Camilla's earthy sensuality. Diana was totally un-sexual. She was pretty enough, but she was a girl just like any number of other girls from the right background you would meet fresh out of school. She had very little finesse, she had no sex appeal. All that, of course, would appear in the future. Anyone who looked at Diana back in those those days would have filed her away under the category of "Must come back later; has potential".'

In fact, Diana *did*, surprisingly, captivate the Prince for the first time as she sat there chattering away on the hay bale. After the usual exchanges, she changed the tone of the conversation to a new level. Staring deep into his eyes, she talked about the death of his beloved Uncle 'Dickie' Mountbatten and his funeral at Westminster Abbey the year before.

She said: 'You looked so sad when you walked up the aisle at the funeral. It was the most tragic thing I'd ever seen. My heart bled for you when I watched it. I thought, "It is wrong. You are lonely, you should be with somebody to look after you." '

Her words struck deep into Charles's heart – and he looked at her with new eyes. Perhaps Camilla and his grandmother were right. There might be more to this girl than he had assumed at first.

A former member of the royal household says: 'At this point he was not in love with Diana, but he was certainly feeling something for her. The Prince is a complete idealist, sensitive and rather protective of his feelings. In his judgement, he was starting to believe a union with Diana could work. She seemed to agree with everything he wanted. He said she understood how he *felt*. For someone as "feeling" as Charles, that was an important plus in favour of Diana.'

A few days after the weekend in Sussex, Charles invited Diana and her grandmother Ruth, Lady Fermoy, to the Royal Albert Hall for a performance of Verdi's Requiem followed by a private dinner at Buckingham Palace.

After that dinner, his first thought was to call Camilla. No sooner had Lady Fermoy's Daimler glided through the gates of the Palace to drop Diana back off home at her bachelor flat in

Coleherne Court than he was on the phone to his mistress.

Charles explained he had spent the evening with Diana and that she had been rather reserved and shy.

Camilla replied: 'Perfect. She's quite perfect. Quiet as a mouse. No bother there.'

With Camilla's wholehearted approval, Charles invited Diana to join him on the royal yacht *Britannia* during Cowes Week on the Isle of Wight.

A fellow guest on board says: 'Diana was still completely in his awe. He would call her Diana and she would call him "Sir". It was like a young girl talking to her mentor or even her teacher. She was clearly thrilled to be there, but she hardly said a word. She was pretty intimidated by everyone. She was a pretty enough little thing, though, and several of us wondered whether there was more to her and Charles than met the eye. They'd clearly not exchanged more than a few conversations at that stage. But he was quite kind towards her. He smiled in her direction once or twice. Of course, he spent hours every evening on the phone to Camilla.'

Diana was later to recall: 'It just seemed natural to call him "Sir" during those early days. It was obviously right to do so because I was never corrected.

In early September, Diana travelled to Balmoral to spend the weekend of the Highland Games with Charles and the rest of the royal family. Again, she was surprised to find that Camilla Parker Bowles was there.

It was during that weekend that *The Sun* photographer Arthur Edwards first spotted 'Shy Di' on a riverbank waiting patiently as Charles indulged his passion for fishing in the River Dee. In his best-selling book, *I'll Tell The Jokes, Arthur*, the top photographer remembers: 'I saw a boyish figure hidden in an old green Barbour jacket, wellington boots and peaked cap. When she heard our car arrive, she ran and hid behind a tree. Then she started to climb a hill away from the river without once turning her head to look back. In a minute or so, she had taken cover in the car.

'In fact, no-one pictured them together until the day of

their engagement nearly six months later.

'But I knew something was up. I'd taken a picture of Diana at a polo match five weeks earlier. I took the picture on a hunch. She was just standing there watching the game, but I just felt she was watching it with a special type of interest. I just had a gut feeling about that girl.

'After seeing her at Balmoral, something twigged. It was like warning bells went off in my head. I rang the office and told them I just knew that Lady Diana Spencer was "The One".

'I'd been hearing her name mentioned by my royal sources for several weeks as the girl who was being groomed for greater things.

'We decided to go with the story.'

The following morning, the first story about Di and Charles appeared in *The Sun* under the headline: HE'S IN LOVE AGAIN . . . LADY DI IS THE NEW GIRL FOR CHARLES.

From the moment the first edition left the presses, the rest of Fleet Street were in hot pursuit. Reporters and photographers camped outside Diana's flat and she was caught in the glare of the public spotlight which was soon to become such an enormous part of her life.

Later that month, the now famous picture of Diana standing holding two children in the grounds of the Young England nursery school in Pimlico where she worked part-time appeared on the front pages – and captured the heart of the nation. Wearing just a flimsy summer dress with her back to the sun, Diana's lovely long legs could be clearly seen. Naively, she had forgotten to wear a petticoat. As the sun shone through the dress, Lady Diana Spencer's undoubted charms were on display for all to see.

Charles would later remark: 'I knew you had good legs, but did you really have to show them off to the entire world?' It was a comment which Diana said wounded her greatly.

But the Prince's half-hearted courtship continued. In October 1980, Diana was invited down to Highgrove, Charles's eight-bedroomed mansion on a 395-acre Gloucestershire estate, which was in the process of being renovated. She was to spend the weekend with Charles at nearby Bolehyde Manor – as guests of Andrew and Camilla Parker Bowles.

She later told a friend: 'I was young and naïve, but I was beginning to feel this was not the normal way one conducted a romance. Camilla Parker Bowles was *always* there.'

That first Saturday morning, Andrew and Charles went shooting, leaving Diana alone with Camilla. As the two women walked through the gardens of the seventeenth-century manor house, Camilla quizzed Diana about her plans.

'Do you hunt?' she asked.

Diana replied that she was terrified of horses after breaking her arm as a child in a fall. Camilla smiled, knowing she would always be able to meet her Prince in the safety of the hunting field.

The two women never enjoyed any kind of friendship.

In earlier accounts of the 'wooing' of Diana Spencer by her Prince, it was suggested that the marriage proposal took place in the cabbage patch at Camilla's home. This is untrue. In fact, the Prince *did* have a long conversation with Diana about marriage in the cabbage patch at Bolehyde Manor.

A close friend of the Prince says: 'He didn't propose, he didn't even make a declaration. But they did speak for well over an hour about their feelings on marriage. Diana said all the right things about wanting children and believing a woman's place was in the home, supporting her husband. She was very frank with him that, if he were to propose, she fully understood what she was getting into. He was pleasantly surprised by that conversation. He felt Diana had shown a maturity beyond her years.'

A few days later, Camilla accompanied Diana to Ludlow Races. The Prince, a keen amateur jockey, was to ride his horse Allibar in the Clun Handicap steeplechase. While Camilla looked relaxed and smiling, Diana appeared tense and on edge. The two women were photographed leaning over a fence, watching the Prince's every move – absorbed in their own individual and separate loves for the same man.

Diana later told a friend: 'I felt so vulnerable. It was clear that I was the outsider in that friendship. Charles was much keener to talk to Camilla than to me. He practically ignored me. I felt that, throughout that whole time, Camilla was simply sizing me up. When Charles finished racing, it was Camilla he ran towards and started talking to. He all but ignored me. You could tell by the way they were looking at each other that something was going on.'

The friend added: 'She was beginning to feel like a lamb going to the slaughter.'

A friend of Camilla's says: 'In those early days, Camilla was a king-pin in the budding relationship, but Diana never realized it. Diana was so naïve, she thought the Prince was pursuing her because he was madly in love with her. Charles was fond of the girl, of course, but his main reason for continuing the relationship was that Camilla was so positive about Diana. Diana failed to realize how strong an ally Camilla would be if she became friends with her. Diana was scared of Camilla; to be honest, she always has been.

'Diana knew from very early on that Camilla had a relationship with Charles on a deeper level of intimacy than she could ever hope to achieve.

'Camilla knew everything. She tried to be friendly to Diana, but Diana always saw her as a threat. The problem with that girl was that she wasn't clever enough to play the game. If Diana had seen Camilla as an ally, as someone who knew the Prince so well she could have offered invaluable advice to Diana on how to handle him, things might have worked out very differently.

'But Diana always thought that once she'd bagged her man, Camilla would simply disappear out of the picture. Of course, that was never going to happen.

'For her part, Camilla thought Diana sweet enough, but rather dense and stupid.'

But Diana was not so stupid that the terrible reality of Charles's ongoing infatuation for Camilla did not dawn on her. When Diana, living under siege from the press in Coleherne Court, sought sympathy from Charles, he responded: 'Yes, yes dear. But Mrs Parker Bowles is going through precisely the same thing. Just hold your head up, smile bravely and say nothing. Camilla's going through it too, you know. You mustn't feel too sorry for yourself. It will soon be over.'

Diana, in an uncharacteristic outburst, told a friend: 'Why does he care more about her than he does about me? I'm the one he's supposed to be marrying, for God's sake.'

But what infuriated Diana more was that Camilla knew even the most intimate details of her romance with Charles, down to their most private conversations. Diana told a friend in exasperation: 'I feel like Camilla is watching over my shoulder, even when Charles and I are having dinner in private – which doesn't happen very often.'

In later years, Diana was to say: 'I remember I asked him once why he spent so much time with Camilla, a married woman. He just shrugged his shoulders and said: "Because she is safe."

'At the time, I thought the friendship was what he was talking about; that it was safe for them to be friends because she was married and no-one would gossip. What I quickly came to realize was that he meant Camilla was safe because he could carry on sleeping with her and no-one would suspect a thing, presumably, least of all, me.

'What really infuriated me was that the next time I saw Camilla, she patted me on the shoulder and told me "not to worry" about her.

'I thought about it later and it was obvious Charles had told her I was worried about her. He told that woman everything. I didn't just marry Charles, I married his mistress too. There was nothing that went on in my marriage she didn't know about.'

But the event which almost prompted Di to end the romance with Charles took place in November 1980. The *Sunday Mirror* ran a front-page story claiming that, on 5 November, Diana had enjoyed a secret romantic rendezvous with her lover aboard the royal train in a siding in Holt, Wiltshire.

Diana, who had been at home in her flat that night nursing a hangover from Princess Margaret's fiftieth birthday party the night before, knew the mystery blonde woman spotted slipping on to the train could not possibly have been her.

The Palace issued an instant denial. However, the story had been fundamentally correct. The Prince *had* enjoyed a late-night rendezvous with his blonde lover – but it had been Camilla, not Diana, who had slipped aboard the train that night.

The train's telephone log revealed Charles had made a late-night call to Camilla's home, Bolehyde Manor – less than fifteen miles away.

Only three people knew the truth – Diana, Charles and Camilla.

Camilla and Charles were never going to reveal the truth –- and Diana chose to ignore it. She was close to realizing her main ambition in life, winning the Prince's hand in marriage, and she was not prepared to jeopardize it at this stage.

By January 1981 speculation was at fever pitch that Diana was 'the chosen one'.

Charles, meanwhile, continued his relationship with Camilla. Just days before leaving to spend Christmas at Sandringham, he drove down to Wiltshire to give Camilla her present, a gold necklace. Diana received a book and a jumper.

In the New Year, Charles went skiing in Klosters, Switzerland. Although he still had serious doubts that Diana would make a suitable wife, his mind was made up in a late-night phone call to Camilla. She told him that even if he married Diana, she would be there for him 'always'.

He took a deep breath and replied: 'In that case, I shall allow my head to rule my heart.'

Charles telephoned his future bride and informed her he would be returning on 3 February and would like to see her three days later.

The proposal took place on 6 February in the nursery at Windsor Castle. When Charles first asked her to marry him, Diana collapsed in a fit of giggles. When he explained the seriousness of his proposal, she went quiet – and said, 'Yes please.'

She had agreed to become the *second* woman in Prince Charles's life.

Two days later, Diana joined her mother on her last private holiday. Her mother, Frances Shand Kydd, was living with her then husband Peter on a sheep ranch outside Canberra in New South Wales, Australia.

Diana, blinded by love and thinking Charles was in love with her, became worried when she had not heard from her fiancé two days into her ten-day stay. She telephoned his private offices at Buckingham Palace only to be told the Prince was not there. Disappointed, she hung up. She tried again a dozen times in the next twenty-four hours. No reply.

What Diana did not realize was that Charles, on the eve of his engagement, was in the arms of the only woman he has ever truly loved: Camilla Parker Bowles.

Stephen Barry was amazed no-one close to the Prince was taking his growing reservations about his marriage seriously. Barry said: 'The Prince was becoming more agitated by the day. The engagement was imminent, but he knew then that he was being forced into a marriage he really didn't want with a woman he really didn't know or love.

'I remember one day, just before the engagement was announced, I found him in his study. He was clearly worried. He said: "I'm making an awful bloody mistake."

'It was a terrible thing to hear him say. The whole country was captivated by Diana, everyone loved her – except the man she was going to marry. But Sir's problem was always that he felt he had to put duty first. He was thirty-three years old; marriage was inevitable. And Diana was the girl who had been chosen for him. If he ducked out now, there would be an almighty row. And he couldn't face that. Perhaps in his heart, he thought he might grow to love Diana. But he already knew in his heart who he truly loved, and that was Camilla. I thought of it rather like a Greek tragedy. Here was the man who appeared to have everything, yet the one thing he truly wanted was the one thing he could not have. And that was Camilla Parker Bowles.'

During their first post-engagement interviews with Press Association reporter Grania Forbes, Charles made a telling comment in response to the question: 'Are you in love?'

He replied: 'Whatever that may mean.'

During the interview, the couple barely exchanged glances and sat at opposite ends of a sofa.

Prince Andrew was heard to say a few days later: 'He's not in love with her, you know. Let's keep our fingers crossed that he will learn to love her – or at least learn to live with her in a civilized manner.'

On 26 February, Diana was examined by the Queen's loyal gynaecologist Dr George Pinker and was pronounced fully fit – and a virgin.

The engagement was announced to a jubilant country at eleven in the morning, 28 February 1981.

The previous evening, Di had packed her bags at Coleherne Court, the beloved flat she shared with old schoolpals Virginia Pitman, Carolyn Bartholomew and Anne Bolton. As she bade her loyal friends farewell, she begged them to stay in touch 'because I shall need you'.

Escorted away from the flat by her new Scotland Yard bodyguard Paul Officer, he quipped: 'This is the last night of freedom in your life, so make the most of it.'

She would later remark: 'Those words felt like a sword through my heart.'

Diana arrived at Clarence House, the Queen Mother's London home, later that evening. No sooner had the footman closed the door on her as she entered her new temporary home for the first time than Diana spotted a white envelope resting in the middle of the bed.

She later told a friend: 'I could not imagine what it could be. I naturally assumed it would be a welcoming note from Charles. I tore it open and then my heart sank. It was from Camilla. How the hell did she know where I was going to be unless Charles had told her in advance exactly what our plans were?

'For God's sake, I only knew the engagement was going to be announced on 28 February when the Palace called earlier that morning and told me I was moving to Clarence House that night in preparation for the announcement the following day.

'Camilla's note was dated three days earlier. That bloody woman knew before me.'

A friend of Camilla's says: 'Of course Camilla knew. The Prince tells her everything, always has. He keeps no secrets back from Camilla. She is his best friend so, of course, he rang her and told her that the engagement was imminent.'

In the note, Camilla invited Diana to join her for lunch. The pair met at Buckingham Palace three days later. It was a tense lunch. Camilla tried to talk to the nervous bride-to-be, but Diana clammed up.

According to a friend of Camilla's: 'It is unfair to see Camilla as the wicked witch in all of this. She truly wanted to help and guide Diana. But Diana was already being a stubborn little thing. Her back was up. She distrusted Camilla. Most importantly, she misjudged Camilla. What she failed to grasp was that Camilla's loyalty has always been to the Prince. Camilla hoped she would get along well with his new bride. If Diana was not exactly rude to Camilla, she certainly did not go out of her way to be friendly. Camilla left that lunch a little dejected. For the first time, she questioned herself about whether Diana *was* emotionally secure enough to cope with the mammoth task that lay ahead of her.'

Shortly afterwards, Charles left for a five-week visit to Australia. The world watched as Diana clutched at his arm at the airport and broke down sobbing.

What the world did not know was that Diana was heartbroken about an incident which had occurred just thirty minutes before they left for the airport. Diana was at his side in his private office in Buckingham Palace as he sorted out some last-minute paperwork.

The phone rang – and it was Camilla. Diana later claimed

her fiancé asked her to leave the room so he could say goodbye to his mistress. She told friends her heart was 'broken into a hundred pieces' that morning.

But Charles's friends tell a very different story.

According to one: 'The phone went and it was Camilla calling to bid HRH farewell, as was quite within her rights as an old friend of twenty years to do.

'As soon as Charles picked up the phone, Diana flew into one of her tantrums. Charles didn't know how to handle her. She was like a petulant schoolgirl.

'He put his hand over the receiver and tried to talk to Diana. She was getting hysterical and saying something along the lines of "I suppose you want me to leave now?"

'He replied: "Of course not. You can stay here, I'll only be a minute." But he barely had time to get the words out of his mouth than Diana stormed out of the door, slamming it behind her.

'Charles was distressed by her behaviour. It was irrational and uncalled for. Camilla had simply called up to wish him well. Diana blew up the significance of the call out of all proportion. And it left Charles feeling perturbed. Even back then, he did not know what to do when Diana went into one of her rages. As their marriage progressed, she flew off the handle more and more.

'Of course, by this stage Diana was already suffering from bulimia, when she binged on food and then threw up. But Charles had no idea of her illness. He'd never encountered anything like that before. He knew the Spencer girls were volatile; he'd dated Diana's sister Sarah a couple of years before. But it worried him that the girl he had picked to be his future queen was acting in such a way.

'I remember him saying some time later: "I don't know what to do. Diana flies into a rage at the slightest thing. It worries me sometimes. Either I am so old and fuddy-duddy that I don't know what's going on – or she has some kind of psychological problem. I hope, for all our sakes, that the former is true. For if the latter is correct, I dread to think what might happen." '

Just five days before the wedding, Charles voiced his fears to John Barratt.

Barratt said: 'I knew Charles was still very much in love with Camilla and was having difficulties with Diana. Literally the week before the wedding he told myself and Lord Romsey that Camilla was the only woman he had ever loved. He told us: "I could never feel the same way about Diana as I do about Camilla."

'Lord Romsey simply assured him that his feelings would, most likely, change.

'The Prince was fascinated by the fact that Diana was still a virgin and he knew it was his duty to get married. But I knew that once that his physical urges had been satisfied by getting Diana into bed, the marriage had no chance of lasting.

'Diana was very beautiful, but she lacked intelligence. Charles could talk to Camilla about anything, but that wasn't the case with Diana. She was young and had totally different interests. She hated hunting, shooting and fishing. She loathed his boring friends. She despised standing around for hours on freezing grouse moors. They had absolutely nothing what-soever in common.

'It was only a matter of time before Charles gave up on her – and went back to Camilla. I knew Camilla well, and she clearly knew this too.'

In July, less than a week before the biggest day of her life, Diana entered the private offices at Buckingham Palace she shared with Michael Coleborne, the man in charge of the Prince's finances. She spotted a small package on his desk, beautifully wrapped up and tied with a small, pink bow. Unable to resist, she looked at the label. It was addressed to Camilla – from Charles. With trembling fingers, Diana opened the box. Inside, nestling on blue velvet, was a small gold bracelet with a blue enamel disc and the initials 'GF'. The initials stood for Fred and Gladys, Charles's and Camilla's nicknames for each other.

When a tearful Diana confronted Charles about the

'inappropriate gift' he replied: 'What's inappropriate about it? It's just a little thank-you to a dear friend.'

But Diana was not so sure. Just two days before she discovered the bracelet, she had overheard Charles ordering a bouquet of flowers to be delivered to Camilla – who was suffering a bad dose of the 'flu. She heard Charles instruct the florist to sign the accompanying card: 'To Gladys. Get well soon, old girl, love Fred.'

Diana was already harbouring grave suspicions that Camilla was more than just a friend.

Although she did not realize it at the time, her worst nightmare was only just beginning. She voiced her fears to her closest friends and family, but they told her it was too late – the country was in the grip of royal wedding fever.

Diana's sister Sarah used Diana's childhood nickname when she told her: 'Bad luck, Duch. Your face is on the tea towels, so it's too late.'

Both Charles and Diana wanted to call the whole thing off. Just the week before the wedding, Charles told a friend: 'I feel like the whole thing is out of my control. I have not had time to even get to know this girl I am marrying. I will do my duty – and I pray for all of us that this thing works out.'

It was too late for both of them. The date had been set. St Paul's Cathedral was being prepared.

The Greatest Show of All was about to begin.

Happiness Lost

'KISS HER! KISS HER! KISS HER!' The chant of half a million people packed into the Mall could be heard a mile away. It was the greatest day for decades in the history of the British monarchy.

The Big Day, 29 July 1981, dawned fair and sunny. The hopes and expectations of the country rose to the occasion. Only two people were harbouring last minute fears that this wedding might not be all it appeared. And they were the bride and groom.

As the crowd begged for the kiss to seal the perfect day, Prince Charles leaned back slightly and whispered to his mother, 'May I?' After a nod of approval from the Queen, Charles leaned forward and planted a kiss full on the lips of Diana, Princess of Wales. It was a picture beamed across the world as the final seal of 'love' on a perfect union. But what no-one knew as they watched the fairy-tale marriage unfold before their eyes that day was what had taken place just twenty-four hours before.

As he nervously awaited his fate, Charles stole his last moment of happiness – in the arms of Camilla. As the world thrilled to the impending wedding of Charles to Diana, he was in bed with his long-time mistress.

He had attended a dinner party hosted by the Queen in the Palace on the Monday night before the wedding. Earlier in the day he had arranged a secret rendezvous with Camilla in the London 'safe house' of a friend to present his mistress with the 'Fred and Gladys' bracelet – the same gift which had sent Diana into a blazing rage just a few days before.

After the small dinner party that night, the group moved on to a nearby ballroom for a bigger and more formal wedding dance. It was a memorable night, packed with eight hundred of Diana's and Charles's friends. The bar staff handed out a cocktail called 'A Long Slow Comfortable Screw Against the Throne'.

Charles danced twice with Camilla and then discreetly mingled with the other guests. Diana danced the night away too, before leaving shortly after one in the morning to spend the night at Clarence House. As she left the party, Charles's valet handed her a small package. Inside was a gold signet ring engraved with the Prince of Wales feathers and a card which read: 'I am so proud of you. When you come up, I'll be there at the altar for you tomorrow. Just look 'em in the eye and knock 'em dead.'

The note and the present made Diana feel more secure than she had in weeks. Before she fell asleep, she took a final look at her stunning £25,000 wedding gown, designed by Elizabeth and David Emmanuel, and smiled. Whatever fears she held were over-shadowed by her hopes and expectations for the greatest day of her young life.

Camilla's husband Andrew retired early. He was preparing for duty – riding alongside the royal carriage the following day on its way back from the wedding ceremony at St Paul's.

As the party reached its end, around half past two that Tuesday morning, the day before the wedding, Charles and Camilla slipped away.

As the Prince's valet Stephen Barry said: 'We all knew how he felt about Camilla. It was a very emotional last assignation for them both. But to do it on that night was truly incredible. Certainly incredibly daring, if not incredibly stupid.'

Another guest said: 'It was fairly obvious what was going on. Both Charles and Camilla had had a bit to drink, but neither was drunk. He left the room first and she seemed to be hanging on in a corner on her own. There was only a handful of people left in the room. Everyone was preparing to go home.

'Someone brought Camilla's coat in for her and she put it on. Then she said she had to nip to the loo. She left the room with her coat on. She never returned. Presumably, the idea was to give those of us who still remained there the impression that she had gone to the loo and then got into her car to go home.

'But no-one was that naïve. We waited for her by the main entrance for a while. But she had disappeared from sight. Everyone naturally assumed that she had been secretly escorted upstairs to the Prince's quarters.

'It seemed a rather foolhardy thing to do, but no-one really thought that much about it. I mean everyone needs to have a final fling.'

On the morning of the wedding, a select group of guests enjoyed a breakfast banquet at the Palace. Camilla had left by private car at around five o'clock.

It came as a surprise to most of the assembled guests that Camilla, the Prince's oldest and dearest friend, had not received an invitation. It was Diana's first act of defiance. According to one guest, Diana had absolutely refused to issue an invitation to Camilla on this, the biggest day of her life.

The guest says: 'Diana was adamant that Camilla should not be at the breakfast. When the list was being drawn up a month earlier, she simply put her foot down. She told Charles that "nothing and no-one" was going to spoil her wedding day. And she struck Camilla's name from the list. Charles was surprised, but he relented.'

The wedding was a glorious success.

Diana's brother Charles told author Andrew Morton:

'My sister was transformed that day. She was never one for make-up but she did look fantastic. It was the first time in my life I ever thought of Diana as beautiful. She really did look stunning that day and very composed, not showing any nerves, although she was slightly pale. She was happy and calm.'

As she walked down the aisle, her father leaning heavily on her arm, Diana had ample time to spot the assembled guests – including Camilla Parker Bowles. As she recited her wedding vows, 750 million people worldwide watched in awe.

Diana was later to say, with detached emotion: 'I had tremendous hope in my heart that day.'

As Charles and Diana rode back to the Palace for their reception, they were escorted by twenty-four horsemen of the Blues and Royals, dressed magnificently in their plumed hats and bright-blue jackets. Among them was Andrew Parker Bowles, the husband of the groom's mistress.

Camilla, who was among the guests at St Paul's, was again snubbed by not being invited to the reception. She celebrated with friends at a private dinner party.

Stephen Barry later recalled: 'The Prince told me he had stayed up the night before listening to the crowds singing "Rule Britannia" on the pavement beneath his window. He said he had found himself with tears pouring down his face. At the time, I thought they were tears of emotion at the tidal wave of patriotism that was sweeping everyone. Perhaps, though, those tears were tinged with sadness at the realization that he was marrying the wrong woman.'

At Waterloo Station, as the day drew to a close, Diana and Charles boarded the royal train which was to take them down to Lord Romsey's Broadlands estate for the first three days of their honeymoon. The couple spent their first night in the Portico Room, the place where Charles had made love to Camilla for the first time, fifteen years earlier.

Charles, used to the mature affections of Camilla, was later to confide to a friend: 'That first night was nothing special. It was pleasant enough, of course. But she really was painfully naïve. It was clear she had absolutely no experience whatsoever in the bedroom.'

The friend commented that the words were spoken in a dull, emotionless voice.

He says: 'As for any man, Charles's big prize was Diana's virginity. But that was achieved without so much as a bang or a whimper. I was left with the impression that the whole accomplishment was rather an anti-climax for Charles. He was an experienced lover. He was used to sleeping with a woman who knew what to do. Diana hadn't a clue. In retrospect, it's jolly sad, but Charles would have preferred a night with Camilla any day of the week.'

Diana herself later complained of her husband's 'insatiable' sexual appetite. She said: 'He wants it all the time. I don't know what to do with him. I don't particularly care for it all that much.'

The newly-weds then flew to join the royal yacht *Britannia*, moored in Gibraltar, for a two-week cruise around the Mediterranean.

The honeymoon was a disaster from the start. Diana, already stricken by the bingeing and purging disorder bulimia, was already looking painfully thin. She gorged and vomited every day of what was supposed to be the most romantic time of her life.

One night she devoured an entire steak and kidney pie followed by a huge bowl of custard. While crew members marvelled at her ability to 'eat like a pig and stay skinny as a rake', as one put it, Diana rushed to the bathroom and made herself sick in secret.

Charles was later to tell Camilla: 'During the honeymoon, she smelled of sick the whole time. It turned my stomach. Of course I knew what she was doing. You only had to spend a few days with her to realize what was going on. She must be thick to think I don't know what she's doing.'

Diana, on an emotional rollercoaster after the wedding, made herself sick five or six times a day during her honeymoon.

Her mental condition worsened when, alone in their stateroom during the first week of the cruise, Diana picked up Charles's official engagement book – the diary which listed all royal visits for the coming three months. As she moved the weighty book, two pieces of paper fluttered to the floor. Picking them up, Diana discovered to her horror that they were two private snapshots of Camilla. Diana stormed up to the main deck and confronted her husband of less than seven days.

Through her tears, she screamed: 'Why don't you just face up to the truth and tell me it's her you love and not me?'

Charles simply blushed and explained they were old pictures of a friend which he had forgotten to remove. Diana had thrown the photographs into a rubbish bin. Charles later sneaked downstairs and retrieved the crumpled snaps.

A few days later, during a state dinner aboard for Anwar Sadat, the Egyptian President, Diana noticed her husband was wearing a pair of gold cufflinks intertwined with two gold 'C's. Charles admitted they were a wedding gift from Camilla, but said rather hesitantly: 'Don't start getting ideas. Please, let's not start this marriage with any bother.'

But again his words did nothing to soothe Diana's troubled mind. She locked herself in their bathroom after the dinner and sobbed loudly. Emerging an hour later with red-rimmed eyes, she asked him: 'Why do you need these constant reminders of that woman? Why can you not forget her and concentrate on me? I am your wife now, she is nothing to do with us.'

Charles replied: 'But she *is* something to do with us. She is my oldest friend. If only you would realize that and try to become friends with her too. If you bothered to get to know her, you would get to like her.'

Diana simply shook her head and burst into tears.

By the time they returned to Balmoral, Charles was having his own doubts about the marriage.

He asked Stephen Barry: 'Is it normal for wives to be so obsessed by one's past?'

Barry was later to reflect: 'I told him it was quite normal. But I wanted to add that it was not normal for a man to make contact with his mistress so soon after marriage.'

For Charles had already decided not to give up Camilla's charms. He placed a ship-to-shore phone call to his mistress from *Britannia* on the fifth day of his honeymoon. He also secretly sent her a three-page letter describing his feelings.

Once back in Britain, their old routine of calling each other every day began again.

Barry said: 'Sir would be more discreet than he had to be in his bachelor days. He would make a point of calling Camilla direct from his office most days. If it was impossible to call, he would write a letter which would be smuggled out without the Princess's knowledge. It was extraordinary. The Prince simply had to be in constant contact with Camilla or he could not function properly. If he went without his daily phone call, he would become tetchy and ill-tempered. Camilla was a habit he could not break, an obsession he did not wish to conquer.'

Diana's fears and paranoia only worsened when, on the final leg of the honeymoon in Balmoral, she discovered two love letters from Camilla to Charles in his private quarters. According to a staff member, the letters 'were so intimate they revealed a long-term commitment between the two. Diana knew from the tone of the letters that Charles fully intended to continue his relationship with Camilla.

'She copied both letters. She had only been married a few weeks, but she was already thinking ahead. Diana still has those letters in her possession. They are signed and dated. In all that has happened since, she has used those letters as a threat against her husband on more than one occasion. She once told him: "Wouldn't it be embarrassing if those *billets doux* somehow ended up in the wrong hands?" Diana knows they are an ace up her sleeve.'

The Balmoral leg of the honeymoon left Diana depressed and miserable. Charles left her for hours on end to tramp the moors and spend endless days fishing. Diana became bored and fed up. He encouraged her to join him during his hunting trips. She refused. She begged Charles to cut short the trip and return to London with her, but he was in his element and refused point blank. He said: 'Who on earth ever heard of anyone cutting short their honeymoon?'

Diana plunged deeper and deeper into depression – and she began heaping the blame for her anger and unhappiness squarely on the shoulders of Camilla Parker Bowles.

Indeed, from the moment she discovered the secret love letters, Diana vowed never to use Camilla's name again. From that moment on, she always referred to Camilla in private as 'The Rottweiler'.

She would tell friends: 'The Rottweiler is the main reason I'm going through this hell. I honestly believe if she disappeared, I would at least have a chance to try and make Charles love me. But with that woman around, I have no chance. He's not even thinking about me; all he cares about is Camilla.'

But Camilla refused to turn her back on Charles – or allow his young wife's outbursts to affect their friendship.

A friend says: 'In the early days of the marriage, Camilla had no axe to grind against Diana. She truly hoped the marriage would work. But she could not give up on her friendship with the Prince. As the months went on, Camilla realized Diana was not making Charles happy. As he told her more and more about Diana's increasingly erratic behaviour, Camilla, in turn, came up with her own phrase for the Princess – she would refer to her as "that ridiculous creature".

'You have to realize, Camilla is not a malicious woman. But her loyalties lie firmly on the side of the Prince. Camilla has always been his most trusted friend. If it comes to taking sides, there is no doubt in Camilla's mind who she will side with. It is always Charles.

'At the very beginning, the two viewed each other with distrust. Within a very short period of time, that distrust degenerated into mutual loathing.'

The Spectre of Camilla

Diana was later to tell friends, when the fairy-tale marriage was finally exposed as the sham it had been from the beginning, that the 'spectre' of Camilla Parker Bowles had haunted her life from the start.

When she emerged from her honeymoon into the harsh glare of the public spotlight, everyone was shocked at how thin and frail the Princess had become.

By September 1981, Diana was convinced her husband was secretly telephoning Camilla behind her back. She was absolutely correct. What she did not know was that Camilla and her Prince had made a 'gentleman's agreement' between them – that, although there was no question of them giving up their friendship, that was all it would be after his marriage.

A friend of Camilla's says: 'After the wedding, Camilla was quite prepared to stand back and allow Charles and Diana to get on with their lives. She told the prince that a continuing physical relationship was out of the question. He accepted that sex ban. He genuinely wanted to make the marriage work.

'But Charles quickly realized he had a major problem with

his new wife. They simply had nothing in common, and he had no-one to voice his fears to. His family were still congratulating themselves on the morale-boosting wedding. He found it impossible to have rational conversations with Diana. There was only one person he could confide in and trust – and that was Camilla.

'He began telephoning her regularly. Camilla, being a devoted friend, willingly offered her advice.

'Diana would fly off the handle at the slightest thing. She was always provoking screaming rows with Charles about Camilla. She accused Charles of the most outrageous things. She was quite paranoid. She would scream at him that he was still "fucking Camilla". Diana looked like this sweet little girl – but she had a foul mouth on her.

'She put him through the third degree. Charles had hoped that after the excitement and chaos of the wedding, life would settle down into some kind of normality. But Diana was having none of it. She became paranoid and erratic. If he left the room to make a phone call, she would accuse him of ringing "that fucking woman".

'He was in a no-win situation. Of course he telephoned Camilla, she was his dearest friend. But they were not having any kind of a physical relationship at that stage. That was something Camilla was adamant about. Charles would probably have happily gone back to having a physical affair straight away. But Camilla wanted him to do everything he could to make the marriage work.

'Increasingly, even she became more and more dismayed by Diana's outbursts.'

At the beginning of October, Charles was convinced his new bride had deep-rooted psychological troubles. Just eighteen months earlier, she had been a fun-loving kindergarten teacher. Now, she was the most famous woman in the world. And the pressures of her new high-profile life were clearly getting to her.

He telephoned Camilla and she sensibly recommended he seek professional help for Diana. She told him: 'She needs proper help. This is something you cannot deal with alone.'

Throughout October 1981, Diana was visited dozens of times at the Palace by a succession of psychiatrists and therapists. Charles's own doctor, Michael Linnett, was called in to help the tormented Princess. He in turn called in top psychiatrist Dr Michael Pare – an expert in the field of depression.

Charles and his wife attended joint counselling sessions on at least three occasions. The Prince also met the experts separately in a bid to 'understand more' about Diana's torments.

But it was all to no avail.

Said a senior courtier: 'Charles did not fully understand his wife's problems. He believed it was something she would grow out of. Diana was getting more and more depressed. She even began making suicidal threats. But the psychiatrists assessed the possibility of her *actually* committing suicide as "low-risk". They explained her outbursts and threats were more because of her acute loneliness.'

Diana was also counselled by experts in the field of eating disorders. Mostly, they prescribed her tranquillizers, but Diana refused to take them. For, just fourteen weeks after the wedding, she learned she was pregnant.

The pregnancy served only to make Diana's behaviour more erratic.

Lady Colin Campbell, herself the author of two best-selling books about the royal family, says: 'Diana was and is the consummate performer. To the public, she was this wonderful, fairy-tale goddess when she first burst on to the scene. She smiled sweetly for the cameras and looked like a movie star. The cameras adored her, and, of course, the public fell in love with her.

'But, in private, she put Charles through hell. Her mental problems were kept secret from all but those closest to the family. But I was hearing tales of her bizarre outbursts right from the start. Diana was an unpleasant shock to the whole family. The royals were not used to dealing with a young girl who was moody and quiet one moment and then a screaming banshee the next. They simply did not know what to do with her.

'Of course Charles sought advice from Camilla. Camilla has always been a port in a storm to him. When Diana started going mad, Charles sought the sanity of his friendship with Camilla.'

During her first Christmas at Sandringham, Diana suffered a minor nervous breakdown.

In Andrew Morton's best-selling book *Diana – Her True Story*, the Princess authorized friends to provide details of a string of alleged suicide attempts. She instructed them to portray her as a girl suffering deep depression, who received no help or support from her husband or his family in her hour of need.

According to Morton's book, Diana – by now three months pregnant with Prince William – first tried to kill herself by hurling herself down a flight of stairs at Sandringham in January 1982. Diana told chums that Charles looked at her with disdain as she lay sprawled on the floor – and then coolly turned on his heel and went off to saddle his horse for a day's riding around the estate.

On another occasion, Morton claims, Diana hurled herself against a glass display cabinet, and on another she tried to cut her wrists with a lemon slicer.

Lady Colin Campbell dismisses the suicide stories as 'absolute nonsense'.

She says: 'It's just Diana trying to go for the sympathy vote again. If the girl was serious about killing herself, she would not have tried to cut her wrists with a lemon slicer, of all things. What was she trying to do, *peel* herself to death? No, those suicide stories were something she made up to gain sympathy from the public. It was just another ploy to turn public opinion against Charles. On another occasion, Diana claims she took an overdose of paracetemol tablets. The Prince was at Highgrove and when he refused to drive back to London to see Diana, as she was insisting he do, she called him back an hour later and said she'd taken an overdose. In fact, the Prince had had a headache the evening before and had gone to the medicine cabinet in search of painkillers. There were four left. He took two and left two. He was disgusted that she'd tried to trick him like that. But he didn't want to take any chances. He got on to their doctor and had him go over to Kensington Palace to check up on Diana. Of course, she was perfectly OK and went out that same evening.'

Indeed, just two weeks after the alleged 'suicide attempt by stairs' Diana and Charles went on holiday to the Bahamas with Lord and Lady Romsey.

Royal watcher James Whitaker says: 'There were no signs that the couple were anything other than blissfully happy. In fact, Diana and Charles behaved like all newly-weds, standing in the water for ages with their arms around each other's necks, kissing constantly. All of which makes the suggestion that, only a couple of weeks earlier, Diana had thrown herself down the stairs at Sandringham completely laughable. I knew about the stairs incident at the time. I spoke to a contact who was on the scene almost immediately Diana had fallen and, far from Prince Charles walking away as she lay there, he was extremely concerned and called a doctor straight away. He waited with her while she was examined and the doctor announced that the foetus was unharmed. He acted with the utmost care and love.'

After the doctor gave Diana the all-clear, Charles took her for a picnic lunch on the Norfolk coast. Her mood instantly improved.

Charles would later say: 'It was amazing how violently her moods would swing. She could be sweet and nice one moment and then terrible the next. She could be dark and gloomy and then happy and smiling a few moments later. I have never, ever, known someone who can change so suddenly, not just day by day, but literally hour by hour.'

Lady Colin Campbell adds: 'Diana's whole life has been a public-relations coup. She knows how to handle the media and she knows precisely what to do to appear to the public as some kind of saint. The girl thinks she's Mother Theresa.

'Charles's friends know the truth. She is a scheming, manipulative little minx.

'She knew she wanted to marry Charles and she conned him right from the start. When he started courting her, she pretended she loved the outdoor country life. She said she "simply adored" hunting and fishing. In fact, she loathed everything about his lifestyle. But Diana wanted one thing more than anything, and that was to win his hand. From the moment she knew she was in with a chance, her mind was made up. She was totally and utterly determined to marry her prince. She successfully managed to con the Queen Mother and Camilla too. They both fell for her little "Shy Di" act.

'Once she had won the main prize, her whole attitude and behaviour towards her husband changed.

'From the start she would chide him for being old and fuddy-duddy. He is a deeply sensitive man who genuinely wanted his marriage to work. But Diana twisted everything. If she broke a fingernail, it was Charles's fault. She blamed her bulimia on Charles. As Charles started drawing away from her, recoiling in horror at this complete loony he had married, she started spreading the word that he was back bonking Camilla. At the time, nothing could have been further from the truth. But, in time, Charles did go back to Camilla. What Diana refuses to accept to this day is that it was her actions which drove him back into Camilla's arms.

'I will always believe, as will everyone who knows the Prince, that he desperately wanted the marriage to work. He has always put duty before anything else. He married out of duty but he also hoped to find a woman who he could walk through life with. Within a few months, Charles realized he had married a woman he wouldn't choose to walk to the corner of the street with. He felt conned.

'But Diana is nothing if not resourceful. Once she had determined in her own mind that Charles was closer to Camilla than he was to her, she was determined to knock Camilla off her perch. Camilla's position as a royal confidante carried an enormous amount of social kudos and clout. Her position was superior to most in the royal household and only marginally below that of Diana herself. Diana knew this and was determined to raise merry hell to get rid of Camilla.'

In fact it was Diana who encouraged Lady Dale 'Kanga' Tryon to renew her friendship with the Prince. Diana invited Kanga – who had known the Prince well in his bachelor days but who had drifted apart from him during his marriage – to lunch at San Lorenzo restaurant.

Subsequent photographs of the two women lunching together gave Kanga's image as a royal confidante a boost. Diana later invited Kanga to join the royal family at Balmoral.

A royal aide says: 'It was Diana's way of trying to dilute Camilla's influence. She thought that by creating the image of Kanga as a confidante, Camilla would feel usurped. Of course, nothing of the sort happened. Camilla knew her position in Charles's life, she knew he considered her his main ally. And Diana's cosy plan backfired. Camilla and Kanga get along famously. Kanga quickly realized Diana was a flighty, mentally-confused young woman. She and Camilla would often discuss the Prince's problems together. They became close and dear friends and they remain so to this day.'

Prince William was born on 21 June 1982. As the country rejoiced at the birth of a son and heir, Diana's behaviour worsened.

A former member of staff recalls: 'She was throwing up ten or twelve times a day. She locked herself away. She was so convinced Charles was back with Camilla that she refused him his marital rights for weeks on end.

'Charles was devoted to William from the start. He adores children and he's quite wonderful with them. But Diana started using the young baby as a foil.

'If Charles wanted to spend time with his son, Diana would say William was sleeping. Diana even instructed William's nursemaid to telephone her every time Charles entered the nursery. Then, she would go upstairs and start a row.

'She was deeply troubled by this point. For example, after her shoes were cleaned she insisted on them being put back in her closet in precisely the straight lines they were in when they were taken away. She was obsessed that everything had to be perfect.

'What had to be perfect above everything else was herself. She started exercising to excess. She was doing 100 sit-ups in the morning and then another 100 at night. She was bingeing and purging all day long. She would go to official functions and pick at a lettuce leaf and then she would binge by eating a whole chocolate cake when she got back home and then throw it straight back up again.'

Charles simply could not cope. He turned more and more to Camilla for advice and comfort.

'I just can't ever have a reasonable conversation with Diana,' he would complain to Camilla.

Camilla, as always, would offer a sympathetic ear and wise advice. In the early years of his marriage, she would counsel Charles to be more understanding and try to explain to him that his new wife was under enormous pressures in her very public role.

'She is young and naïve,' Camilla would say. 'You must be patient with her and allow her to grow into the job. None of us can truly understand what she is going through. The girl's only problem is that she will not listen to anyone's advice.'

Camilla even encouraged Charles to spend more time with his new bride. In the early days of the marriage, he wrote a letter to his closest friends informing them that he intended to devote 'more time' to his family life. He gave up taking so many skiing trips. He stopped going to Iceland to fish every August.

A friend says: 'He was genuinely doing everything he could to make a go of it. He even cut back the amount of time he devoted to his friendship with Camilla. But he had to keep in contact with Camilla. He was living with a whirlwind, a flighty woman he simply did not understand. Camilla always understood. She was the only person he could confide in and know he was totally safe with. He would phone Camilla in tears sometimes, beside himself with anger and frustration. He knew the marriage was a disaster. The only friend he had in the world was Camilla.'

The situation came to a head when Diana overheard her husband making a phone call on a portable telephone from his bath. She heard her husband whisper: 'Whatever happens, I will always love you.' Enraged, Diana stormed into the bathroom and screamed hysterically at her husband for a full ten minutes as he lay in the bathwater.

A former royal aide says: 'The story of Charles's dressing down in the bath soon went around like wildfire. People thought the mental image of the future king sitting stark naked in the bath tub as he had a strip torn off him was rather amusing. In retrospect, it was rather sad. Most of us felt quite sorry for the Prince. He really had no idea how to handle the situation. He started spending more and more time alone. He simply retreated into his shell.'

In fact, Camilla too bore the brunt of Diana's growing obsession with the fact that she believed Charles was having a new affair with his old love.

A friend of Camilla's says: 'As Diana became more erratic, she would take to calling Camilla's house at all times of the day or night. If the Prince was out on official business and dared be even a few minutes late, Diana would call Camilla's home every half an hour, hanging up as soon as Camilla answered.

'Of course, Camilla knew who it was. But it was horrid for her. Most of the time, Prince Charles wasn't even there. But she'd have to put up with the nuisance calls – constantly.'

Dame Barbara Cartland, Diana's step-grandmother, recalls her frequent tantrums.

She says: 'I always got along well with the Prince. One day, as he told me, Diana asked him, or rather ordered him, to pour her a cup of tea.

'He has a dry sense of humour and he quipped back: "We have people to do that for you here, darling. Why don't you simply ring the bell and get one of the servants to oblige you?"

'She was so boiling mad at him, she picked up the entire teapot and hurled it across the room at him! Can you imagine!'

On another occasion at Sandringham, Charles drove off mid-row with Diana to have lunch with the Queen.

As he stepped into his car in the courtyard, Diana opened an upstairs window and screamed: 'That's right, go and have lunch with your mother and leave me here all alone! You're so bloody selfish.'

Then she ran downstairs and ran alongside him as he drove off in his Land Rover, yelling: 'Yes, dump me like garbage! Leave me on my own again – go on!'

Tales of their frequent rows soon became the talk of the household staff.

Late one evening, raised voices were heard coming from the couple's private quarters.

Diana's voice reached screaming pitch: 'What am I supposed to do all day while you're off enjoying yourself – die of boredom? Call yourself a husband? All you want is to be a husband in the bedroom when it suits you. You and go fuck Camilla if that's all you're interested in.'

One retired staff member says: 'Diana was always ranting and raving. She never cared who heard their rows. She would be forever criticizing her husband to the staff, something we found slightly improper. I remember after one particularly nasty row, she asked me: "It's wrong what he's doing, isn't it?"

'I replied: "I simply could not say, Ma'am." It was embarrassing. Diana was breaking the golden rule of never discussing your personal problems with the staff. When Charles found out she was talking to everyone, he tried to gently explain to her that her behaviour was "inappropriate" for a woman in her position.

'She merely threw another fit and screamed: "Well, who the hell would you like me to talk to? You never talk to me any more!" '

In September 1982, Diana came face to face with her main rival when she and Charles attended a housewarming party at the Parker Bowleses' new residence. The couple had sold Bolehyde Manor and moved into Middlewick House near Corsham, Wiltshire, just twelve miles from Highgrove.

Another guest says: 'Diana was quite rude and objectionable. She arrived, had a glass of water and then started moaning about how she didn't feel well and wanted to leave. Charles was publicly embarrassed. He apologized to Camilla and drove Diana back to Highgrove. He went to his study to work and Diana, who was supposed to be feeling sick, went into the kitchen and ate a huge tub of ice cream. Then she went upstairs and threw up. She refused to talk to Charles for twenty-four hours. She wanted to punish him for dragging her along to the party.'

Charles began seeing Camilla regularly again. They often met on the hunting field as they both rode out with the Beaufort Hunt or crossed paths when he spent the weekend at Highgrove.

Camilla's old friend Carolyn Benson remembers: 'After Charles married Diana and their marriage got into problems, Charles turned to Camilla for help. I think Camilla found herself in a position which got more and more involved without realizing what was happening. Wales was a naughty boy.'

Diana, by this stage, decided she was 'bored' with life in the country, and began spending many more of her weekends in London, meeting friends from her carefree bachelor-girl days at private dinner parties or going out with them to her favourite Knightsbridge restaurant San Lorenzo.

But despite the fact that Charles and Camilla were again growing close, friends insist there was no physical relationship between them.

Camilla told a friend: 'He just needed someone to talk to. By this stage, he could barely stand being alone with Diana. She made his life totally miserable with her antics.'

At the beginning of 1984, Diana became pregnant again – with Prince Harry. As her pregnancy continued, Prince

Charles was growing ever closer to Camilla.

A friend says: 'The Prince could not stay away. When Diana was pregnant with Harry, he was on the phone to Camilla five or six times a day and seeing her at every opportunity. It was clear to everyone that the inevitable was going to happen.'

Harry was born on 15 September, 1984. Not long afterwards, Charles went to bed with Camilla again. Their 'gentleman's agreement' not to have a physical affair was over.

He knew Diana had used Harry's birth to score another 'publicity coup'. She had allowed friends to leak a story to the newspapers that Charles was so anxious for the baby to be a girl that when he saw the new baby boy, he said: 'Oh, it's a boy – and it's got rusty hair' and then went off to play polo.

Diana was later to tell Andrew Morton: 'Something inside me died. I knew it was the beginning of the end.'

Charles, for his part, knew it was the end too. He angrily telephoned Camilla to tell her how yet another untrue story had somehow been 'leaked' to the press and arranged to see her late one night during that first week after Harry's birth.

After she had consoled him over Diana's publicity stunt, Charles leaned over and kissed Camilla for the first time since they had met up for that final night of passion on the eve of his wedding. Then he led her by the hand upstairs – and into the marital bed he had shared with Diana.

Lady Colin Campbell says: 'It was inevitable that Charles would end up back in Camilla's arms and that she would end up in his bed. Charles was livid about the way Diana had used Harry's birth to score points. In fact, Charles was thrilled at Prince Harry. He stayed with Diana at the hospital for hours. He did play polo, but that was the following day. It was hardly as she portrayed it, with him running out of the hospital to go and play.'

The couple's sex life had become non-existent. Diana told one friend: 'He's seldom here to notice me.' And a friend of the Prince would later say: 'Diana may have this image of a sex goddess, but she was as cold as a fish in the bedroom.

Top: Charles and Camilla in 1975 during the first flush of their romance. They were captured together on a polo field, of course.
Below: The young lovebirds after a night out in London's West End in 1975.

Camilla and sister Annabel as bridesmaids at a friend's wedding in 1952.

Camilla and her mother, the Honourable Rosalind Shand, at Camilla's coming out party in 1965.

A smiling Camilla in the early days of her marriage.

Camilla enjoys a chat with a fellow deb at another coming out party.

Andrew and Camilla Parker Bowles' wedding day at the Guards Chapel, July 1973.

Top: Lt. Col. Andrew Parker Bowles and family at Buckingham Palace, when he received his OBE.
Below: Andrew and Camilla in the early, happy days of marriage.

Top: Camilla & Andrew's first family home – Bolehyde Manor, Wiltshire.
Below: Andrew Parker Bowles with former lover, Princess Anne.

The fairytale that never was – Charles and Diana on their way to Waterloo station to begin their honeymoon.

The two women in Charles' life – Diana and Camilla at Ludlow Races in 1980. Camilla told Charles she approved of the young Lady Diana because she was "quiet as a mouse."

The way things could have been. An artist's reconstruction of the wedding of Charles and Camilla.

Diana with William and Harry – her "greatest joys" throughout the turbulent years of marriage.

Andrew Parker Bowles escorts the royal carriage during the fairytale royal wedding of Charles and Di.

"An understanding marriage" – the couple at Windsor Great Park recently.

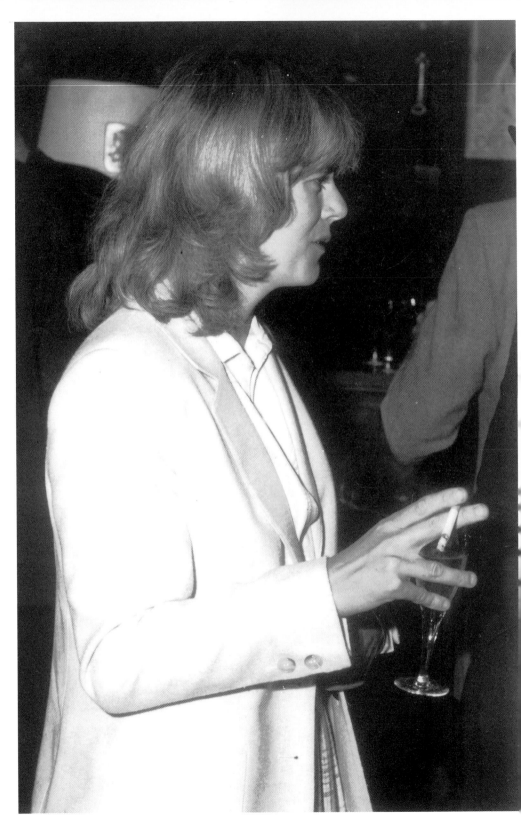

Camilla in relaxed mood before news of the scandal hit the press.

The Prince once joked that his wife was so cold, he didn't close his eyes and think of England – he would close his eyes and think of Camilla.'

In fact, it was Diana who initiated the end of their sexual life together. As a bulimic, she was already dissatisfied with her body. A former maid once told how she walked into Diana's bedroom one day to find the Princess standing stark naked in front of a full-length mirror. She was pulling on her flat tummy, trying to pinch any fat that remained.

'It was quite strange,' the maid said. 'The poor girl had nothing there, but she was looking for any minor lump or bump. She always wanted reassurance that she looked lovely before she would leave the Palace. Everyone thought she was beautiful. But she always thought she was fat.'

Convinced that she was overweight, and suffering the headaches and sore throats which accompany violent bingeing and purging, Diana began to push Charles away. When he tried to make the first overtures of love to her at night, she would turn her back and pretend to fall asleep.

A friend of the Prince says: 'He tolerated it for a while, but he soon became peeved by her behaviour. He found it insulting, to say the least. He would often complain in private that his wife was "as cold as a fish". Diana did nothing to encourage him. In fact, her bulimia was a total turn-off for Charles. He would often hear her making herself sick behind the locked bathroom door. Then she would clean her teeth and crawl back into bed. He could smell the sickly combination of toothpaste and vomit on her breath. It was hardly a combination conducive to a night of passion.'

The couple began sleeping apart in their private rooms at Kensington Palace.

Shortly before he died, Diana's father Earl Spencer admitted: 'My daughter was pure when she married. To my knowledge, she has only ever slept with one man in her life – and that is her husband.

'In any case, the trouble with her is that she tells me she doesn't like sex.'

Her brother Charles confirmed: 'Hand on heart, the only man my sister has slept with is the Prince of Wales.'

Diana would often retire to bed at nine in the evening, a habit which irritated Charles.

One member of staff said: 'She'd go off and he'd retire to his study, staying up until all hours listening to opera at full blast. When he'd finished for the night, he'd slip upstairs and began sleeping in a single bed which was prepared for him in his dressing room, which adjoined the master bedroom.

'Diana didn't seem bothered by this arrangement. She knew the marriage was on the rocks.'

While Charles's friends knew he was again having a full-blown affair with Camilla, they maintained a discreet silence. The couple had several 'safe' houses in which they would meet.

One of their closest circle says: 'Once the affair was back on again, there was no problem in Charles and Camilla meeting. They know lots of people who are more than willing to put themselves out to allow them to meet up in their homes. Everyone knew how Diana had behaved to the Prince and they felt sympathetic towards both him and Camilla.'

But Diana did have some sympathizers.

Lord Beaverbrook, a former lord-in-waiting to the Queen and a first cousin of Andrew Parker Bowles, said: 'It was Charles who ran to Camilla when things began to go wrong with Diana. And once Camilla was ensconced, she started throwing her weight around. When she saw the romance was a runner, she simply took a proactive role. Of course Diana was upset; she had every right to be.'

The unsettled Princess even began behaving erratically in public. At the 1984 State Opening of Parliament, she turned up late with a brand new hair-do which bared her neck for the first time. The Queen was reported to be 'furious' that her daughter-in-law had turned an important state occasion into a front-page fashion statement.

The royal family were, by now, fully aware they had a

major problem on their hands. The future king and queen were barely speaking to each other. They were spending weekends apart and the only times their paths crossed were on official engagements planned several months before.

The press had leapt on the story of their bitter feuding and the ongoing 'War of the Windsors' was making almost daily headlines.

Prince Philip was angry at his son for placing the future of the monarchy in jeopardy by continuing his friendship with Camilla. He summoned Charles to a one-on-one meeting at the Palace. Tough-talking and blunt, Philip held nothing back. His face red with rage, he criticized Charles for acting selfishly and told him to 'get his bloody act together'.

Charles, who had never enjoyed a close bond with his father, was flabbergasted. He tried to explain that he was living with a woman who had irrational outbursts and who was suffering from a physical illness.

'Well, bloody well learn to deal with it,' was his father's curt reply. 'This situation cannot go on. It is up to you to put an end to all this nonsense.'

'It's not my fault,' responded Charles.

'I don't care whose bloody fault it is, just end this idiotic situation *now!*' replied his father.

The row did nothing to improve Charles's mood. He began to realize he had only one true friend who genuinely cared for him – and that was Camilla.

By the end of 1984, Diana began carrying out official engagements on her own. It gave her a chance to enjoy the mass adoration she thrived on, and Charles was not forced to take a back seat to his wife's latest fashion statements as he had done so many times in the past.

Charles continued to meet regularly with Camilla after she had moved to Middlewick House in Corsham, Wiltshire, a magnificent manor house set in 500 acres and just a ten-minute drive from the Prince's home at Highgrove.

Diana's main comfort in 1985 was the arrival of Sarah Ferguson. The bubbly redhead was an old friend and when she appeared on the scene as Prince Andrew's girlfriend and then wife, Diana was initially pleased.

But having fun-loving Fergie around soon turned into a chore for the Princess. Charles would say to her: 'Why can't you be more like Sarah?'

The royal family instantly warmed to Fergie, who shared their love of outdoor pursuits and was relaxed and comfortable with the rest of the family. Diana soon began to resent Sarah. She tried to imitate Fergie's fun-loving personality by poking a friend's bottom with the end of an umbrella at the Ascot races and by giggling with her friend during serious state occasions, but her childish behaviour merely served to irritate her husband further.

'I wanted a wife, but I've married a bloody schoolgirl,' he would complain to friends.

After Fergie married Andrew that July in Westminster Abbey, Diana and Charles embarked on a bucket-and-spade holiday to Majorca as the guests of King Juan Carlos of Spain at his Marivent Palace.

During this holiday, the rift between Charles and Di became public. They barely spoke to one another and seemed keen to put as much distance between them as possible.

As James Whitaker recalls: 'When Charles came up from his air-conditioned quarters to go windsurfing, she walked off in the opposite direction. When she went diving off the boat, he deliberately looked the other way. They never once addressed a single word to each other.

'The five-year-old marriage was dead.'

The final death knell was sounded when Charles cut short his holiday by two days – and flew straight into Camilla's arms. He headed for Balmoral, where Camilla was a guest of the Queen.

By now, Diana was in no doubt that her husband was again sleeping with Camilla.

She said to a friend: 'What I simply cannot understand is

what he sees in her. I mean, she's hardly an oil painting. And she is so blunt and rude. What the hell has she got that I haven't?'

What Camilla had was a deep understanding of Diana's husband, something Diana had never been able to attain.

By the beginning of 1986, the fairy-tale marriage was a sham. Diana moved her personal possessions out of Highgrove and into her own rooms at Kensington Palace.

Highgrove had a new mistress – Camilla.

Falling Apart

At the beginning of 1987, it was clear to the select few who were invited to spend weekends at Highgrove that Camilla was firmly ensconced as the mistress of the household.

It was Camilla, not Diana, who would greet weekend guests at the door. It was Camilla, not Diana, who would sit at the opposite end of the table from Charles at dinner. It was Camilla, not Diana, who would share his bed at the end of the night.

One member of Charles's inner circle says: 'If Diana's name ever came up during those weekends, which it rarely did, Charles would simply say she had chosen to spend the weekend in London.

'Quite frankly, it was clear by this stage that he'd all but given up on the marriage. Diana never fitted in at Highgrove the way Camilla did. She loathed the conversations at the dinner table, which were often philosophical and highbrow. Camilla revelled in them. She is far more intelligent than Diana; she and Charles are always finding obscure writers to read. They are both prolific bookworms. They never run out of things to say to each other.

'They are one of those couples who seem to know what the other is thinking before any words are spoken. They share private little jokes together. Camilla can say something and then give Charles a secret look and he'll smile back knowingly. They are in absolute unison.

'Camilla's body language gave it all away. She was so relaxed at Highgrove. Had one not known that both she and Charles were married to other people, one would quite happily have concluded they were an old married couple.

'Camilla was always fussing over Charles. She isn't a wimp, don't get me wrong. It's just that she clearly has a deep affection for him. She would always be plumping up the cushions on the sofa, fixing a picture frame which was wonky on the wall. Just small things like that, things which the lady of the house would normally do.

'She would often talk with pride about the roses she was growing in the garden. Very often, she would sunbathe in the rose garden in her bikini. They were, to all intents and purposes, living as husband and wife.

'Camilla, unlike Diana, was quite prepared to change her diary to fit in with the Prince's plans. On the weekends he was at Highgrove, she was there all the time for him. To be frank, the food was not always the best – but the conversation was always sparkling and the company very exclusive. The conversations about history were always first-class.'

People invited to Highgrove included dozens of Camilla's and Charles's oldest friends.

One visitor was Lady Sarah Keswick, wife of a banker and daughter of the Earl of Dalhousie. She too shared the Prince's love of music and laughter. Like Camilla, Sarah became a target of Diana's wrath.

One night, Charles invited Sarah to a night at the opera in the royal box at Covent Garden. Diana walked in late and began screaming at them both.

A person sitting in a nearby box said: 'It was quite something. She didn't give a damn who heard her. She behaved more like a fishwife from Billingsgate than a royal princess. I'll never forget it. I had no idea she had such a foul mouth on her.'

Diana contemptuously described her husband's friends as 'that fuddy Highgrove Set' or 'the wrinklies'. But their company suited Charles. They shared his interests: country pursuits, painting, environmental issues, architecture, politics, literature, classical music. Diana, by contrast, liked loud pop music, dancing and the noisy London life – something Charles longed to escape.

His Georgian manor house became his refuge during those darkest days of his marriage – when he knew it was on the rocks, but when he was desperately trying to keep up the pretence of the fairy-tale for the world – and the monarchy. He was never happier than when he was working in his garden at Highgrove or walking around the estate with his gamekeeper – or with Camilla.

He and Camilla even hired portrait painter Neil Forster, who lived a few miles away in Sherston, Wiltshire, to give them painting lessons. They would spend hours in the garden at Highgrove, sketching and painting and talking.

And it was at Highgrove that he was able to enjoy his children. *The Sun*'s top royal photographer Arthur Edwards disputes claims put out by Diana's friends that Charles is a cold and distant father.

Arthur says: 'Nothing could be further from the truth. The thing is, he doesn't push himself forward as a loving parent the way Diana does. I've seen him many, many times with the boys and they both adore him. I've seen both William and Harry spontaneously fling their arms around their dad and tell him how much they love him.

'He's a wonderful father. At Highgrove, he could relax with his sons away from public scrutiny. He spends hours with them, talking to them about their lives and what lies ahead. He has a great rapport with both boys. He is forever taking them out cycling, fishing or even hunting. They both admire their father enormously. But, most importantly, they love him very much too. Any talk of Charles being a cold dad is nonsense. He is a fine father. Considering the cold upbringing he himself endured, it is remarkable that he is so relaxed and open with his own children. Perhaps that is why he is such a good father. He knows what it felt like to have a cold, tough father and a mother who was rarely there. He is determined to have a much closer friendship with his own children. And he has succeeded.'

Arthur told how, in November 1991, he watched Charles say goodbye to his sons, who were flying home after joining him and Diana aboard the royal yacht *Britannia* on an official visit to Canada.

He said: 'The little Princes were clearly upset to be leaving to go home to England without their parents. Charles took it the worst. As Prince Charles watched his two boys walk away, there were tears rolling down his cheeks. It was obvious how he felt.'

Diana would still pay the occasional visit to Highgrove during early 1987. She would tell her friends: 'I have to go down to the prison this weekend – unfortunately.'

In one of her rare visits to the estate, on a weekend during which Charles spent most of his time fishing in a bid to avoid any more fighting, Diana pushed the last-number-recall button on his mobile phone. Her call went straight through to Middlewick House, Camilla's Wiltshire home. She flung the phone to the floor in anger.

She also discovered a secret stash of letters from Camilla in the drawer of the Prince's dressing table in his bedroom.

Camilla and Charles have exchanged hundreds of letters through the years. It is a habit they continued until only recently. Some of the letters are loving and intimate. Others are friendly and chatty. They are a relaxed form of correspondence both enjoy.

The discovery of the letters infuriated Diana. She already had in her possession the 'love notes' she had discovered on honeymoon, but a former staff member says she pocketed another letter. Later, she would tell friends, 'I plan to use them in any divorce action.'

She dined alone that night in her private study and left

early the next morning to drive back to London.

Her worst fears were realized when she turned up at Highgrove again three weeks later. Arriving early in the morning, around eight o'clock, with just her detective accompanying her, Diana saw a car driving out of the front gates in the opposite direction. Inside, the Princess saw the familiar blonde head of Camilla.

Storming into the downstairs family room, she discovered her husband having breakfast. 'What was Camilla doing leaving here this early?' she demanded.

Charles simply ignored her and carried on reading his newspaper.

Diana went upstairs to the main bedroom. The four-poster bed she and Charles had shared was unmade, the sheets crumpled and slept in. The Princess then ran into the spare bedrooms; none was disturbed.

She later said to a friend: 'I was hysterical. It was clear the main bed, *our* bed, *my* marital bed, had been slept in by two people. I went downstairs and screamed at him for sleeping with that woman in my bed. He wouldn't answer. I was shouting at him and crying but he wouldn't say anything. I kept asking him why he was bonking her. It was the worst moment ever. I felt like it was all over. I knew for sure he was sleeping with that bitch. I seriously thought about topping myself there and then. I knew there was no chance. I knew he loved her and not me – and always had done.'

A friend said: 'Right the way through the difficult time, when the marriage was deep in the mire, Diana always secretly nursed the hope that Charles would realize the error of his ways and run back to her. When it was confirmed to her that day that Charles was sleeping with Camilla, she knew it was over.

'Charles had had enough. He was sick and tired of her antics. He became stubborn. Don't forget, this is a man who has grown up being told everything he does is wonderful. His surroundings have always been controlled. Diana was like a mad bull in a china shop.

'At first he couldn't cope or understand. Eventually, he gave up even wanting to understand what was wrong with her or their marriage.

'The fundamental problem has always been that Charles wanted to be loved. Camilla always loved him. Diana was happy to be loved and worshipped by the masses. She never understood Charles, she never will.'

In *Diana: Her True Story*, Andrew Morton spoke extensively to used-car salesman James Gilbey – a man whose name was linked with Diana's in the infamous 'Squidgey' tapes.

Gilbey told Morton: 'Diana was never able to get Camilla out of her mind. As a result, their marriage was a charade. The whole prospect of Camilla drives her spare. I can understand it. I mean what the hell was that woman doing in *her* house? Diana sees the whole thing as a gross injustice.'

In April 1987, Charles went on a solo painting holiday to Italy. Camilla stayed in a neighbouring villa. They used the holiday to continue their secret affair. When word leaked to the press that Camilla had been staying less than ten minutes away from the Prince, her family rushed to her defence.

Andrew's brother Simon said: 'It's nonsense to even suggest any impropriety. Camilla was there with her husband.'

Former Highgrove police officer Andrew Jacques revealed the extent of Camilla's relationship with the Prince in a devastating story in *The Sun*.

Under the headline SEPARATE HOMES, Jacques told how he had once sneaked a peep through the living-room window of Highgrove when Charles was home alone with Camilla.

He said: 'I was patrolling outside the house when I noticed a light on in Princess Diana's private sitting room. The curtains were closed, but through a chink between the drapes, I spied Camilla and Charles dancing cheek to cheek. They were smooching to very romantic music. Then I saw them sitting side by side on the sofa. Then they embraced. They disappeared behind the sofa for a few moments. I could see the Prince's face, but Camilla ducked out of my sight. It was as if she was on her hands and knees. A few minutes later, they re-emerged from behind the sofa and the Prince appeared to be doing up his trousers. Camilla was adjusting her dress. They had obviously been engaged in an intimate sexual act.'

Jacques added: 'The fights and rows erupted frequently between Diana and Charles. Their marriage grew more distant by the day. At the start of their marriage, they were like an ordinary couple. But within a couple of years, they seemed to want as little contact with each other as possible. They never laughed or did anything together.

'The only time they would meet up was if Diana brought the boys down for the weekend. They would meet at mealtimes and very often those meals ended with a blazing row for all to hear.

'They stopped sleeping together. Charles moved his favourite brass bed from Kensington and had it installed in his private dressing room. It was a very masculine room, with no feminine touches.

'The main bedroom with the four-poster was Diana's when she was there. It had her mark all over it. There was a row of forty or fifty cuddly toys like My Pet Monster propped up on a settee. She would bring books with her like the *Relate Guide to Marital Problems*.

'They barely spoke to each other. They were living a lie and it was clear to see. Sir was besotted by Mrs Parker Bowles and the Princess knew it.'

The 1987 marriage of the Marquess of Worcester to actress Tracy Ward showed the depths to which the Waleses' marriage had floundered.

Charles spent the night locked in conversation with Camilla, leaving early. Diana stayed up all night furiously dancing with a succession of men. One of the men she lavished attention on that night was Philip Dunne, a handsome Old Etonian. In full view of the assembled crowd, Diana ran her fingers through Philip's hair and pecked him on the cheek.

Dunne was twenty-eight years old and, according to a friend of the Princess, 'exactly her type'. His father was the Lord Lieutenant of Hereford and Worcester. His long-time girlfriend was the Honourable Katya Grenfell.

Dunne and Diana were soon spotted enjoying dinner at London's exclusive Menage à Trois restaurant together. Rumours quickly circulated that Diana was enjoying her own fling with Dunne. The rumour reached epic proportions when Dunne was photographed sitting by Di's side at a David Bowie concert that summer.

A couple of weeks later, it was revealed that Diana had spent the night at Dunne's family home in Herefordshire, Gatley Park. His parents were away for the weekend. Charles was alone at Highgrove. Days later, Philip was invited to be a member of the royal party – at Diana's specific request – at the Ascot races. He was photographed sharing a joke with Di in the winners' enclosure.

When news of the non-existent 'affair' hit the newspapers, Dunne received a telephone call from Prince Charles's private secretary. He was told, in no uncertain terms, to stop seeing Diana.

To this day, Diana's friends deny any affair. 'She was simply using Dunne to get back at Charles,' says one. 'He was never a serious contender. But he was fun, and he amused her greatly. She never did anything more than flirt with him.'

During an official trip to Madrid in April 1987, Diana made light of rumours of her alleged affairs. She quipped: 'When we first got married, we were everybody's idea of the world's most perfect couple. Now they say we are leading separate lives. The next thing is I'll start reading that I've got a black Catholic lover.'

It was a joke that fell flat, for, by this stage, dozens of rumours were circulating that the Princess did indeed have a few male friends of whom her husband did not approve.

Lady Colin Campbell says: 'Diana embarked on a string of flirtations with chaps from the right background. If, as she claims, she was not sleeping with them, she certainly gave all the right signals. She was trying to rattle her husband's chains. Unfortunately for her, he was beyond caring.'

In 1988, Diana met the Life Guards officer Major James Hewitt. He began giving the Princess and her sons riding lessons at Conermere Barracks near Windsor. Hewitt was young, sexy and fun, and again, 'exactly her type', according to friends.

Within a short space of time, William and Harry began treating Hewitt as an 'uncle' figure. Diana regularly took her sons to spend weekends at Hewitt's parents' home in Devon – something the Prince voiced his 'strongest objections' to.

In his book *Diana v Charles*, royal expert James Whitaker interviewed Hewitt's former personal valet Lance-Corporal Malcolm Leete at length.

Leete told him: 'One particular morning I got a call at 3.30am to say that Diana was coming to ride at seven. The usual happened, she arrived, gave Hewitt a peck on the cheek and said hello. But I remember from that day they became much more friendly towards each other. Princess Diana's visits changed from once a week to three days a week, regularly – Mondays, Wednesdays and Fridays.

'They always went into the Park, but this particular morning there was no lady-in-waiting. They went out by themselves. I thought it was quite peculiar. She would have had someone with her like a detective. They became closer and closer to each other.

'She started sending him presents, buying him things, always in a flash carrier bag – Harrods or other big stores. I never paid much attention to it all, but I always had to press the clothes before he wore them and that made me think that whenever he wore them, he was always going to see her.'

Leete told how one morning, the couple disappeared inside the indoor riding arena. Overcome by curiosity, he stood on a mounting block and looked through a window.

He said: 'The pair of them were in the corner. I wasn't quite sure what I saw, but they were certainly cuddling.'

Lady Colin Campbell says: 'It was far more than that.

Leete said he saw Hewitt put his hand up the Princess's blouse. Her blouse was outside her jodhpurs and his hand was clearly up inside it. There was nothing innocent about that encounter at all.'

When Hewitt was sent to serve in the Gulf, Diana wrote him long, intimate letters and watched TV newscasts of the unfolding war for hours on end. She would sign all her letters 'Dibbs', Hewitt's affectionate pet name for her. She also kept a photograph of him in her bedside locker drawer. She told a friend she was 'frantic about James' when he failed to telephone her one night as planned.

Hewitt's girlfriend, Emma Stewardson, also received letters. She later told the story of how he had spurned her affections in favour of the Princess to a Sunday newspaper. She told how Hewitt became 'infatuated' by the Princess and regularly arranged to meet her at weekends.

Pictures of the Princess with Hewitt soon appeared. In one, she throws her head back in laughter and thrusts her hips forward as she presents him with a polo trophy. In another, she leans provocatively back against a Land Rover while she talks to him.

Lady Colin says: 'The body language is there for all to see. This was a woman sending out *all* the signals.'

When Hewitt's girlfriend spilled the beans about the relationship, Diana was furious. She called a friend, saying: 'Why the hell can't I have my own life when no-one seems to care that my husband is having his way with the Rottweiler?'

In fact, Diana had not chosen her friend wisely. In March 1994, Hewitt was to betray her by selling his story of their 'intimate' friendship to the *Daily Express*. Just a few months earlier, the dashing Major caused further embarrassment to the Princess when he was cited in the divorce papers of TV weathergirl Sally Faber and her husband, the Conservative MP David Faber.

In the words of one former friend of Hewitt's: 'He always did have a problem keeping his flies done up in the company of pretty girls. He was a flash so-and-so, he loved the chase, if not the kill. God gave him a pretty smile, lovely eyes and a big dick, but not much up top in the old brains department.'

In fact, Hewitt's revelations about Diana were a big disappointment. Despite receiving a reported six-figure sum from the newspaper, Hewitt shied away from the facts, hinting at an affair with the Princess, but giving no details.

He said: 'When we first met, we started talking about riding and she told me how she had lost her nerve a long time ago and had always thought about trying to regain it. I said that I thought I could help and I started giving her lessons.

'Naturally, I had to clear our meetings through the army and we began riding together. It was all very surreptitious. Yes, we built up a rapport easily. I think she is great fun, with a good sense of humour. I found her interesting and intriguing. She is terribly loyal, affectionate and caring.

'Obviously, when I first met her, I was as unaware as anyone who wasn't a close friend how unhappy she was with her marriage. But as you become friendly with people, you get a feeling as to what upsets them and what makes them happy. Occasionally, she was upset, and occasionally she was happy. She wanted friendship.

'She was in a situation where it is very difficult to make friends. Remember, she was still developing and was interested in meeting a variety of people. She is the sort of person that, once she feels she has your trust, she opens up very quickly because she is a very giving person.

'I'd defy any man not to find her attractive.'

Talking about how the friendship developed to 'another level', he added: 'All the time, in my gut was the warning bell of the fear of getting too close.'

Hewitt was forced to lie low in Switzerland when his 'kiss and tell' appeared.

As one royal observer says: 'It was so, well, *tacky*. Honestly, one would have thought the Princess of Wales could have chosen a man with a little more class. One wonders how she felt when this chap she invested so much faith and hope in turns up the next minute plastered all over some downmarket newspaper selling his rather boring little stories about her. To be frank, it just confirmed what everyone thought – that the Princess had her head turned by a small amount of flattery from a chap who is clearly on the same intellectual level as her. It was a rather mucky affair. He just came out of it rather like a bimbo prepared to tell all for a nice fat cheque. Everyone refers to him as a *him*-bo now.'

At the same time as Hewitt's kiss-and-yawn was appearing, the *Sun* carried a far racier interview with Paula Campbell, a busty blonde telephone operator who readily admitted enjoying Hewitt's 'notable assets' while he was stationed in Germany.

She said: 'He used to call up and tell me he wanted to lick my body all over from the toes upwards and then he'd ask me to talk the same way to him.

'He arrived at the telephone exchange and there was just me on night duty. The switchboard office had a small room off it. It was about eight foot square. There was room in there to lie down. He just put into practice all we'd been talking about on the telephone.

'It was all rather disappointing. His talk was better than his performance. But he is big where it matters.

'He told me he had never slept with Princess Diana. He said they had a very special relationship, but I believe him when he says he never slept with her.

'But I don't think he could love anyone else except himself, not even the Princess of Wales.'

But back in 1988, when the Princess's friendship with Hewitt first became public, it was the breaking point for Prince Charles.

On 22 September 1988 the Prince flew to Balmoral.

For thirty-seven days, he did not see his wife. He spent his time painting, fishing and hunting. His only company were his old friends Lord and Lady Tryon – and Camilla. He and

Camilla happily spent days alone, away from the prying public gaze, walking through the heather and sharing their love of painting.

A friend of Camilla's says: 'Camilla spent a couple of weeks up there, then she returned home for a few days and then she flew back up to Scotland. The Prince was very depressed at the start of the trip. He told Camilla he was at "breaking point". He would only refer to Diana by this stage as "the mad woman".

'The Prince was fed up with everything. But mostly, he was fed up at his silly airhead wife and his miserable marriage. Camilla was seriously concerned by his unhappy mental state. She spent hours and hours talking to him. She consoled him and comforted him. Camilla felt an enormous amount of guilt at this time, because she had been the one who had been so forthright about Diana being the right girl for Charles. But it wasn't Camilla's fault. At first glance, Diana did appear to be the best on offer at the time Charles was looking for a bride. Charles felt he had done everything he could. But his pride made him feel there was always more he could do. He'd never failed in his life before, but slowly, it was dawning on him that he was failing in the most important things of all: his marriage and his family.

'Camilla never passed judgement. She was never particularly nasty about Diana. She was just a great, great friend, someone who would listen for hours and never get bored.'

Her greatest test came in June 1990, when the Prince broke his right arm badly in two places when he crashed from his pony during a polo match at Cirencester Park, Gloucestershire. The fall was so bad that spectators who were standing more than fifty yards away heard the bone snap.

An initial operation was unsuccessful. The Prince was moved to Nottingham General Hospital, where he spent three long weeks in his own room.

The recuperation was long and painful. He spent months recovering at Balmoral or Highgrove. His normally full diary of public engagements was empty, cancelled on the advice of his doctors.

Loyal Camilla hardly left his side. As the break took more time than expected to heal, Camilla buoyed his spirits. Camilla was given her own suite of rooms at Balmoral, adjoining the Prince's. She developed a close friendship with Sarah Key, the pretty Australian physiotherapist hired to help the Prince rebuild the strength in his arm.

According to one visitor who went to Balmoral during that time: 'Camilla did everything for the Prince. She would sit there for hours reading to him, she helped him with the exercises he was given to do, she would cut up his food and help him eat it. She comforted him when the pain was bad. She was devoted to him. She was always fussing around him. In the evening, they would sit in his private drawing room together for hours. Sometimes they would talk, other times they would listen to classical music. On other occasions, they would sit there in silence for ages. But it was never a painful silence. It was the silence of a couple so secure in the love they share that they do not need words to fill the gaps.'

Diana was furious that Charles did not wish to see her – preferring to be nursed by Camilla. Diana remained at Kensington Palace.

But seeing Diana was the last thing the Prince wanted. The accident gave him ample time to consider the state of his marriage. And he decided he could not stand it.

As he later told a friend: 'That time was bad for me. The fracture left me in permanent pain and I felt useless and helpless. There was nothing I could do to speed up the healing process. I wanted to get back to work. Camilla was an absolute rock.

'But what the accident did give me was more time to reflect on my life. And I decided it wasn't going the way I wanted it to.'

Charles was deeply troubled. For the first time, he told his mother he feared he 'could not stick out' the marriage.

Their most poignant meeting came over lunch at Balmoral

one day. The Queen tried to offer some wise advice. Her own marriage to Prince Philip had not been without difficulties. She knew Philip had enjoyed his own 'discreet liaisons' through the years.

She told her son: 'Divorce is out of the question. We must come to some arrangement with Diana. I am not asking you to give up Mrs Parker Bowles. As you know, I am extremely fond of her myself. But Diana must be kept in check. She is a flighty girl; who knows what she might do?'

The Queen wrote Diana a long letter. She invited the Princess to dine with her privately on her return to Buckingham Palace.

Recalling that dinner, Diana told a friend: 'The Queen stressed the importance of making the marriage work. She told me Charles was willing to give it another go. I promised I would do my best. But I insisted he end his friendship with Camilla. I remember the Queen looking at me over her glasses and saying: "Why are you so concerned about Camilla? All men have certain urges. Camilla is married, she is no threat to you. Try to put her out of your head. You have nothing to concern yourself with there, my dear." '

Diana realized at that moment that Camilla had more than one powerful ally inside the royal family.

Privately, the Queen confided to her aides that she feared Diana was 'a bolter' – someone who would bolt from the family, leaving them in turmoil if she could not get her own way.

Diana's chop-and-change past did nothing to allay those fears. Even as a teenager, Diana had had difficulty committing herself to anything.

After leaving her Swiss finishing school, she enrolled on a cordon bleu cookery course under teacher Elizabeth Russell, but lasted only ten weeks. Then she decided she fancied training as a dance teacher, so she signed up on a three-year teaching course with Madame Betty Vacani, who had taught the Queen and Princess Margaret to dance. A month later, Diana went on a skiing holiday – and never returned to the dancing school.

Madame Vacani says: 'She never gave a reason or an explanation, but I think she felt the course was too all-embracing. I imagine she thought teaching at a kindergarten would be less demanding.'

Diana began teaching at the Young England kindergarten, but only part-time. She said: 'I prefer only being a part-time worker. It leaves me free to do my own thing. I loathe being tied down by restrictions.'

But in 1988, Diana felt suffocated by restrictions.

Another death knell was sounded in the marriage during the terrible Klosters skiing tragedy on 10 March 1988. Diana, Charles, Fergie and Charles's friends Major Hugh Lindsay and Charles and Patti Palmer-Tomkinson were sharing a small, secluded chalet at Wolfgang, near Charles's favourite Swiss resort of Klosters.

One day, after a morning on the slopes, Di and Fergie returned to the chalet while the Prince and his party ventured further up the mountain to pursue their favourite off-piste skiing.

An hour later, the two women heard a helicopter fly overhead. Shortly afterwards, Charles's press secretary Philip Mackie entered the chalet stony-faced. He told them there had been a terrible accident. The Prince's party had been engulfed in an avalanche. He said no further details were known except that a male member of the party was dead.

A few minutes later, a clearly shaken and upset Prince Charles telephoned. Major Hugh Lindsay, a former equerry to the Queen, had been killed outright. Patti Palmer-Tomkinson had been revived by mouth-to-mouth resuscitation. She had suffered severe injuries and was, at that moment, undergoing a seven-hour operation at a local hospital to save her shattered legs.

Diana and Fergie packed Hugh's belongings into a suitcase. Prince Charles accompanied Patti to a nearby hospital. He stayed at the hospital late into the night until Patti left the operating theatre. He was by her side as she came around. He then paid a sombre last visit to see Hugh's body in the hospital morgue, where he spent more than twenty minutes alone in the room with his old friend, saying his final farewells.

The following day, the tearful royal party flew back to RAF Northolt. Diana comforted Hugh Lindsay's wife Sarah, a member of the Palace press office, who was six months pregnant.

Those close to Diana circulated the story that 'cold-hearted' Charles did not even want to return to England with his friend's body; that he suggested they were all over-reacting and should continue their skiing holiday.

In fact, nothing could be further from the truth. Charles was heartbroken by the tragedy. For the first month after the accident, he would called Sarah Lindsay on a daily basis. He still contacts her regularly to make sure she is doing well. A friend says: 'It was Charles, not Diana, who offered Sarah her greatest strength in her hour of need. He was a rock. He telephoned her constantly, he sorted out all the financial arrangements for the funeral. He did absolutely everything he could, and more, to help her. She will be forever grateful to the Prince for what he did for her in those dark days after Hugh's death.

'The Princess was there the day of the accident. She looked suitably miserable for the cameras at the airport. But she hardly went out of her way in the months to come. She probably telephoned Sarah once or twice. Charles was on the phone constantly.'

The accident also brought the Prince and the Palmer-Tomkinsons even closer together. Today, they are still among his closest circle of friends.

Lady Colin Campbell says: 'The Prince's circle of friends is small, elite and utterly devoted to him.

'They know the true character of the man and they all stick together through thick and thin. Charles was deeply affected by the loss of Hugh. He was totally supportive of Patti Palmer-Tomkinson as she recuperated. He visited her many times in hospital and again at home as she recovered. Far from wanting to stay on in the resort skiing, it was Charles who stayed up throughout the night making arrangements to fly the body and the rest of the party home. For Diana to try and cash in on that incident was shameful. Charles's friends never forgave her.'

At this time Diana was receiving treatment for her bulimia, now at a critical stage, from Dr Maurice Lipsedge, a world-renowned expert on eating disorders, at Guy's Hospital in London. The Princess would pay three one-hour visits to Dr Lipsedge's office each week. She was asked to fill out a special eating-diary, logging the high points and low points of each day and monitoring each morsel of food which passed her lips.

It was during this time that Diana is said to have confronted Camilla during the fortieth birthday party of Camilla's sister Annabel Elliot. According to one witness, Diana stormed up to Camilla and said: 'Why don't you just leave my husband alone?' Camilla turned on her heel and left the room. Charles followed closely behind.

A friend of Camilla's says: 'The incident only served to make Camilla even more contemptuous of Diana. Camilla has never spoken to the Princess since that day. Any pity or sympathy she may have had at the back of her mind for her had died. From that moment on, it was all-out war over the affections of the Prince. And it was pretty clear who was going to win.'

Diana Fights Back

Andrew Parker Bowles was admiring the fillies being paraded before him at Ascot. It was June 1992, and Andrew was now a brigadier with the illustrious title of Silver Stick in Waiting to the Queen. He was also in charge of the Army Veterinary Corps.

He and Camilla had been invited to Ascot as the personal guests of the Queen that year. His wife's affair with Charles was now so commonly known among their own circle that people rarely commented on it any more.

The Duke of Marlborough's younger brother, Lord Charles Spencer-Churchill, having enjoyed several glasses of champagne, caught sight of Andrew as he walked across the Royal Enclosure. Churchill called over to his friend: 'Ernest Simpson! Hey, Ernest Simpson! Why don't you come over here?'

Andrew's back stiffened. He of course fully condoned his wife's extra-marital affair, but to be mocked publicly and referred to in the same breath as the cuckolded husband Wallis Simpson had ditched half a century earlier to marry the Duke of Windsor, was something he would not tolerate.

In front of dozens of witnesses, he calmly turned around to face Churchill. 'Come over here,' he commanded. A rather shaky Churchill lurched across the paddock.

Andrew grasped him by the arm and thrust his face towards him. 'I don't *ever* want to hear you talk to me again like that, do you hear? NEVER!'

Spencer-Churchill himself told best-selling royal author Nigel Dempster in his book 'Behind Palace Doors': 'He was very, very angry indeed. He pummelled my right arm and shoulder extremely hard. The next day I was black and blue with bruises. I thought it was just a tease, a bit of a giggle. But Andrew didn't find it amusing at all.'

Spencer-Churchill added ominously: 'I told him, "Mark my words, it will end in tears. When you play around with the monarchy, you play around with fire."'

A few months later, Parker Bowles was sitting in his favourite chair at his gentleman's club, Whites in St James. Lord Soames, one of Andrew's oldest friends and the father of Andrew's former 'flame' Charlotte Hambro, sat down beside him and proceeded loudly to chastize him for his 'ungentlemanly' behaviour.

Parker Bowles was so upset by the old man's criticism that he immediately stood up and left the club. As he walked towards the exit, he overheard a fellow club member whisper: 'There goes the finest man in Britain. He is so loyal to the Crown that he is prepared to lay down his wife for the sake of his country.'

Although he was happy with his unconventional marriage, these snide jibes wounded him deeply.

At home, the Parker Bowles marriage was much as it had been for years. Camilla was still deeply devoted to both the Prince and her husband. She loyally ran her own household – and the Prince's household at Highgrove. She and her husband enjoyed a passionate, if volatile, relationship.

A family member says: 'Camilla and Andrew have always loved each other very deeply. They have an enormously strong marriage, despite the opinion of others. The marriage is an open one; they both have other partners, but when they are together they are very happy with each other's company. They still are today, despite all the chaos and upset of the past few years.

'Camilla and Andrew have an equal partnership. She gives as good as she gets. I have heard them have the most almighty rows about the silliest things, real stand-up screamers. They are just a very passionate couple. But the rows never simmer on for long. And they both seem perfectly content with their lives. Andrew truly admires the Prince of Wales. As a man who enjoyed his own freedom within marriage, he always approved of his wife's friendship.'

Within the royal family itself, the ranks were divided. Princess Anne, who never liked Diana, sided with her brother. She steadfastly refused even to talk to the Princess. She believed some of the negative stories about Charles which were appearing in the newspapers had been planted by Diana's allies.

Diana had built up her own circle of trusted friends who would call sympathetic reporters almost daily with new tales of the Princess's anguish – and fresh sordid stories about Charles's heartlessness.

One prominent Fleet Street royal watcher says: 'When the Princess came on the scene it was the first time any of us began getting inside scoops from a source within the royal family itself. Of course, none of the boys in the pack were complaining. We were all sympathetic to Diana. Her side did all the talking. You never got a peep out of Charles's cronies. They still simply couldn't bring themselves to break their vow of silence. But Diana's lot were far more open. Diana had wooed the press. She knew the full value of the tabloids in getting her story across to the people. And she milked the tabloids for everything they had.

'If there was even the slightest chance of getting on to the front pages, Diana could turn a routine visit to a children's hospital into a front-page story simply by giving a great quote. She learned that early on. As the marriage started crumbling, she started consolidating her public position through the newspaper columns. She wanted to make sure that if, and when, the walls came tumbling down, she would emerge as the victim in the whole sorry saga.

'The phone would go at all times of the day and night. The tipsters were all Diana's friends and their information would be spot on.'

On one memorable occasion, one of Diana's tipsters told photographers the Prince was enjoying a 'romantic boat trip with a mystery blonde'. It was enough to send Fleet Street's photographers into a feeding frenzy. When the pack arrived at the location, they managed to get several good pictures of a relaxed and unsuspecting Charles, aboard a small dingy with his 'mystery blonde': Camilla Parker Bowles.

On another occasion, Diana's friends tipped off the press that Camilla was spending the weekend at the Queen Mother's Deeside Lodge with the Prince. After a three-day stake-out, the photographers got their picture – of Charles leaving the house with Camilla a few steps behind. What no-one mentioned was that a few paces behind Camilla was her husband.

In May 1988, when Charles was on another painting holiday in Italy, he was informed on the flight out that Prince Harry had been taken to hospital for an emergency hernia operation. He immediately wanted to fly to his son's side, but Diana said no.

She told him it 'was only a little op' and that there was 'absolutely no need' for him to return. Charles checked in with the hospital every hour from then on, so great was his concern for his son.

The next day's headlines said it all. Diana's informants painted the Prince as a cold-hearted father who ignored his son's illness while 'saint' Diana had spent the night sitting on a hard chair at the end of Harry's hospital bed at Great Ormond Street Children's Hospital in London.

Later, in June 1991, when Prince William was acciden-tally hit by a fellow pupil swinging a golf club at Ludgrove School, it was again Diana who scored the 'good parenting' points. When the accident occurred, Diana was having lunch at San Lorenzo and Charles was at home at Highgrove.

The pair both raced to the Royal Berkshire Hospital in Reading where William was undergoing X-rays. When a compressed fracture of the skull was discovered, the child was rushed to Great Ormond Street Hospital.

Later that day, the Prince was due to attend a charity gala performance of the opera *Tosca* at Covent Garden. It was an important meeting of European and British ministers. The event had already been postponed once because of the Prince's broken arm.

William's surgeons told Charles it would be 'fine' for him to go. But Prince Charles insisted on carrying a pager so he could be alerted immediately if there was any worsening of his son's condition.

Diana, meanwhile, talked to her 'friendly' journalists. She told them that while she had slept in a small chair at the end of William's bed all night, hard-hearted Charles had gallivanted around town.

The following morning's headlines said it all. WHAT SORT OF DAD ARE YOU? asked *The Sun*.

A former staff member at Great Ormond Street says: 'The Princess asked for all that morning's newspapers to be delivered to William's room. She spent ages reading through them. She seemed quite pleased at the favourable press coverage she had received.'

Charles – and the rest of his family – were becoming increasingly angry at the continuous smear campaign against him. First, it was unfair. Second, it was untrue.

As one former royal aide says: 'The constant diet of negative stories about the Prince which appeared in the press greatly wounded him. He is someone who takes his position in life and his family very seriously. But Diana was much cleverer than him at media manipulation. It took the Prince years before he could catch up. His problem was that he'd been brought up to believe that *anything* was better than airing one's dirty laundry in public. Now he had this wife who was washing her smalls in public on a daily basis. It infuriated and maddened him.'

Another woman close to the Prince says: 'Diana proved herself to be extraordinarily difficult. Her behaviour did, and continues to endanger the future of her marriage, the monarchy and the country itself. Many people who got to know her during her marriage to HRH have come to the conclusion she is very unpleasant. It is not in the Prince's nature to answer back. He has not been brought up like that. There was always an intellectual gap between them, but Diana was the one who went running to the press.

'Right from the start, it was the Prince who worked hard to try and make that marriage work. He hired all manner of psychiatrists and eating-disorder doctors to try and help his wife. But she always wanted more. What she really wanted was to take over. She loved being the Princess of Wales, she loved all the attention and the glory. But she wanted to be the Princess of Wales without the Prince of Wales. And that is an utterly ridiculous notion. But Diana believed her own press. She thought she was above and beyond anyone else in the family. Newspaper polls were constantly deeming her the most popular royal. She thought she could get away with anything.'

Princess Anne once confronted Diana about the daily diet of royal tittle-tattle which was appearing. 'It is astonishing,' she told Diana during one of Anne's rare visits to Kensington Palace. 'Before you joined, there were hardly any leaks. Now the ship is so full of holes, it's no wonder that it's sinking.'

Diana looked back at her, dumbstruck. 'I wouldn't go telling too many tall tales if I were you,' Anne added. 'They might just come back to haunt you one day.'

Princess Anne had never had anything in common with Diana. She despised Diana's constant dieting and her cover-girl image. Anne, who had spent years rebuilding her reputation into a woman now considered Britain's most hard-working royal, felt put out of place when Diana came along and stole her thunder simply by wearing a new outfit or flaunting her trim body in a bikini at the beach.

Anne was overhead saying: 'She's nothing more than a horse, a clothes horse. If she were a real horse, I might like her more. At least horses have a brain.'

One another occasion, Anne observed that Diana's dresser in the early days of her marriage, Evelyn Dagley, had eight O level passes. Diana had none. It was a passing comment made flippantly at dinner, in full earshot of the Princess of Wales. The jibe did not go unnoticed.

Diana was later to say: 'She never liked me. She was jealous.'

Anne purposely did all she could to avoid meeting Diana. On state occasions, she would stand as far away from the Princess as she could, literally putting distance between herself and Diana.

In private, the Princess spent most of her time at Gatcombe Park, her estate in Gloucestershire. Once, when Diana was due to arrive to pick up Prince William – who had spent the day at a birthday party at Gatcombe for Anne's daughter Zara – Anne saddled up her horse and rode off, returning only later that night when the Princess had come and gone.

A handful of Charles's friends decided, unilaterally, to fight back on his behalf.

One says: 'Diana's manipulation of the media was so unfair and so unbalanced it was getting ridiculous. The Prince is not as photogenic as she is, but he is the future king and he still has a massive groundswell of support in the country.

'It is no coincidence that we see pictures of Princess Diana and the boys at Alton Towers and Thorpe Park. *She* is the one who makes sure the photographers know where she will be. *She* is the one with the eye for the main photo opportunity. Prince Charles has always taken the boys to school, and he is constantly taking them on outings. He spends hours fishing, cycling and walking with them. But you hardly ever see a picture of it because it is not his style to cash in on his children to boost his public image. In fact, not only is it not in his nature to push the boys forward, the exact opposite is true. The Prince wants to shield the children. He doesn't want them to constantly be in the public eye. The constant stream of pictures of them being squired around by their mother upsets him.

'Several of us made the decision that, whether he liked it or not, we simply had to counter this relentless onslaught in the media that he was being subjected to on an almost daily basis by Diana.'

The Princess's thirtieth birthday party provided Charles's friends with their first chance to strike back publicly.

Diana had 'let it be known' to her circle of press informants that Charles was so aloof and uncaring that he could not be bothered to attend her birthday celebrations. In fact, for several months, the Prince had been begging Diana to allow him to throw a lavish party in her honour at Highgrove.

'I don't want to go to any party you might organize for me,' she had said. 'I'd rather be on my own.'

Charles had insisted he would foot the bill and invite only her friends, not his, but 'she rejected him out of hand', according to a close friend of the Prince.

This story was leaked to the press by someone very close to the Prince. The subsequent story, splashed all over the front page of *The Sun* under the headline: DI DON'T WANT TO DANCE, enraged the Princess.

Like a petulant child who had failed to get her own way, she stamped her foot and shouted: 'He can't do this! He can't do this to *me*!"

In the end, Diana spent the day alone with Prince Harry, joining her sister Jane in the evening for a quiet dinner. Diana 'leaked' her own quote-of-the-day to the press, telling a friend to instruct Fleet Street's finest that she 'had spent the evening quietly at home, with the only man in my life – Prince Harry'.

The Prince's friend said: 'She preferred to sit around being bored and miserable than to give her husband even the slightest joy at organizing a party for her. It was small-minded and petty.

Charles was upset, but it said more about Diana than anything else. She was prepared to bite off her nose to spite her face.'

While Charles's friends fought back, he found an enemy within his own camp, in the shape of his father. Prince Philip was at war with everyone. He viewed Diana as a 'silly little girl' but he was furious at Charles for not taking a firmer stand against her.

Philip and Charles had never enjoyed a close relationship. From childhood, Philip had been determined that his eldest son should be 'a man's man'. It was Philip who insisted Charles went to his old school, Gordonstoun, a rigidly tough boarding school in Scotland. Charles loathed the cold-shower mentality of the place and still refers to it as 'an institution rather than a school'.

It was Philip who decided, when Charles was barely a teenager, that his son should follow his footsteps into the Royal Navy. It has always been Philip who has drummed into Charles the importance of his future position in life, as head of the British monarchy and of the Church of England.

A former equerry says: 'Philip was the one who was forcing Charles to get married. Charles would happily have stayed a bachelor all his life. But Philip kept insisting he should get married and would goad Charles that people would begin to think he was a queer if he didn't hurry up and walk down the aisle. Philip has always ruled his son with a rod of iron. Privately, Charles is still frightened of his father. When Philip added his voice to the growing call for Charles to marry Di, the Prince felt he had no doors left open to run through.

'The whole philosophy that Philip drummed into Charles's head was to put duty and the Crown before everything else. Philip has spent *his* life putting duty and the Crown before everything else. He found it very difficult, in the early days of his marriage to the Queen, to take a back seat and allow her to be centre stage. But he always remembered his sense of duty. Philip's deep-rooted loyalty has never wavered.

'Philip was always shockingly blunt to Charles, who was always too sensitive for the old man's liking.

'Prince Philip knew what it was like to put up and shut up. He'd done it all his life. And he understood Charles's need to take a mistress. But he was enraged that Charles and Camilla were being openly discussed in the newspapers.'

For several months, Philip tried to broach the subject of his son's affair with Camilla. He even wrote Charles several letters, expressing his 'fears' that his personal life was becoming 'increasingly complicated'. But each time Philip tried to talk to his son, Charles would change the subject or avoid it altogether.

Finally, Philip cornered Charles on a shooting field at Sandringham. According to witnesses the conversation went along the following lines: 'What the hell is going on?' the older man enquired. 'The whole bloody court is talking about you and Camilla. You're playing with fire. I don't care if you want to have a shag on the side, but for God's sake, deal with Diana. That's your problem. You always avoid problems until they become so enormous they overwhelm you. You have *got* to stand up and be a man.'

Charles, red-faced with annoyance, tried to turn away.

Philip physically grabbed him by the arm. 'You are *not* going to walk away this time,' he shouted.

Charles began to try and explain his predicament: 'Diana is impossible. We have absolutely nothing in common. I would dearly love to get out. Why the hell did no-one do anything to stop me getting into this situation in the first place?' he exploded.

Philip was furious. To him, it was just his weak son trying to make yet more excuses. He shook Charles by the arm: 'For God's sake, grow up,' he yelled.

Then Philip jumped into his Land Rover and drove off.

It was the last conversation between the two for more than four months.

A former equerry says: 'From that moment on, every time Charles walked into a room, Philip would walk out.'

Charles's only ally was the Queen Mother. He began spending a considerable amount of time with her, both at her London home, Clarence House, and at her Scottish estate, Birkinhall.

An insider says: 'Charles has always been closer to his grandmother than he has to his parents. When Camilla was not around, he would talk to the Queen Mother. She tried to intercede in the growing feud between Charles and Diana. She even tried to play matchmaker by inviting them both to Clarence House one Friday evening. But Diana could not face the old lady. She always felt terribly uncomfortable around the Queen Mum. She cried off at the last minute, claiming she had a migraine.'

Nothing, it appeared, was going to happen to prevent the inevitable. The fairy-tale marriage was so badly damaged that no-one and nothing could save it.

Prince Charles himself sought help and guidance from a professional. He began visiting the officers of one of Britain's top psychotherapists, Dr Allan McGlashan. The Prince would arrive at the doctor's Sloane Street offices at 6.30pm at least once a week during this difficult time. Dr McGlashan proved 'enormously helpful' to the Prince, according to a friend.

She says: 'They would discuss Diana's eating disorders and the best ways for the Prince to react to and deal with those. The Prince fundamentally blames all the problems in his marriage on the bulimia and on deep-rooted, long-term psychological problems he believes Diana has suffered from since childhood.'

The Queen herself tried to smooth the waters. She would often personally call Diana to try and resolve problems. One such problem occurred when Diana's beloved father Johnnie Spencer died on 29 March 1992.

The couple were in Lech, Austria, on a skiing holiday. The year before, Charles had taken a solo skiing trip and had been widely criticized for not taking Diana and the boys. Buckingham Palace had decreed that this year they should, for all intents and purposes, put up the pretence of playing Happy Families.

Both Charles and Diana had agreed to go on the holiday for the sake of their sons. The announcement that Charles was to accompany his family on their skiing trip was made at the last minute. He had planned to spend the week at Balmoral – with Camilla. But two days before Diana and the

Princes flew to stay at the Arlberg Hotel in Lech, Charles bowed to the wishes of the Palace and announced he would go too.

But the couple barely spoke to each other in private. Charles flew into Lech separately and very publicly greeted his two sons outside the hotel. It was later revealed that Diana had been banned from the photocall for the world's media.

A Palace insider said: 'The Prince wasn't wild about having his picture taken with the boys, but he agreed to do it on the advice of his staff. They told him he simply had to start redressing the balance. He had to start projecting himself in a positive light. Reluctantly, he agreed.'

The following day, Charles had an impromptu snowball fight with his sons in full view of the Schneiderhof Hotel, where most of the photographers and reporters were staying. The candid and happy snaps were published all over the papers the next day. Charles, who had for so long allowed Diana to manipulate the media, was fighting back. And Diana was livid.

When the news came that Spencer had died, Diana instantly packed her bags. She intended to fly home, leaving her husband and sons behind. A specially-ordered Queen's Flight was despatched to bring her home.

But the Palace was adamant it would look terrible if Charles was seen to be ignoring his wife in her hour of need.

'Why are they bothering about him ignoring me now?' said a grim Diana. 'He's been ignoring me for years already.'

Finally, a call was put in to the Queen, who was at Windsor Castle. She telephoned Diana directly, and spoke to the upset Princess for more than twenty minutes. When the call ended, Diana agreed, reluctantly, to bow to her mother-in-law's wishes and allow Charles to travel back with her.

The couple did not exchange a single word on the plane. A witness said: 'Charles, at one stage, tried to put his hand on her arm, but she brushed it away.'

When the plane touched down, Diana scored her own publicity coup. Despite professing to be devastated by her father's death, she refused her husband's offer to carry her suitcases off the plane at RAF Northolt. The subsequent photographs and stories condemned the Prince for allowing Diana to struggle with her own bags in her darkest hour of grief.

But one of Charles's aides says: 'It simply wasn't like that at all. It was so unfair what she did that day. The Prince offered to carry her bags, but she had insisted on carrying them herself. It seemed astonishing to all of us that day that Diana was still out to score brownie points.'

The pair travelled to Kensington Palace together. Later that night, Charles drove down to Highgrove to see Camilla. They remained together throughout the next forty-eight hours.

A former staff member at Highgrove says: 'They barely emerged. The Prince and Camilla locked themselves away for hours. There was clearly something serious going on. When anyone entered his private living room to bring in food or drink, they would be talking about Diana and the problem she had become. But they would become quiet when the servants entered. Both of them have too much style to wash their dirty linen in public.'

The Prince did fly to Northamptonshire for the funeral on 1 April aboard a red Wessex helicopter of the Queen's Flight. But he left before the cremation service. His aides said he had 'prior, important business' to attend to. He actually went to meet Camilla.

By this stage, Charles was taking the most extraordinary risks to be with the woman he loved. Most Friday afternoons, he would drive down from London in his gleaming Aston Martin and leave the M4 motorway by Exit 17. On the drive down, he would be followed by a police back-up car containing two sergeants from the royal protection squad. His own personal protection officer would follow on behind.

The Prince believed his security detail thought he was leaving the motorway to take a back-road route to Highgrove; he would instruct the protection officers to leave him at the motorway exit and allow him to continue alone.

But his affair with Camilla was known to all of those close to the royal circle.

One former aide says: 'The Prince, of course, never knew we'd twigged what was going on. He would tell us he wished to make the final short drive home alone and would only allow his personal protection officer to follow him from Exit 17 onwards. That officer would then follow him to the gates of Camilla's home and would wait there. Sometimes he would wait for an hour, sometimes two – sometimes he would sit in his car at the gates throughout the night.

'Of course we all knew what was going on. As the Prince would drive off, we'd all sing in unison, "We know where you're going!"'

On other occasions, when Charles was staying at Highgrove, he would drive an unmarked Ford estate car the twelve miles between his estate and Camilla's home, Middlewick House.

An estate worker says: 'It was a fairly scruffy car, dirty on the inside from carrying machinery and dogs, and it smelled to high heaven. But Charles used it because it offered him anonymity.

'I remember talking to a friend over at Middlewick and they told me the first time the car appeared in the driveway, they were contemplating towing it away because it was so filthy. Then they were told it was the Prince's vehicle, which surprised everyone, since they were all used to seeing his Aston Martin parked outside Mrs Parker Bowles's house. But the Ford was what he preferred to use. There were often reporters hanging around outside both places. I guess the Prince believed they would never think to keep an eye out for him in a scruffy old car.

'The car was so filthy that we cleaned it up one day before the Prince arrived that Friday night. When he saw it had been washed, he wasn't too happy. He left instructions that it was to remain dirty. He preferred it that way because it didn't draw attention to itself – or him. But everyone knew what was going on.

'It was common knowledge to everyone even remotely attached to the royal family that the marriage of Charles and Diana was over.

'And it was common knowledge that Charles was very much in love with Camilla. You only had to look at his eyes when they were together to tell he was besotted with her.

'The only people who didn't know were the British public. And it was only a matter of time before they found out.'

The Devil
and the
Deep Blue Sea

Princess Diana first demanded a separation from her husband as early as November 1989. Fed up with 'living a lie', as she would later tell friends, she confronted Charles in his study at Kensington Palace and told him she wanted out of the marriage.

He dismissed her demands as 'ridiculous'.

He told her: 'There is absolutely no way a separation would be acceptable either to me, my family or the palace. If you find me intolerable, you do not have to see me. But the marriage remains. I shall never, ever allow a separation to occur.'

For Charles knew that no matter how bad the marriage was, any separation would spark a constitutional crisis on a level with the devastating crisis which had rocked the monarchy some fifty years earlier when his great-uncle Edward VIII had abdicated the Crown for the love of American divorcee Wallis Simpson.

To those inside the royal household, history could not be

allowed to repeat itself in such a damning way. The House of Windsor had survived one crisis – it could not survive another.

Edward VIII became king on the death of his father George V in January 1936. Within twelve months, he had created the biggest scandal in British history and was banished to live out the rest of his days in exile – all for the love of a woman.

The comparisons between Edward and Mrs Simpson and Charles and Camilla are almost eerie. Both were long-time love affairs. Both involved strong women who captivated the heir to the throne. Both were affairs which remained secret from the British public for years – while they were openly gossiped about and discussed in aristocratic circles. Both caused a scandal which rocked the monarchy to its foundations when they first burst into the public arena.

One ended with the then monarch renouncing the throne and living out his days in a lonely, self-imposed exile with the woman he loved, but who was never accepted or embraced by the royal family. The other involved a woman who *had* been embraced by the royal family – but who could never be allowed to marry the man she loved.

History could not be allowed to repeat itself.

The affair of Edward and Wallis Simpson began in 1931 when both were invited to a house party hosted by the society 'grande dame' Thelma, Viscountess Furness. According to one royal biographer, 'Wallis set her sights on Edward immediately. She knew what she wanted, and that was the ultimate prize. Nothing was going to stop her.'

She was totally unsuitable as a partner for the future king. Divorced from her first husband, a US naval officer Earl Winfield Spencer, she was separated from her second husband Ernest Simpson when she met Edward.

From their very first meeting, she captivated Edward. In his personal ledger, Edward was to write shortly after their affair began in June 1931: 'She is the most intriguing, fascinating, unpredictable creature I have ever met. I fear I am falling . . .'

The similarities between Wallis and Camilla are uncanny.

Neither was a raving beauty in the conventional sense, but both had an earthy quality which captured the heart of the heir to the throne. Wallis was strong, confident and self-assured, just like Camilla. According to friends, Wallis 'could always muster a turn of phrase to banish Edward's dark clouds of depression and make him feel loved, wanted and needed' – the same qualities which attracted Charles to Camilla. Both have been described with words like 'rock-solid, trustworthy, loyal'.

Between Charles and his great-uncle too, there were similarities. Both were sensitive men, craving affection after a childhood of loneliness.

Edward told a previous mistress, Freda Dudley Ward, 'In my childhood I never ever knew love. There were servants who seemed to love me but I could never forget it might be because I was heir to the throne. I never knew real affection from my own parents.'

Charles too would say: 'Growing up, I never knew the comforts of a loving family environment. My nannies seemed to love me, but I did not know if it was because of who I was or who I would become.'

Like Camilla, Wallis soon became the 'accepted' mistress. She played hostess at Edward's private home, Fort Belvedere, near Ascot. She would sit at the head of his table and would refer to Edward quite openly as 'my boy'.

In his book *Fall of the House of Windsor*, author Nigel Blundell gave the account of a guest who attended a dinner party at Belvedere: 'It was a very lively evening with a great deal of conversation and jollity. The party went on until around 2am. As a house guest, I retired to my bedroom. I do know that night Edward went to Wallis's room. Those of us who knew him well enough could see that he, and all of us, were heading for trouble. The man whom I admired so much was going to destroy his great heritage. He was blinded and astounded by Wallis and nothing could move him from the path he was taking. He believed, in his distorted thought, that he could make everything work out in a way that would suit everyone, that he could take Mrs Simpson as his wife and she would sit beside him when he became king. That was how the infatuation with her had taken over his thoughts. I think sometimes he did allow himself to consider the worst, that he would be prevented from marrying her. And I think in those moments, he had decided long before the abdication that he would quit his royal life for her. Sad, but true.'

Yet while London society was abuzz with talk of Edward's 'inappropriate' affair, the British public knew nothing of the growing scandal. The British papers studiously avoided any mention of the affair – only announcing it like a bombshell just days before the abdication.

The British public felt cheated and conned when they learned the devastating truth. As one newspaper editor of the time said: 'They had the wool pulled over their eyes. The American press and the European press had been writing about the affair between Edward and Mrs Simpson for years. But the British public knew nothing of it. When they found out they had been deceived, the public outcry was enormous. Edward was personally hugely popular. The public outcry on his abdication was unprecedented.'

Edward and Wallis would openly attend parties around London, she lavishly dressed in the latest fashions, dripping with jewels. Like Camilla and Charles half a century later, they seemed oblivious to the constant criticism of their relationship from within their own circle.

Edward's mother, Queen Mary, begged her son to 'rid yourself of that woman for the sake of the country – and the Crown'.

Like Charles all those years later, Edward replied: 'I cannot do so, Mama. She is the woman I love.'

In September 1935, Edward and Wallis holidayed in Europe. It was then that Edward made the decision to renounce the throne. He was implored to change his mind by the Prime Minister of the day, Stanley Baldwin, and by his own family – but his mind was made up.

'I cannot live without the woman I love,' he would say, over and over again.

But in the 1930s, the idea of a twice-divorced American on the throne of England as the country faced up to war was unthinkable. The crisis built up over a period of months. Finally, the decision was taken. On 10 December 1936, Edward signed the abdication papers and George VI, the present Queen's father, was announced as the next king.

In an emotion-packed radio broadcast the next day, the nation listened in stunned silence as Edward revealed the true reason he had placed the Crown and the country in crisis. He said: 'It is impossible to carry the heavy burden of responsibility and discharge my duties as king as I would wish to do without the help and support of the woman I love.'

Two days later, Edward went into exile in France. On 3 June 1937, he married Wallis at their new home, the Chateau Le Cande outside Paris. The royal family allowed them to use the courtesy title of the Duke and Duchess of Windsor, but always denied Wallis her greatest dream – to have the honour of being addressed as Your Royal Highness.

Only on his death on 28 May 1972 was the Duke of Windsor accepted back by his family. The Queen arranged for his body to be flown back to London and then on to the royal graveyard at Frogmore in Windsor Great Park for burial.

For the remainder of her days, Wallis remained in France. When she died on 2 April, 1986, her body was flown back to Frogmore, to rest beside the man who had paid the ultimate price for loving her. Her simple headstone reads: 'Wallis: Duchess of Windsor, 1896-1986'. Even in death, the royal family denied her that which she most craved: the letters HRH.

To the present royal family, the abdication crisis has always been regarded as a story of how one man's selfishness and weakness almost destroyed the House of Windsor. The present Queen Mother loathed Wallis for causing a situation which meant her 'beloved Bertie' was forced to take the Crown, a position she believed his poor health and nervous disposition made him unsuitable for. When he died early, aged just fifty-four, she blamed 'that terrible woman' for placing him under a burden which wrecked his health. Even today, the

Queen Mother never refers to Wallis by name. On the rare occasions the abdication crisis is referred to in the royal household, Mrs Simpson is simply 'that dreadful woman'.

When the crisis between Camilla, Charles and Diana became evident, Elizabeth, the Queen Mother, said curtly: 'History will not be allowed to repeat itself. Absolutely not. Never, *never*, NEVER!'

But, by 1989, history *was* repeating itself.

Charles was to tell friends he was haunted by one particular statement which reverberated down through the years.

Sir Alan Lascalles, an adviser to Edward VIII, told the King at the height of the abdication crisis: 'Sir, you can have the throne, or you can have the woman. You cannot have both.'

Prince Charles was to confide to his closest circle of friends: 'That statement went round and round my head. I was in the same damnable situation. And I did not know what to do.

'I was trapped between the devil and the deep blue sea.'

After Diana had made her first demand for a separation, Charles informed his mother. The Queen summoned Diana and the Prince to a private lunch at Buckingham Palace. She implored them to try and make their marriage work, at least in the eyes of the public.

According to Palace insiders, Diana listened as the Queen stressed the importance of maintaining 'an outward sense of propriety' for the sake of the Crown. At the end of the meeting, Diana said calmly: 'I know where my duty lies.' But while Diana outwardly agreed to the Queen's demands, inwardly she was already plotting her escape.

Diana was further outraged when, in June 1992, at the height of speculation about the state of her marriage, Camilla was invited to the Queen's Cup polo match at Smith's Lawn in Windsor Great Park. She was a personal guest of the Queen and was warmly welcomed by Her Majesty in the royal box.

With typical humour, Camilla loyally wore a two-piece

Prince of Wales check suit.

A fellow guest says: 'Camilla made a joke that it was the only suit she had clean that day, but the irony wasn't lost on anyone. Camilla's always had a very dry wit. That suit was her way of making a silent statement. The Princess of Wales was furious.'

It was a public declaration of the Queen's continuing support for Camilla – and a public rebuke for Diana. The wind of change was blowing against the Princess.

Lady Colin Campbell says: 'Diana knew she needed something so devastating that it would give her the clout and power to demand anything of the family. She was firmly ostracized by this stage and she knew she needed a powerful weapon on her side.

'She knew that no-one inside the royal inner circle would knowingly do anything to harm the Crown.

'So she conned a top security adviser. She told the man she wanted to *save* her marriage to the Prince, but that she needed some proof of his affair with Camilla in order to do so. Diana played her finest little-girl act. The whole idea, she said, was to trap Charles on the phone to Camilla and then use that to force him into giving Camilla up.

'Of course, the master plan was to entrap Charles and use any taped evidence to blackmail him into meeting her every demand.

'The security adviser used a call-tracking device which was locked on to Charles's mobile phone.'

The notorious Camillagate conversation was recorded on 17 December 1989. The conversation, which is examined in detail later in this book, was the bombshell Diana needed.

She arranged to have the conversation broadcast repeatedly over a mobile phone line. It was a blatant act of 'treason' by Diana which was later to backfire horribly. The conversation *was* picked up and recorded by a member of the public. But it was to remain private and unpublished for another two years.

Diana reneged on her promise to use the tape to save her

marriage – in fact, she wanted to use it to sabotage what was left of the marriage.

Days later, Diana went to see her husband again.

A source close to the Prince says: 'She walked into his office cool as anything and said: "I have been sent this tape. It proves you and Camilla are having an affair. I want a separation – *now*!"

'Charles told her what he had told her a few weeks earlier, that a separation between a Prince and Princess of Wales was "unthinkable". He refused to give in to her demands. He ridiculed her threats as "the rantings of a deranged mind".'

But although the Prince believed his wife was calling his bluff, he informed his private secretary and his other closest advisers. They took the news of the secret tape far more seriously. For they knew Diana, unstable and angry, would stop at nothing to win what was now viewed as her full-scale war, not only against her husband – but against the entire royal family.

They decided to fight fire with fire.

They knew all about Diana's own 'liaisons' outside the marriage. By this stage, it was common knowledge at the Palace that she was enjoying an intimate friendship with the used-car salesman James Gilbey.

When Diana arrived to spend Christmas at Sandringham just two days before Christmas Day, she had no idea that *her* private phone inside her bedroom was being tapped.

The Palace did not have to wait long to get exactly what they wanted. On New Year's Eve, Diana and Gilbey duly provided Charles's side with the infamous 'Squidgey' tape.

Telephone Sex

It was the bombshell which exploded the myth of 'the perfect Princess'.

'And so, darling, what other lows today?' asks James Gilbey.

The unmistakable voice of the Princess of Wales replies: 'I was very bad at lunch. And I nearly started blubbing. I just felt really sad and empty and I thought: "Bloody hell, after all I've done for that fucking family."'

The infamous 'Squidgey' tapes had been sitting in the safe at *The Sun*'s offices in Wapping for more than two years. The sensational recording had been made by amateur radio buff Cyril Reenan at his home in Abingdon, Oxfordshire, during the New Year of 1990. A £900 scanner on the roof of his house had picked up the conversation which had been secretly recorded and broadcast by Prince Charles's aides.

Reenan, a highly respectable retired bank manager, instantly recognizing the value and importance of what he had overheard, turned the tapes over to *The Sun*. The paper knew it had a ticking timebomb which would explode the fairy-tale image of the woman regularly voted the most popular royal by its readers.

During the rambling, rather cringe-making twenty-three-minute conversation, Gilbey calls Diana 'darling' fifty-three times. He calls her 'Squidgey' fourteen times. She gushes and blows kisses down the phone to him. They talk about masturbation and her fears of getting pregnant.

In one memorable exchange, Gilbey says: 'Oh Squidgey, I love you, love you, love you, love you,' to which she replies: 'You are the nicest person in the whole wide world.'

In fact, within ten days of receiving the tapes in 1990, *The Sun* sent a reporter to Gilbey's London flat in Lennox Gardens, near Kensington Palace. When the reporter asked him directly about the 'Squidgey' tape and repeated a few of the choice phrases from the tape, his mouth fell open and he turned white.

'He just stood there looking stunned,' says a witness. 'He knew the game was up. He didn't say a word. Once he'd got his act together he just ran into his car and drove off at high speed. It was pretty obvious he knew we had him bang to rights.' To this day Gilbey has steadfastly refused to comment on the tapes.

The decision was taken that the tapes could not be published at the time, because, according to one top executive at the paper: 'We knew the tapes could cause enormous damage to the Princess of Wales and the entire royal family. And we were not prepared to do that. We had the tapes checked out and authenticated, but we did not publish them. To be frank, we wondered whether they would ever be made public. They were simply devastating. The idea that the Princess of Wales would be talking so intimately to a man other than her husband, a man who repeatedly whispered that he loved her and was so relaxed with her that he was calling her "Squidgey" was a bombshell which could possibly have destroyed Diana's image for ever.'

But, by the summer of 1992, the royal family seemed intent on destroying itself. Princess Anne was divorced and embroiled in a new love affair with Commander Timothy Laurence. Fergie was estranged from Prince Andrew and the infamous 'toe-sucking' pictures of her in the south of France with her 'financial adviser' Johnny Bryan had just been splashed all over the newspapers. Prince Edward, for his part, was making headline news by declaring: 'I'm not gay!' in response to a question which was not even asked. The marriage of Charles and Diana was clearly a sham – and both sides had been regularly 'informing' on each other to their favourite Fleet Street contacts for years. Diana had openly co-operated with author Andrew Morton on his devastating exposé of her unhappy marriage, *Diana: Her True Story.*

The 'Squidgeygate' tape, which just two years earlier had been deemed too racy for publication, was now justifiably newsworthy, for it showed the full extent of the depths to which the marriage of the Prince and Princess of Wales, future king and queen, had sunk. It also showed the hypocrisy of the advisers at the Palace. For years, Fleet Street had known the marriage was over. For years, the Palace had consistently denied there was even a hint of discord. It was almost laughable.

Those within the royal circle knew Diana and Charles were leading separate lives. Everyone in Fleet Street knew the marriage was over. Diana's friends were calling up on an almost weekly basis to throw some more 'dirt' at the Prince. And yet the Palace doggedly released hollow press statements to try and perpetuate the myth that the Waleses were a couple.

In reality, the pair had not slept together for more than five years. They never spoke to each other unless they were arguing. It was a sham marriage – and the public had a right to know.

On 24 August 1992, *The Sun* decided to run the 'Squidgey' tapes. An American newspaper, the *National Enquirer*, was planning to publish the full transcript.

Unlike fifty years earlier, when the British public were the last to know about the affair between Edward and Mrs Simpson because of a blanket ban on coverage in the British press, the public would not be duped again.

Four million readers woke up the next day to the headline: MY LIFE IS TORTURE. DIANAGATE TAPE OF LOVE CALL REVEALS MARRIAGE MISERY.

The tape had been made while Diana was alone in her bedroom at Sandringham shortly after Christmas 1989, lonely and bored during one of what she described as the 'interminably boring' Christmases with the royal family. Gilbey was stationary in his car in an Oxfordshire lay-by – talking on his mobile phone, number 0860 354661.

In fact, Diana was later to say the publication of the taped conversation was 'a great relief' to her, because, for the first time, the full extent of Diana's loathing for her husband and the break-up of the marriage was out in the open.

She later told a friend: 'It was a huge weight off my shoulders. For the first time, everyone knew the hell I was going through. I'd known about the existence of the tapes for two years. I felt like the Sword of Damocles was hanging over my head. Once they came out, it was a nightmare, but it was also a big relief.'

Prince Charles was furious. He felt that publication of the Princess's rather painfully naïve conversation with her admirer, packed with innuendo and crude sexual references, had embarrassed the royal family immeasurably. He was seen as the cuckolded husband and he believed it showed his wife 'as a total airhead'.

The question of whether Diana ever slept with Gilbey is one still hotly debated among their friends. Most tend to concur with the view that the relationship never went beyond the heavy petting stage. Yet certain extracts of the tape suggest the relationship was more intimate. On the tape, Diana is heard saying: 'I don't want to get pregnant.'

Gilbey replies: 'Darling, it's not going to happen. You won't get pregnant.'

Diana: 'Yeah.'

Gilbey: 'Don't get like that. It's not going to happen, darling. You won't get pregnant.'

Diana: 'I watched "EastEnders" today. One of the main characters had a baby. They thought it was by her husband. It was by another man.'

Gilbey: 'Squidgey, kiss me. Oh God, it's so wonderful, isn't it, this sort of feeling. Don't you just love it?'

Diana: 'I love it. I love it. Never had it before. I've never had it before.'

Gilbey: 'Darling, it's so nice being able to help you.'

Diana: 'You do. You'll never know how much. You'll never know how much.'

Gilbey: 'Oh, I will, darling. I just feel so close to you, so wrapped up in you. I'm wrapping you up, protecting.'

Diana: 'Yes please . . . yes please . . . '

One part of the conversation was omitted from the original *Sun* story as being too personal and intimate for a family newspaper.

Gilbey says: 'Darling, umm, it's just like, umm, sort of...'

'Playing with yourself?' replies Diana.

'What? No I'm not, actually,' says Gilbey.

'I said it's just like . . . just like,' she says.

'Playing with yourself,' he says.

'Yes,' says Diana.

Gilbey responds: 'Not quite as nice. No, I haven't played with myself actually. Not for a full forty-eight hours. Not for a full forty-eight hours. Ummm, tell me some more . . . '

Diana: 'I haven't for a day.'

Gilbey: 'You haven't?'

Diana: 'Not for a day.'

Some royal watchers believe Diana *did* engage in a full-blown affair. Lady Colin Campbell says: 'Diana keeps putting out these stories that her relationship with Gilbey was nothing more than an innocent flirtation. It sounds rather more than that when you listen to the tapes. If Diana is talking about getting pregnant, it pretty much leaves it clear that they were sleeping together.'

Gilbey, at first sight, seemed an unlikely suitor. He ran the Holbein Motor Company, an upmarket used-car dealership in Battersea. That company finally ended up in liquidation, crashing with heavy losses.

Gilbey had, in fact, known Diana from her carefree bachelor-girl days at Coleherne Court.

A friend of Gilbey's says: 'James has always had an eye for a pretty girl and another eye on the main chance. When he was reintroduced at a party to Diana in the late eighties, he was straight in there, like a rat up a drainpipe, so to speak.'

Their friendship first hit the headlines in October 1989 when the Princess was photographed coming out of Gilbey's rented one-bedroomed apartment in Lennox Gardens, Knightsbridge. It was later revealed she had dismissed her private detective, Sergeant David Sharp, some two hours earlier. Gilbey later said: 'We were simply playing bridge. It's hard for the Princess to keep up old friendships.' He said the Princess made up a foursome at bridge that night. But that was impossible: she was the only visitor to his apartment the whole evening.

In fact, according to aides close to Prince Charles, Diana's friendship with the rather unsuitable car dealer was common knowledge at the Palace.

One says: 'Everyone thought it rather amusing that Diana had finally found someone of her own class. Of course, everyone knew she was having this thing with him. They met up all the time, and she couldn't dismiss her royal protection officer without us knowing. The first thing he did was radio back to the Palace to alert us that Diana was in this man's rather modest flat, unguarded. A second car was sent out there without her knowledge. There was no way we were going to leave her unguarded. Don't be ridiculous.'

Perhaps the most worrying thing for the Palace was Gilbey's co-operation with Andrew Morton on *Diana: Her True Story*. Gilbey was quoted extensively in the book and was the person responsible for telling Morton some of the juicier stories about Diana.

A Palace aide says: 'What was of great concern was that Gilbey was considered an unsuitable confidant for the future queen. He'd already proved that by co-operating with Andrew Morton. Even the Princess was privately concerned that he'd gone "over the top" in some of the stories he gave Morton. Claiming the Sandringham stairs incident was a serious suicide attempt when, in fact, Diana had simply taken an accidental slip was over the top, to say the least.'

But Diana was determined to pursue her friendship – to spite those at the Palace who warned her of Gilbey's unsuitability.

Diana's main ally in her growing 'friendship' with Gilbey was Mara Berni, the owner of the fashionable Knightsbridge restaurant San Lorenzo. Mara would allow Gilbey to drop off letters for Diana at the restaurant, which she would pass on to the Princess discreetly at a later date. She also allowed Diana and Gilbey to dine alone in a private room in the restaurant.

A former waitress says: 'They would go in there, the order would be taken and delivered and then no-one was allowed to go into the room apart from Mara. It was quite strange. They often stayed in there alone for hours. You'd never hear a peep out of them apart from the occasional high-pitched giggle from the Princess.'

On the 'Squidgey' tapes, Gilbey says: 'Darling, forgetting that for a moment, how is Mara?'

Diana replies: 'She's all right. No she's fine. Can't wait to get back [from holiday].'

Gilbey: 'Can't she? When's she coming back?'

Diana: 'Saturday.'

Later on, the conversation returns to Mara and a planned meeting at her restaurant.

Gilbey: ' . . . I love it when I hear you laughing. It makes me really happy when you laugh. Do you know I am happy when you are happy?'

Diana: 'I know you are.'

Gilbey: 'And I cry when you cry.'

Diana: 'I know. So sweet. The rate we are going, we won't need any dinner on Tuesday.'

Gilbey: 'No, I won't need any dinner, actually. Just seeing you will be all I need.'

In fact, Charles's friends knew all about the Mara Berni connection.

One says: 'Of course he knew. Diana would go over to San Lorenzo all the time to meet Gilbey. The Prince was hardly going to complain. The more time Diana spent away, the more freedom it gave him. He didn't want her anywhere near. His only objection was that she chose someone so clearly not of her class. He thought it shameful that she should have a fling with Gilbey, a used-car salesman, of all people. It just confirmed to the Prince that Diana's head was turned by anyone with a good line in chat and a sympathetic ear to listen to her whingeing.'

Those who believe Diana's explanation that Gilbey was simply infatuated by her point to the fact that, throughout the entire conversation, it is he who continually professes love for her – while she remains quietly detached and aloof.

A friend of Gilbey's says: 'James put Diana up on a pedestal. It's rather like listening to one of those pathetic sex phone-in lines. Diana's never been much interested in the down-and-dirty of real sex. To her, the idea of some chap sitting in a lay-by getting all steamed up about her was about as close as she gets to a sexual thrill. She just loved leading him on and flirting.'

In another portion of the tape, Diana talks about another of her former admirers, James Hewitt. She talks about how she 'spent a fortune' kitting the guardsman out with a new wardrobe.

Gilbey: 'I like those ordinary Italian things that last a couple of years and then I chuck them out. It was a sort of devotion to duty. I was seeking an identity when I bought my first pair of Guccis twelve years ago.'

Diana: 'Golly!'

Gilbey: 'And I've still got them. Still doing me proud like.'

Diana: 'Good.'

Gilbey: 'I'm going to take you up on that, darling. I will give you some money. You can go off and spend it for me.'

Diana: 'I will. Yah.'

Gilbey: 'Will you?'

Diana: 'I'm a connoisseur in that department.'

Gilbey: 'Are you?'

Diana: 'Yes.'

Gilbey: 'Well, you think you are.'

Diana: 'Well, I've decked people out in my time.'

Gilbey: 'Who did you deck out? Not many, I hope.'

Diana: 'James Hewitt . . . entirely, dressed him from head to foot, that man. Cost me a lot, that man. Cost me quite a bit.'

Gilbey: 'I bet it did. At your expense?'

Diana: 'Yah.'

Gilbey: 'He didn't even pay you to do it?'

Diana: 'No!'

Gilbey: 'What an ext . . . very extravagant, darling.'

Diana: 'Well, I am, aren't I? Anything that will make people happy.'

Gilbey: 'You mustn't do it for that, darling, because you make people happy. It's what you give them . . . '

Publication of the tapes came as a complete shock to one woman: Gilbey's long-time girlfriend Lady Alethea Savile. The daughter of the Earl of Mexborough was totally unaware of the relationship between her boyfriend of two years and the Princess. In fact, up until the day the tapes were published, Lady Alethea was planning to marry Gilbey.

After the publication of Andrew Morton's book a few weeks earlier, Alethea had accompanied Gilbey on holiday to Italy – with Diana's brother Earl Spencer and his wife Victoria Lockwood. But the romantic holiday could not save the relationship.

Lady Alethea refused to comment on her boyfriend's 'betrayal', saying only: 'The whole thing is mind-blowing.'

One of her friends says: 'She went crazy. She felt completely betrayed. Whether James was or was not sleeping with the Princess, the fact was he bloody well wanted to. And that was appalling to Alethea. Just a couple of days before the tapes appeared in the *Sun*, he'd been in her bed, making love to her. The next thing she knows, he's all over the newspapers making verbal love to another woman – and the Princess of Wales to boot. Alethea was appalled. She is a lovely woman from a good family. Her family had been dismayed when she'd taken up with Gilbey in the first place. Once those tapes appeared, it was curtains for him as far as the Savile family went.

'James tried calling Alethea, but she simply refused to even talk to him. She was distraught over the whole affair. She went to pieces.'

In fact, a year later, Alethea wrote a piece for the *Daily Mail* which talked about how she was admitted to the Sierra Tuscon rehabilitation clinic in Arizona suffering from severe depression. Alethea admitted being 'in floods of tears' after the publication of the tapes and she underwent therapy at the clinic to ease her heartache and 'enormous depression'.

A close friend of Alethea's says: 'She could not cope with the publicity. All the press attention and the endless speculation sent her crazy. It was Alethea who dumped James.'

Gilbey refused to talk about the tapes, switching jobs shortly afterwards to work in the promotions department of the Lotus Formula One team based in Norfolk. According to someone who knew him well: 'James arrived at Lotus rather shell-shocked by the whole experience. For a few weeks, he would stiffen and leave the room if the Princess's name came up. But after a while he became more relaxed. He actually seemed rather proud of his royal connections. He's not the most attractive of men, rather slight of form and balding. To him, it was a massive ego boost that the most gorgeous girl in the world spoke so intimately to him.'

Close friends say that Diana has not spoken to Gilbey since the end of 1993.

Dianagate, as *The Sun* dubbed the affair, left Diana even more anxious to break away from the royal family.

She was also devastated to learn of the existence of a second tape – one which recorded her speaking from her bedroom at Kensington Palace to one of her 'friendly' journalists. The tape, which still remains in the hands of Prince Charles's advisers, is damning proof that not only did Diana co-operate directly with Andrew Morton on his book – but that she was continuing to 'feed' unflattering stories to the newspapers about her husband.

On this second tape, Diana and Gilbey discuss the Morton book. Diana instructs Gilbey to continue to 'keep up the good work' – supplying pro-Diana stories to the papers.

A Palace insider says: 'Diana was actually made aware of this tape at the time. It proved, conclusively, that she co-operated with the Morton book. No-one knows for certain where that tape is, but you can rest assured it is somewhere safe in the Palace and Diana knows it could be used against her if the powers-that-be chose to do so.'

The situation reached crisis point three days after the 'Squidgey' tapes were published.

Diana, in Balmoral with the rest of the royal family, again demanded a separation. She wanted out of the marriage.

An emergency closed-door meeting was held at Balmoral between Diana, Charles, the Queen and Prince Philip. The Queen, sympathetic to Diana's cause, advised her that it would be wise for her to accompany Prince Charles on a planned visit to Korea in November 1992. She said that if Diana did not go on the trip, it would only lead to a greater press feeding frenzy about the state of the marriage. Diana agreed. The Queen suggested a three-month 'cooling off' period for both Charles and Diana to 'give serious consideration' to their future plans.

The possibility of an informal separation was also discussed. Prince Philip explained a full-blown divorce was out of the question. He explained to her, in no uncertain terms, that if she were to go for a divorce, she would lose custody of the two young Princes. Since they were second and third in line to the throne, custody would remain with the royal family. It was unthinkable for it to be otherwise. Diana realized the family meant it.

Despite all that had happened, Diana now saw her only trump card was the role she played as mother to the future king and to the second in line to the throne: Wills and Harry.

She told a friend: 'It'll be over my dead body that they try to take the boys away.'

She therefore made an agreement. She would stick with the marriage until the end of the year. She would accompany the Prince and her sons on a summer cruise to the

Mediterranean. She would go on the tour of Korea. But if, when she came back, she still felt the same way, a separation would be announced. It was agreed that Diana would be allowed to remain in her own private quarters at Kensington Palace while the Prince would be set up in a new London home at St James's Palace. He would also retain his main home at Highgrove, a place the Princess 'loathed' anyway.

In fact, Charles met with Camilla shortly afterwards to seek her advice about a major refurbishment of Highgrove. Camilla oversaw the whole redecoration process as the pretty pastels and flowery prints of the Diana-era were removed and a more 'manly' style was introduced to the house.

An estate worker says: 'It was as if the Prince wanted to erase any memory of Diana from the house. Camilla oversaw all the renovations and redecorations. She was at the house the whole time, even when the Prince was away. She masterminded the whole thing. And he was thrilled with the result. Camilla's taste in decor and furnishings is completely in line with his. As a result, the house is a lot more comfortable than it was in Diana's day, when it was full of chintz and flowery things.'

The Queen, meanwhile, still lived in hope that Diana would not 'bolt' from the family.

A royal aide says: 'Even at that stage, after the publication of the "Squidgey" tapes, the Queen was doing all she could to preserve the marriage and the dignity of the monarchy. She was always sympathetic to Diana and she hoped against hope that Diana would stick it out. I think in her heart, though, she knew all was lost. It was something she could not even bring herself to think about.

'But the Queen was always more than fair to Diana. She was always sympathetic and she personally intervened when the marriage broke down. She still talks to Diana to this day. They are in contact far more regularly than people would imagine. Of the whole family, the Queen is the one who has bent over backwards to be fair and supportive to the Princess.'

A few days later, a clothes rack was unceremoniously placed in the office of the Prince of Wales at St James's Palace.

The metal rack on wheels contained grey and black clothes bags crammed from end to end. Inside, the Prince of Wales's uniforms were stacked up high. A small box also appeared. It was crammed with personal papers and small items of jewellery, including the Prince's modest collection of cufflinks – among them the pair with the intertwining 'C's which Camilla had given him as a wedding gift.

A Palace aide says: 'It was a clear signal that the Prince of Wales was moving all his stuff out of Kensington Palace. The uniforms and cases of his other personal possessions were later taken by car down to Highgrove. Some were taken to his new quarters at St James's Palace.

'It was very sad. It was like seeing the Prince of Wales thrown out on the street. Very sad indeed.

'He refused to even go back into the Kensington Palace rooms while Diana was there. He waited until she'd gone out for the day and then went back and packed a few more personal possessions. He took all his letters, all his personal journals. He didn't want to leave anything behind which Diana might find and use against him in the future.'

In the summer of 1992, Diana went on a cruise of the Mediterranean with Prince Charles on a luxury yacht owned by Greek shipping tycoon John Latsis. The media hyped the holiday as 'a second honeymoon'. It was wishful thinking.

The couple were accompanied by Princess Alexandra and her husband Sir Angus Ogilvy, Lord and Lady Romsey and their children and Princes William and Harry.

Sadly, the Prince and Princess hardly exchanged a single word. Diana preferred to eat separately from the main party, she spent mealtimes with the children, and slept in a small cabin at the other end of the yacht from her husband.

One day, they passed each other in the ship's galley. He simply ignored her. He fetched a glass of milk and then left.

In an updated chapter in his book *Diana: Her True Story,* author Andrew Morton later revealed that Diana went into the stateroom to make a phone call back to England to check on the condition of her AIDS-stricken friend Adrian Ward-

Jackson. She picked up an extension and heard her husband in the middle of a long ship-to-shore call to Camilla from the main ship's satellite phone.

Morton says: 'It merely provided further fuel for Diana's suspicions regarding her husband's relationship with Camilla, if any were needed.'

In October 1992, Diana was to come face to face with Camilla once more. The setting was Westminster Abbey; the occasion, a service to mark the fiftieth anniversary of the Battle of El Alamein.

Camilla, dressed in black, went to the service with her father Major Bruce Shand, a Military Cross winner. She had considered backing out at the last minute, knowing Diana would be there and the press interest would thus be 'overpowering', but out of love and devotion to her father, she went.

An audible buzz went through the Abbey as Camilla entered, her head held high, and walked slowly with her father to their allocated seats. A few moments later, Diana walked in with Prince Charles. As she walked down the centre of the Abbey to the front pew, Diana turned and gave Camilla a frosty stare.

Said one witness: 'It was enough to chill you out. Camilla, being Camilla, did what she always does when Diana is being a petulant child: she just ignored her.'

Afterwards, Camilla was rushed by a crowd of photographers outside the church. She later quipped: 'It was like going into the lion's den. But I guess all they're going to care about was the fact that my hair was in a mess.'

Sure enough, the headlines branded Camilla a 'frump' and repeated the question: how could Charles possibly dump the most beautiful woman in the world for a woman so remarkably *plain*?

Later that evening, the Prince phoned Camilla to apologize for his wife's 'childish' behaviour and for the 'barrage of abuse' she had been subjected to.

According to a family friend, Camilla replied: 'There is no use in apologizing, darling, it's not your fault. I'm afraid Diana is not in the best of health these days. I know people want to see me as the wicked woman in all of this, but you know the truth – and that is all I care about. If I have your support, I can endure anything.'

The publication of Andrew Morton's book that summer and its subsequent serialization in *The Sunday Times* had caused Camilla enormous pain, and incredibly, Diana was still 'cashing in' on the book even after the furore blew up.

Just a few days after the first extract of the book was serialized in *The Sunday Times,* a well-spoken woman telephoned a top executive at *The Sun*. The executive was advised to 'get' a photographer around to the house of Carolyn Bartholomew, one of Diana's friends who had fully co-operated with the Morton book. Bartholomew's obscure address in Fulham was given.

When the photographers arrived, they were greeted by the sight of the Princess of Wales leaving Carolyn's house. The two women hugged and embraced for a full five minutes. It was Diana's way of showing that she stood by what was in the book.

The Princess steadfastly refused to sign a statement confirming she had not co-operated with the book. She refused to disown either the contents or her friends who had co-operated with the publication.

Prince Charles was devastated by this blatant act of betrayal.

He later told Camilla: 'From this moment on, I shall never forgive her – and I shall never forgive or forget what she has done.'

He immediately launched a 'counter-attack'.

Several 'positive' articles about the Prince appeared. The author Penny Junor, who had become close to the Prince and his circle of friends when she produced a biography of him, wrote a piece for the *Today* newspaper under the headline: CHARLES: HIS TRUE STORY.

The article told of the Prince's 'extreme disappointment' with his marriage and of his 'sense of betrayal' by his wife's behaviour. Junor was quoted as saying: 'It is time to put the record straight once and for all. The Prince has suffered in silence long enough.'

She added: 'It would take a miracle for the marriage to survive. I fear too much damage has been done. As heir to the throne, Charles will one day be Defender of the Faith. One of the cornerstones of the Anglican faith is the sanctity of marriage. Charles acknowledges that to live a publicly dishonest marriage is incompatible with his faith and position.

'On the other hand, this marriage has come to this state because of Diana's illness and for no other reason. If she could be treated and cured, I am sure that Charles would be willing to work to repair the damage.

'The trouble is, Diana is a very sick woman. In public, she is a wonderful princess, charming and beautiful.

'But Charles has lived with a very different woman. She screams, shouts, is vitriolic and unreasonable with him.'

While Charles's aides attempted damage control, Camilla's life was made 'a living hell' by the mounting crisis. Reporters were camped out at the door of Middlewick House. Camilla lost more than a stone in weight through the upset. She also began chain-smoking.

A close confidante says: 'Camilla went through hell. But she would never even think to go public with her side of things. As ever, she remained steadfastly loyal and quiet. She was being subjected to the most awful abuse. She was branded a scarlet woman and every other name under the sun. In the end, she left and went to stay at a friend's house for a few weeks. She simply could not cope with all the fuss. I am sure Camilla would love to have set the record straight. But she maintained her dignity and silence.

'But she never stopped speaking to the Prince. Throughout the whole scandal of the Morton book, when Diana's so-called friends put the blame for the Prince's marriage failure firmly on her doorstep, Camilla remained firm friends with the Prince.

'Throughout it all, Camilla showed she had one thing in which the Princess of Wales was sadly lacking: class.'

One member of Camilla's immediate family says: 'She believes the old adage that silence is golden. If you look at what Diana's side have said and done, you would think Camilla is the Wicked Witch of the West, the woman who "stole" the Prince from the fairy-tale Princess.

'It wasn't like that at all. The Prince was the one who refused to give Camilla up. Truth is, she's the only woman he's ever loved, always will be. You cannot blame Camilla for everything. The marriage was a disaster from the start. The only person who has helped the Prince survive over the past few years has been Camilla. After the Morton book, even after the 'Squidgey' tapes, Camilla was always there for him. He knew he had a true friend in Camilla.'

The four-day trip to South Korea undertaken by the Prince and Princess of Wales that November was an unmitigated disaster from start to finish. The trip had been planned by the Prince's deputy private secretary Peter Westmacott two months earlier – but even he did not know that Diana intended to accompany Charles on the trip until seventy-two hours before they were due to leave.

Another Palace insider said: 'It was chaos. Everything was up in the air. No-one really knew what was going to happen. Diana was still threatening to duck out three days before they were due to set off.'

The pair had a blazing row on the Queen's Flight on the way over to Seoul and were clearly not speaking to each other from the moment their VC-10 plane touched down on the runway after the fourteen-hour flight.

On the eve of the trip, Diana put out a press release denying that there was any truth in reports that a rift had developed between her and the Queen, but adding the tell-tale line that there were 'difficulties' in her marriage.

Hopes by the Palace for a 'love tour' bit the dust. The Prince and Princess could barely stand to look at each other. At joint functions, their body language made it clear for the world to see that theirs was a mutual hatred and loathing. They would purposely stand as far away from each other as possible. Diana frequently rolled her eyes skyward when her husband spoke in public. She physically turned her shoulders away from him when they were forced to sit or stand side by side.

A friend of Diana's says: 'She was clearly unhappy to be there. She felt she had been pressurized into going to fulfil her part of the deal she'd made with the Queen. But she knew from the start it was a big mistake. Just seeing Charles there made her mad. And knowing he was going back and telephoning Camilla made her even madder.'

At a cocktail party at the British Embassy, the pair walked to opposite sides of the room and refused to say a word to each other.

One observer says: 'They kept as far apart from each other as they could. They didn't even exchange glances across the room.'

When they were apart on that trip, both relaxed and smiled for the cameras. Diana returned to her 'normal' cheerful self and the Prince visibly cheered up. But when they were together, the stony silence and long faces returned.

The headline writers back home summed them up as THE GLUMS.

In a car taking them to a state dinner, both looked solemn and grim. They purposely fixed their eyes firmly in opposite directions and turned their bodies away from one another. The Prince then spoke the only words to his wife anyone was to hear during the next four days: 'You get out of that side', he said as the car arrived at its destination.

The diplomatic mission of Britain's royal ambassadors had turned into a cruel, crude farce. Said one witness: 'It was like the War of the Roses. They both had their own camps of people and their own agendas. When they were together, you could have cut the tension with a knife. It was appalling. Their Korean hosts simply could not work it out. They had expected this wonderful fairy-tale couple, and they got the *Nightmare on Elm Street*.'

In a desperate attempt to salvage something from the trip, Westmacott called James Whitaker to one side. He explained to the royal correspondent that the Prince and Princess were 'distressed' by what they considered 'gross' intrusions into their private life through the constant reports about the unhappy state of their marriage.

Whitaker replied: 'Peter, are you trying to tell me this is a happy marriage?'

Westmacott replied: 'No, I am not trying to say that. But I am saying it has been unfair and exaggerated.'

The story made the headlines on that night's television news back in Britain – it was the first time a Buckingham Palace official had recognized, on the record, that the marriage was in trouble.

The couple did not even travel home together. Diana returned to London alone, while Charles continued on for a private trip to Hong Kong.

An aide says: 'The Prince knew the Korean trip had been a disaster. He said one day: "She is impossible. She won't even make the effort any more. And, to be frank, I don't think I can be bothered any more. It's time for things to take their natural course. I'll be damned if I have to put up with that woman any more."'

Shortly after she returned home, Diana told a friend that she had inadvertently picked up the telephone at a hotel in Korea – to find her husband in the middle of an affectionate late-night call to Camilla.

She said: 'It's all over. I want out of that bloody family and I don't care what the repercussions are.'

Prince Charles celebrated his forty-fourth birthday on 15 November 1992. His wife ignored the event, choosing not even to buy him a card or a present.

Camilla telephoned him to wish him many happy returns. She and Charles spent more than an hour on the phone together.

Twenty-four days later, on 9 December, the Palace issued a terse statement: the Prince and Princess of Wales were announcing their official separation.

Over At Last

It was Prime Minister John Major who finally made the announcement the world had been waiting for.

Standing on the floor of the House of Commons on 9 December 1992, he said: 'It is announced from Buckingham Palace that, with regret, the Prince and Princess of Wales have decided to separate. Their Royal Highnesses have no plans to divorce and their constitutional positions are unaffected. This decision has been reached amicably, and they will both continue to participate fully in the upbringing of their children.

'Their Royal Highnesses will continue to carry out full and separate programmes of public engagements and will, from time to time, attend family occasions and national events together.

'The Queen and the Duke of Edinburgh, though saddened, understand and sympathize with the difficulties that have led to this decision. Her Majesty and His Royal Highness particularly hope that the intrusions into the privacy of the Prince and Princess may now cease.

'They believe that a degree of privacy and understanding is essential if Their Royal Highnesses are to provide a happy and secure upbringing for their children, while continuing to give a wholehearted commitment to their public duties.'

In fact, Diana had again 'forced' the royal family into making the announcement.

A few days after she returned from the disastrous South Korean trip the previous month, she went to see solicitor Paul Butner of Wright, Son and Pepper in London. Mr Butner has never spoken of the meeting but it is known Diana asked him to hammer out a separation agreement with the Queen's solicitor Sir Matthew Farrer.

Then she instructed her solicitor to insist the separation announcement be made by the Prime Minister. A royal aide says: 'By this point, everyone knew any attempt to paper over the cracks in the marriage would be worthless. So the Palace allowed Diana to start making the first moves for a separation. But they were aghast when she demanded the Prime Minister make the announcement. It was just Diana attempting to show, once again, how much clout she had. She was being a prima donna right to the end.'

When the Palace initially turned down the Princess's demands, she produced the ace up her sleeve. Princess Anne was to marry Commander Timothy Laurence on 12 December 1992. A petulant Diana threatened to make her *own* announcement of the separation on that day, stealing what little positive publicity the Palace was hoping for from Princess Anne's happy wedding. The Queen was furious – but she backed down. She was determined that no-one, and certainly not the Princess of Wales, would be allowed to ruin Anne's big day.

She told a close aide: 'I suppose we shall have to give that tiresome girl what she wants again. I shall not have anyone ruining Anne's day. Instruct the Prime Minister accordingly.'

Prime Minister Major was due to meet European Union heads of government in Scotland on the day of the announcement. But, in response to a private telephone conversation with the Queen, he abandoned his plans the previous evening and flew back to London.

Diana thus had her separation announced in the House of Commons, just as she had requested.

Lady Colin Campbell says: 'The Palace was livid that they had had to give into the whims of this headstrong young woman yet again. It left a very nasty taste in people's mouths.

'Diana was now openly considered an outsider within the the royal circle. What she had done, in those last months of 1992, had provoked the crisis at the heart of the monarchy which everyone had tried to avoid. Her actions were considered shameful and appalling.

'She was effectively frozen out of the royal circle from that day forth. Of course, in public, as the mother of the future king, she was accorded a certain amount of civility by the other members of the royal household. But in private, she was a social outcast. She had let the side down, and the Queen was not amused.'

For her part, Camilla refused to comment on the separation, saying loyally: 'I will not be making any statement. Obviously, if something has gone wrong I feel very sorry for them.'

Her husband said: 'Like everyone else, one feels sad about what has happened.'

A short time after the official announcement, the Palace instructed Diana that William and Harry would be spending Christmas at Sandringham with their father and the rest of the royal family. Diana tried objecting, but her objections fell on deaf ears. She spent what she later described as 'a lonely and tearful' Christmas with her brother Earl Spencer on the Althorp estate.

Bitterly she told her friends: 'They took the boys off me for Christmas. I try fighting them, but I am weary of the fight. There seems nothing I can do any more. If I complain too much, they take the boys away. And the boys are all I have left now.'

Slowly, Diana was beginning to realize she had won the battle to destroy her marriage and destroy the reputation of the future king – but that she was losing the war.

Thirty-six days later, the 'Camillagate' scandal erupted with the force of a tornado.

The Scandal

'Your great achievement is to love me,' he says.

'Oh darling, easier than falling off a chair,' she replies.

'You suffer all these indignities and tortures and calumnies.'

'Oh darling, don't be so silly. I'd suffer anything for you. That's love. It's the strength of love. Night, night.'

The 'Camillagate' tape, published on 13 January 1993, revealed, for the first time, the full extent of the depth of feeling between Prince Charles and the woman who had been his mistress for nearly a quarter of a century. It was devastating. For the first time, the world heard the most intimate conversation of two people desperately in love – two people each married to someone else.

The bedtime call took place around one in the morning, 18 December 1989 when Charles was staying at the home of an old friend, Anne, Duchess of Westminster. He made the call from his personal mobile phone. Camilla was alone in bed at her home in Wiltshire. Her husband was in London.

She and Charles spoke with the frank openness of lovers secure in the knowledge that the intimate details of their conversation would go no further. Neither could have had any idea that their six-minute, 1,574-word conversation was being secretly bugged and that it would come back to haunt them more than three years later, causing a scandal unparalleled in modern times.

The affair which Prince Charles had denied and tried to hide for more than two decades was about to become known around the globe.

In fact, transcripts of the tapes had been at the offices of both *The Sun* and the *Daily Mirror* for months; in November 1992, both newspapers had written articles which mentioned the existence of the tapes. Andrew Knight, the former chief executive of News International, which owns *The Sun*, had written an article in the *Spectator* magazine as early as July 1992, claiming the newspaper had 'highly damaging material' about the royal family locked in the safe in his offices at Wapping. One element of the 'damaging material' was the 'Squidgey' tape of Diana – the other was the 'Camillagate' tape.

Again, the British press chose not to be the first to publish; the 'Camillagate' scandal was put into motion on the other side of the world when the mass-circulation Australian magazine *New Idea* revealed it had obtained a copy of the tape – and that it was going to publish and be damned.

Prince Charles had actually considered seeking an injunction, banning publication of the tapes. He was fully aware that they were in the possession of British newspapers. But after long discussions with his advisers, he had vetoed any legal action because of the added pressure it would put on the one person he cared about most – Camilla.

A friend says: 'By the time the tapes appeared, the Prince had known about them for at least six months. He knew their content and he knew they would surface eventually. He had discussed the repercussions of them several times with Camilla. She knew the score, too.

'Charles decided he was prepared to stand up and face the public fall-out. If he had attempted to ban publication of the tapes, it would have led to an even greater scandal. People would have wondered what he was trying to hide and he would have been found guilty by default anyway. And he knew if he tried any kind of legal action, Camilla would again be brought into the fray. He wanted to do everything he could to prevent the woman he loved from being subjected to such a nightmare ordeal.

'He knew once the papers had the tape, he was standing on the end of a very short plank. The only question remaining was how long would he have to stand there before he was forced to jump?

'But I don't think even he realized quite how enormous the reaction would be. I think secretly he believed that after the Diana and James Gilbey "Squidgey" tapes, the public might not be so shocked by the conversation between him and Camilla. But, of course, they were.'

The news agencies Reuters and Associated Press had already put out extracts from the tape on the foreign wires. The British papers had no alternative but to run them.

Wednesday, 13 January 1993 was to be forever known within royal circles as 'Black Wednesday'.

Prince Charles was awoken at half past six that morning by the Queen's private secretary Sir Robert Fellowes. It was the start of what he would later describe as 'what felt like the longest bloody day of my life'.

Fellowes, the husband of Diana's sister Lady Jane Spencer, has always been one of the Prince's closest friends. After the scandal of 'Squidgeygate' and the Andrew Morton book, he had effectively cut all links with his sister-in-law. As one of the most 'true blue' royalists, he considered Diana a 'traitor to the cause'.

Charles was in Scotland, visiting the Shetland Islands to help islanders who had suffered horrendously after the *Braer* oil tanker had disgorged 80,000 tons of crude oil on to their shores. Fellowes telephoned the Prince and told him the 'Camillagate' tapes had been made public. The Prince's reaction was a simple and forlorn: 'Oh God.'

The Prince's private secretary Commander Richard Aylard was the next to call. He arranged to meet the Prince later that day 'to discuss damage control'. Damage control was perhaps an understatement of what the Prince would need. The tapes were so intimate, so personal and so embarrassing that, he later told a royal aide, 'It took all the strength I could muster to go downstairs for breakfast that day – I couldn't even face the servants. The thought of facing my own family filled me with dread.'

In fact, his first reaction was to telephone Camilla to forewarn her. She already knew. Her home had been besieged by reporters and photographers since the crack of dawn. She was told the news about the tapes by a reporter from *The Sun* as she emerged from her house in the small hours. Her first reaction was to say: 'Oh my God, I can't believe it. I must speak to my husband.' She then disappeared inside Middlewick House and took the phone off the hook. Ironically, therefore, when the Prince tried repeatedly to call Camilla to warn her of the impending scandal at seven that morning he could not get through.

The blatant passion of the conversation between the Prince and his mistress stunned everyone. According to one aide: 'It was staggering to hear the depths of passion that still existed in their conversation. Everyone close to the Prince knew that he and Camilla had renewed their romantic liaison several years before. But this is a couple who had known each other for nigh on twenty years, and they were talking with the excited passion of newly-weds. It took us all by surprise. It proved they were even more in love and more deeply involved than anyone could have guessed.

'You'd be hard pressed to find a married couple who'd know each other that long and who still had that burning passion between them.

'They speak without any hang-ups or embarrassment. They have no qualms about talking to each other in the most intimate way. They come across as a couple who want and desire each other equally.'

Throughout the conversation, the language is colourful, intimate – and raunchy.

Camilla: 'Mmmm, you're awfully good at feeling your way along.'

Charles: 'Oh stop! I want to feel my way along you, all over you and up and down you and in and out . . .'

Camilla: 'Oh!'

Charles: 'Particularly in and out . . .'

Camilla: 'Oh, that's just what I need at the moment.'

Charles: 'Is it?'

Camilla: 'I know it would revive me. I can't bear a Sunday night without you.'

Charles: 'Oh God.'

Camilla: 'It's like that programme "Start the Week". I can't start the week without you.'

Charles: 'I fill your tank!'

Camilla: 'Yes you do.'

Charles: 'Then you can cope.'

Camilla: 'Then I'm all right.'

Charles: 'What about me? The trouble is I need you several times a week.'

Camilla: 'Mmmm. So do I. I need you all the week, all the time.'

Charles: 'Oh God, I'd just live inside your trousers or something. It would be much easier!'

Camilla: (laughing) 'What are you going to turn into? A pair of knickers? Oh, you're going to come back as a pair of knickers?'

Charles: 'Or God forbid, a Tampax. Just my luck!'

Camilla: 'You are a complete idiot! Oh, what a wonderful idea.'

Charles: 'My luck to be chucked down the lavatory and go on and on for ever, swirling round at the top, never going down!'

Camilla: 'Oh darling!'

Charles: '. . . until the next one comes through.'

Camilla: 'Or perhaps you could come back as a box.'

Charles: 'What sort of box?'

Camilla: 'A box of Tampax, so you could just keep going . . . Oh darling, I just want you now.'

Charles: 'Do you?'

Camilla: 'Mmmm.'

Charles: 'So do I.'

Camilla: 'Desperately, desperately, desperately!'

The couple talk about meeting up at a safe friend's house. Camilla refers to her husband as 'it'.

Part of the conversation revolves around the couple's attempts to link up. They discuss the 'ambulance strike', a bitter dispute which had been going on for six months. Camilla's husband Andrew Parker Bowles played a key role in providing army ambulance services as back-up. Charles and Camilla talk about how they both wish the dispute would continue – to allow them to meet. Furtively.

Charles says: 'Oh God, when am I going to speak to you?'

Camilla: 'I can't bear it. Um . . .'

Charles: 'Wednesday night?'

Camilla: 'Oh, certainly Wednesday night. I'll be alone, um, Wednesday, you know, the evening. Or Tuesday. While you're rushing around doing things I'll be, you know, alone until *it* reappears. And early Wednesday morning. I mean, he'll be leaving at half past eight, quarter past eight. He won't be here Thursday, pray God. Um, that ambulance strike, it's a terrible thing to say this, I suppose it won't have come to an end by Thursday?'

Charles: 'It will have done.'

Camilla: 'Well, I mean, I hope for everybody's sakes it will have done, but I hope for our sakes it's still going on.'

Charles: 'Why?'

Camilla: 'Well, because if it stops, he'll come down here on Thursday night.'

Charles: (*groaning*) 'Oh no.'

Camilla, as well as offering him a passionate physical relationship, also offers him a motherly ear. She asks him for a copy of a speech he has just written which she longs to read.

Charles says: 'I'll be working on the next speech.'

Camilla: 'Oh no, what's the next one?'

Charles: 'A rather important one for Wednesday.'

Camilla: 'Well, at least I'll be behind you.'

Charles: 'I know.'

Camilla: 'Can I have a copy of the one you've just done?'

Charles: 'Yes.'

The couple talk anxiously of 'how wonderful' it would be 'to have just one night together'.

Camilla suggests a number of 'safe houses' where they could rendezvous. It was an anguished conversation for them both – after so many years of intimacy, they are still not free to meet and love each other in the open. They both know they will never be together permanently. But they both agree they cannot face life without meeting regularly.

When they finally hang up on each other, Charles says he will ring off by 'pressing the tit', the button on his mobile phone. Camilla replies: 'I wish you were pressing mine.'

A close friend of Camilla's says: 'Despite the shocking frankness of the conversation, what cannot be denied is the closeness between the two.

'She reassures him throughout, she tells him how much she loves him. She tells him she will always be there for him. She reassures him of how much he is loved and she tells him how clever he is.

'They tell each other they love each other because they truly do, not because they just want to hear the words spoken.

'When the Prince tells Camilla her greatest achievement is to love him, one gets the impression not of arrogance, but that he is enormously grateful that he is deserving of her love.

'The fact that Camilla was anxious to read his speech, shows she genuinely cares about his work and is interested in every aspect of his day. She is constantly bolstering him up, giving him support in all areas of his life.

'A lot of people poured scorn on Camilla, but everyone close to her and the Prince knows what a valuable source of strength she has been to him. He has no-one else to talk to except Camilla. And of course he adores her.

'Everyone who knows Camilla adores her. She's smart, she's very funny and what you see is what you get. She is loyal to a fault and if she is your friend, you know you have a friend for life. Camilla is the one person all of us know we can call for some solid advice. But she is someone who never particularly unburdens herself on others; that is not her style. She is very strong and confident in herself as a woman. Her attitude towards the whole scandal was that, deep in her heart, she knew the truth and those she loved knew the truth. That was all that truly mattered to her.'

Within twenty-four hours of 'Camillagate' first breaking it had appeared on the front pages of fifty-three newspapers around the world – and was being broadcast on television news stations in countries from Japan to South Africa, America to Australia.

The mockery that followed the publication of the 'Camillagate' tapes was almost unbearable for the Prince. He returned to the Queen's estate at Sandringham in shame.

'How can it have all gone wrong so quickly?' he would ask his loyal private secretary Richard Aylard, over and over again.

According to those close to him, he seriously considered leaving Britain, renouncing the throne and 'running away' to his beloved Italy. A friend says: 'It completely knocked him for six. The ridicule was staggering. In Italy, they were referring to Charles as the Prince Tampacchino, the "little Tampax Prince". In stores across Britain and America, girls were asking for "Charlies" instead of tampons.

'The Prince heard all these stories, of course. And he was heartbroken. He felt like he had let down himself, let down the Queen, and more importantly, let down his country.

'He seriously talked about going to Florence. He was at the point of just clearing off. He is someone who has always believed totally in his destiny. But, for once, and for the briefest time, he questioned whether his future was going to be as it had always been mapped out. He was totally disillusioned and fed up. He was as depressed as anyone had ever seen him.'

The Prince even ordered his rooms at St James's Palace and the every single room at Highgrove to be swept for telephone bugs. None was found – but it was too late anyway: the irreparable damage to his reputation had been done.

The Prince started to take sleeping pills to help him rest at night. A friend says: 'He was surviving on one or two hours' sleep a night. He was shattered. In the end, his doctor gave him some mild sleeping pills just to help him get some rest.

'He hardly smiled for months, he went around with this dark gloomy storm cloud above him. He was truly a very sad and pitiful sight. He would lock himself away for hours. He was often red-eyed. It was clear he'd done a lot of crying.'

Another close friend who saw him at a dinner party more than a month after the tapes were published said: 'He was almost on the verge of tears all evening. He tried talking about what he was going through, but it was clear he was deeply distressed. Only when he talked about Diana did he get angry. He felt, indeed he still feels to this day, that he tried to make the marriage work in the early days. He would have stuck in the marriage even when it was clear it wasn't working. It was Diana and her problems which caused the rift. She was the one who forced the separation. She was the one who was determined to get out.

'He kept saying how he never meant any of this to happen, how he couldn't understand "the whole bloody mess".

'He was genuinely confused and miserable. There were a few of us that were seriously concerned about his depression. He was so vulnerable, he felt so alone, anything was possible at that stage.

'He even made a passing joke about suicide. He said: "Perhaps they'd all prefer it if I was six foot under. Then what would they do?"

'He forced himself to laugh when he'd said it. He was making a big joke. But privately, a lot of us were worried. He was about as depressed as anyone had ever seen him. All his life, he had wanted to be taken seriously. Now, in a six-minute phone conversation, he had blown years of hard work. He was being laughed at by everyone – everyone except Camilla. In his darkest hours, it was Camilla he turned to once again. She comforted him and offered him a strong shoulder to lean on. She was constantly giving him advice. She encouraged him to face the battle head on.'

The pair would talk on the phone at least once every day. According to friends, these conversations would sometimes be two or three hours in length.

The Queen Mother, anxious about the welfare of her favourite grandson, invited him to lunch. According to one royal aide: 'The Queen Mother knows the depths to which the Windsor men can sink in despair. After all, it was she who watched as Edward VIII, the former Prince of Wales, sank deeper and deeper into the mire over Wallis Simpson. She knew Charles had always suffered from attacks of deep melancholia. She feared history might be repeating itself.'

The Queen Mother telephoned her grandson almost every day in the weeks following 'Camillagate', and she invited him to lunch at Clarence House at the beginning of April. She asked Charles to tell her all about his visit to see the ageing Duke of Windsor when he was living in exile in France shortly before the Duke's sad and lonely death.

She ended by telling him: 'You have a duty, Charles. You have a duty to your country. Remember what happened before.'

Charles was later to say: 'It was a very clever move. She knew how deeply affected I had been by meeting my great-uncle. Talking about his circumstances helped put mine into perspective. I knew that, no matter what happened, I had to pick myself up by my shoestrings and carry on. History could not repeat itself.'

'She is a wonderful restorer of backbones,' one of the Queen Mother's ladies-in-waiting would later add with a smile. 'She made it clear to Charles, although it took some time for him to fully accept it, that no matter how grim and bleak things appeared, his duty was to the Crown. She told him that no matter how bad he was feeling, he could turn his time of crisis into a strength. He could use the lessons he had learned to rebuild – and look forward.'

Prince Philip was less understanding. He exploded in rage when he first read the 'Camillagate' extracts running in the newspapers.

'Now the whole bloody country knows who you're bonking!' he screamed at his son. 'It's not that you have been bonking the woman for years that bothers me – it's the fact you were so bloody idiotic, you got found out. What the bloody hell are you going to do next?'

Charles sat stony-faced and silent as his father berated him. Without saying a word, Charles left the room and went upstairs.

A courtier says: 'He felt abandoned by his father in his hour of need. On the one occasion when Charles truly needed fatherly advice, Prince Philip just screamed and ranted at him. Their relationship plunged further downward from that day on.'

After the 'Camillagate' tapes were published, Camilla's world was turned upside down. She was under siege at Middlewick while Andrew was in London. But, according to a close friend, publication of the tapes never seriously threatened their marriage.

The friend said: 'Camilla and Andrew always knew where they stood with each other. The publication of the tapes didn't mean anything to that marriage. Camilla had known the tapes were in the public domain for months. Not only had she braced herself for their eventual publication, but she had also warned her husband.

'People who weren't in the know started speculating about whether Andrew would go for a divorce. But he wouldn't do that even if he wanted to, which he doesn't. Andrew's first loyalty has always been to the Crown. He has this deep-rooted sense of duty. And there was, and is, no way he will do anything to embarrass the monarchy.

'When the tapes became public, Andrew's first response

was to race down to Wiltshire to be by his wife's side. He even spoke to the Prince on at least two occasions in the weeks following the scandal breaking.

'Camilla stayed strong throughout. Her nerves were on edge, but she's not the type to crack under pressure, unlike the Princess of Wales. Camilla hated all the attention, but she bore the pressure as well as anyone could. She is a very tough character; you should never underestimate Camilla.

'She maintained a resolute silence throughout. She allowed her name to be blackened without speaking out, because she knew if she spoke out, it would only fan the flames of scandal. She surrounded herself by family and friends and just kept her head down.

'Apart from the Prince of Wales, there are a few friends she trusts implicitly. Her sister Annabel was a rock to her and Annabel's husband Simon was terribly supportive. They rallied round. Camilla even tried to joke about the press pack outside her gate. She loathed all the attention, but, as always, her best defence mechanism was to laugh. She showed incredible strength of character throughout that whole ordeal.'

Carolyn Benson, who was a house guest at Middlewick that first weekend, said sadly: 'Whatever happened, they knew their lives would never be the same again – Andrew and Camilla were trapped.'

Another friend said: 'Andrew and Camilla had reached an impasse in their marriage. But they were still devoted to each other on a level no-one can truly understand. When "Camillagate" broke, Andrew stuck by his wife. It would not be his style to abandon her at a time of crisis. He, like she, knows where his duty lies.'

Camilla showed even more strength of character shortly afterwards when Andrew Parker Bowles was photographed leaving the same Carolyn Benson's London home at quarter to seven in the morning.

Andrew denied any impropriety and simply said: 'Of course I have stayed with Carolyn. I have stayed with a lot of people in a lot of premises and spent the night there as well.'

He told a friend: 'It makes me absolutely bloody mad what they're saying. I'm not standing for any of this much longer.'

Carolyn, who is godmother to Camilla's son Tom, said: 'I am a good friend of both Andrew and Camilla. I am not going to justify any malicious rumours by commenting further on the incident.'

One friend said: 'The whole idea was ridiculous. Camilla told me she spoke to Carolyn later that same day. The two have remained firm friends ever since.'

And Carolyn's father Colonel Gerard Leigh told one writer: 'Carolyn has been friends with Camilla since they were children. Any suggested link between Carolyn and Andrew is ridiculous. If anything, Carolyn is better friends with Camilla than she is with the Brigadier.'

But another friend of the Parker Bowleses says: 'Andrew may or may not have been having an affair with Carolyn. It really doesn't matter. Camilla and Andrew have a rock-solid partnership. Dynamite couldn't blow them apart. They are firm friends with each other and they share the same sense of humour. When you've been through what they've been through, you have to learn to laugh together. Camilla and Andrew may not enjoy the passion between themselves that they both enjoy with others, but they are best friends. And when the chips are down, as they were when the tapes broke, they stick together. There was no way either one of them was going to bolt from that marriage.'

A couple of days after the photographs of Andrew leaving Carolyn's house appeared, he and Camilla put on a show of force by holding a picnic lunch in the grounds of Eton school, where their son Tom was in his final year. Camilla's father Major Bruce Shand and her sister Annabel Elliot joined the family outing.

A friend says: 'They could not say anything about all the scandal, but they put on a dignified show of strength. That is typical of Andrew and Camilla. When things are as bad as they can be, and then get worse, they stick together. They have a stronger marriage than most people I know.

They understand each other totally.'

Andrew's brother Simon said: 'Andrew and Camilla have always said they will never divorce. They may not be in love with each other in the conventional sense, but they get on well and will stick together. They have had a very open marriage and these sophisticated arrangements can blow up in your face, my God, as this has done.'

At the picnic on the green playing fields of Eton, the couple laughed and joked and behaved just like any other proud parents. Their son Tom looked a little less jolly. For weeks, he had been subjected to the cruel taunts of some of his schoolmates calling his mother 'a tart'.

One one occasion, according to a former schoolfriend, Tom became embroiled in a fist-fight in defence of his mother. The friend says: 'The jibes had been going on behind Tom's back for years. It was to his credit that he was popular at Eton. He was a fine sportsman and an immensely likeable chap. He knew about the snide comments which were being made, but he chose to ignore them.

'One day, however, he walked into the changing rooms after rugby practice and one fellow challenged him directly to his face. He pretty much said Tom's mother was a tart who had brought shame on the royal family. Tom snapped: "Shut up. You don't know what you're talking about." But the other chap repeated the accusation. Tom leapt on him and gave him a pretty good working over. After that, the name-calling stopped.'

Incredibly, despite the heartache the 'Camillagate' tapes had caused, the two main players continued to talk regularly.

A former equerry says: 'I walked into the Prince's private study about a week after the tapes had been splashed all over the papers and he was deep in conversation with Camilla. He had his back turned to me and I heard him talking to Camilla in hushed tones. I quietly turned around and went out again. But I was shocked . . . I was truly shocked.'

Bending With the Wind

'Just when I thought it couldn't get any worse, it has.'

Prince Charles was speaking to his grandmother shortly after the most difficult meeting of his life. It took place in his private rooms at Buckingham Palace nine days after 'Camillagate' broke.

Major Bruce Shand, Camilla's elderly father, had written to the Prince demanding a meeting. Shortly after four in the afternoon, the decorated war hero arrived and was ushered into the Prince's study where Charles sat working at his table.

Major Shand first refused to shake the hand of the man who had been his daughter's secret – and now very public – lover for years, then, despite the fact that he was near eighty years old, he refused the Prince's offer of a chair.

Instead, for ninety minutes, the old man became increasingly angry. He started speaking to the Prince in a bewildered and sad voice, but within minutes, he became red-faced with rage.

'My daughter's life has been ruined, her children are the subject of ridicule and contempt. You have brought disgrace on my whole family,' ranted the Major.

The Prince bowed his head in shame. Shand continued in the same vein. He told Charles that his wife was an invalid who had been 'deeply and profoundly upset' by the scandal. He said the Prince had 'made a mockery' of his entire family and their good name.

According to one source close to the Shand family: 'The Prince said nothing. He stood there like a young boy being torn off a strip by his father. He kept trying to murmur a few words under his breath, but the Major was irate. He was beside himself with rage. The Prince had known Major Shand for years, he had stayed at the family home many times in the early days when he had first got to know Camilla in the mid-seventies.

'The Major was like a second father to him. In fact, Charles got on better with Bruce Shand than he did with his own father.

'For him to be so upset by what had happened affected Charles deeply. Bruce demanded Charles sever all links with Camilla. He told Charles to "get out" of her life in no uncertain terms.

'He criticized his abilities as a father and as a husband. He said Charles, in his position and with his background, should have "known better" than to continue the affair with his daughter so publicly.'

'It was,' the Prince said later, 'the worst moment of my life.'

A friend said: 'It was a moment of total humiliation for Charles. The Major was someone who knew the royal family extremely well. He had known Charles for twenty years. He felt perfectly at liberty to tell him exactly what he thought. No-one had ever spoken to Charles in that manner before. He was genuinely shocked at the old man's anger.'

As the Major prepared to leave, his anger abated for a moment. Looking Charles straight in the eye, he said: 'For the sake of my family, for the sake of your family, for the sake of the country – you must stop seeing my daughter. I implore you, please, please put an end to this nonsense for ever.'

Charles nodded his head in silence. Then he promised the

Major he would 'think about it'.

The words made Shand erupt in a final outburst: 'I don't want you to *think* about it, I want you to do what you know is the only course of action left open to you. You must sever all links with Camilla – and you must do it now!'

The Prince responded to the old man's plea by bursting into tears.

On his first official visit to the City of London after the scandal broke, a man shouted from the crowd: 'You should be ashamed of yourself!'

The Prince's face reddened and he turned away.

His private offices at St James's Palace began receiving hate mail from members of the public – the same public he was set to rule over – condemning him for cheating on his beautiful wife. A daily diet of anti-Charles stories appeared in every national newspaper.

It was clear, above all else, that drastic action was needed to counter the anti-Charles sentiment sweeping the nation.

A former courtier says: 'The Prince had wrongly assumed that "Camillagate" would merely cause a small blip in the works. In fact, it soon became apparent to everyone at the Palace that they had a full-blown crisis on their hands. The future of Prince Charles was seriously in jeopardy. Newspaper polls were coming out on a daily basis proving his popularity was at an all-time low.

'Even more serious was the fact that the royal family were embroiled in a scandal just as serious as the abdication crisis more than half a century earlier.'

Shortly after his harrowing meeting with Major Shand, Charles was summoned to a meeting with the Queen, Prince Philip, the Queen's private secretary Sir Richard Fellowes and the Prince's private secretary Commander Richard Aylard – an unstuffy former naval officer who was to become the kingpin in the almost military-style campaign to revamp Charles's image.

In a meeting which lasted more than an hour, the two private secretaries underlined the seriousness of the situation –

and the fact that the future king's reputation and image had sunk to an all-time low. Drastic measures were needed, and they were needed fast. The Queen agreed to a proposal from Commander Aylard that the Prince needed to embark on a 'positive public-relations' campaign.

The following Sunday, for the first time in living memory, photographers waiting outside the church at Sandringham after the royal family's traditional Sunday-morning service were staggered to find Prince Charles walking over to them with his two sons.

One photographer recalls: 'It was the first time anyone could remember that the Prince willingly put himself out and stood and posed for pictures outside the church with the two boys. It was clear a wind of change was sweeping the Palace.'

Charles knew he had important decisions to make to secure his future. There was no question in his mind that his duty lay where it always had done: in succeeding to the throne as King Charles III.

But he fully understood the growing crisis. During the darkest days after 'Camillagate', he was to recount one of his favourite historical quotes to friends, a quote made by the former German Kaiser Wilhelm: 'The monarchy is like virginity, once you have lost it, you can never, ever get it back.'

A close member of the royal circle said: 'He was facing up to the stark reality that his very future, the future of the institution he had been born into and which he had spent forty years in, was in jeopardy. Charles knew the situation was very grave indeed.

'His sense of duty and destiny made him determined to fight back.'

The trouble was that there was more and more very public dissent. A poll in *The Sun* newspaper shortly after 'Camillagate' revealed that, out of a staggering 20,000 readers who responded, the vast majority believed that the Prince's reputation was so tarnished that he would never be king. Seventy per cent of readers said they thought less of him after 'Camillagate'. More than sixty per cent believed he had to end the affair with Camilla.

Even Charles himself said: 'It's a bloody awful time. It's utterly bloody awful.'

The most damaging criticism came from within the ranks of the Church of England. Since Charles was the future Head of the Church, this criticism from churchmen was of great significance to the future of the monarchy.

The Venerable George Austin, Archdeacon of York and a tireless supporter of family values, went on the BBC Radio Four programme 'Today' and made a comment which was to grab the headlines. 'My view,' he said, 'would be that Charles made solemn vows before God in church about his marriage, and it seems, if it is true about Camilla Parker Bowles, that he began to break them almost immediately. He has broken his trust and vows to God on one thing. How can he then go into Westminster Abbey and take his Coronation vows?'

It was a shattering blow. Austin, though not a bishop, was one of the most respected churchmen in the land.

The Archbishop of York, Dr John Habgood, fired a warning shot at the Prince. He said: 'He must resolve his personal problems before becoming king.'

The Bishop of Oxford, the Right Reverend Richard Harris, was a little more understanding. He joined the growing discussion: 'While one of the Queen's titles is Defender of the Faith, I don't think people take that literally now. It's been very good when monarchs have presented themselves as ideal role models, but it is not expected of them these days.'

So great was the growing criticism from the Church that the Queen summoned senior Church leaders to a meeting at Lambeth Palace, the Church of England's headquarters.

She told them: 'Although the misfortunes of the Prince of Wales's private life are a regrettable chapter in the monarchy's history, he will be king. No question about it.'

Although the Archbishop of Canterbury announced publicly that he was 'in full support' of Charles becoming king, the damage was done.

CHARLES NOT FIT TO RULE screamed the headlines.

It was then that Charles, and his advisers, realized their never-before-questioned belief that Charles would one day be king was in serious jeopardy.

The war was on.

But Charles's advisers were new at the game of positive public relations, and at the end of April 1993, the Prince made a massive PR mistake. He decided to fly to the funeral service of King Juan Carlos of Spain's father, Don Juan de Bourbon y Battenberg, in Madrid. At the same time, the British public's attention was firmly focused on the horrendous IRA bombing of a shopping centre in the northern town of Warrington. Two young boys, Jonathan Ball and Tim Parry, had been killed in the bloodbath. The whole of Britain was outraged by the callous slaughter.

Diana had asked permission to go to a memorial service in Warrington for the two young boys. The Palace refused her permission. Diana retaliated by telephoning the mother of twelve-year-old Tim Parry twenty-four hours before the memorial service. She had a long chat with the grieving woman and offered her 'warm words of comfort and condolence'.

Mrs Wendy Parry was later to say she was 'deeply touched' by the Princess's caring and compassionate nature.

Her husband Colin said: 'Wendy answered the phone and I noticed her face go slightly red.

'Then a smile as wide as the Mersey tunnel spread across her face as she said, handing me the phone, "It's the Princess of Wales."

'You could tell by her voice it was her. The Princess said she was terribly sorry about what had happened. She said she just wished she could give Wendy a big hug. They obviously spoke as mother to mother.

'She was just very, very kind and sympathetic with the things she said. She's great and it has meant such a lot to us. I think she feels deeply how much we have lost and she said exactly the same things you would expect any other mother to say.'

Mrs Parry also revealed that Diana had told her she had

wanted to be at the memorial service, but that she had been refused permission from the Palace. It was Diana at her 'magnificent finest', according to the Prince's friends.

The subsequent angry reaction appeared on the front pages of newspapers across Britain the next morning.

SNUBBED DI RINGS BOMB FAMILY ran the front-page headline in *The Sun*. It was another publicity coup for 'Saint' Diana.

In fact, the Prince had visited Warrington a couple of days after the bomb had gone off. He and Commander Aylard studied the television tapes of the visit later. It was a disastrous trip.

Charles was seen on the BBC news saying to a woman who had lost her leg in the blast: 'Your courage has made my day.' He came across as being uncomfortable, unsympathetic – and wildly out of touch. He was bitterly disappointed by his performance.

Diana was still a bigger crowd-puller than Charles. Over a month-long period, in April 1993, Diana drew crowds of more than 10,000 on sixteen public engagements, while Charles's score was an average of just 132 spectators on twenty-five royal engagements. He was working harder, but he was not being *seen* to work harder.

The Palace swung into action. One of the biggest repackaging jobs of all time was about to begin; the Palace realized it had to get its public-relations machine in order.

Even the Queen responded to the call to 'bring the monarchy into shape for the twenty-first century'. First, she announced that she would start paying taxes for the first time ever. It was an announcement hailed as 'long overdue' but 'admirable' by both royalists and critics alike.

Then it was announced that Buckingham Palace would be opened to the public for two months each summer – August and September – for the next five years, beginning in 1993.

It was a tremendous success. Queues stretched for blocks, the Palace gift shop did a roaring trade – and the positive publicity around the world was fantastic. During that first summer a total of 377,000 visitors paid £12 a head to tour the Palace. Two million pounds profit was made from attendance fees and a further £1.2 million was raked in from the sale of souvenirs.

The Queen also agreed to contribute a major part of the rebuilding costs of Windsor Castle, devastated by fire in December 1992.

In June 1993, another meeting was called at St James's Palace. Sir Richard Aylard called on 'professional' help in rebuilding Charles's image after 'Camillagate'.

Among those chosen to revamp his fortunes were pop promoter Harvey Goldsmith, the TV arts presenter Melvyn Bragg and the editor of *The Times* Peter Stothard. While the Prince's image was discussed for more than an hour, Charles himself inexplicably failed to turn up.

Commander Aylard sent a handwritten memo to his boss, stressing the importance of him co-operating 'in the work we have before us'. On the bottom on the memo was the underlined word *please*.

A royal aide says: 'The Prince has not missed a meeting since.'

The marital battles of the eighties had now become a full-scale war for the hearts and minds of the British public – and for the future of the monarchy.

Charles knew he needed to make still more changes if he was seriously to hang on to his chances of becoming king.

Throughout 1993, he continued to talk regularly to Camilla on the phone. A source close to Camilla says: 'Despite all that had happened, the Prince still needed Camilla. There was never a thought in his head that he might have to give her up. They continue to enjoy long conversations, but always on a safe landline. They had learned their lesson the painful way from using mobile phones.

'The relationship was even more secret than ever. Only a handful of people were aware it was still going on. The Prince kept it secret from everyone, including his own father. He knew the process of rebuilding his image would be long and drawn out. He could not afford any negative publicity, and certainly no negative publicity about him and Camilla.

'They met only once or twice, both times at the safe houses of friends. They were meetings shrouded in secrecy. But they were meetings Charles needed. He simply could not live without Camilla. Even when things were at their lowest ebb, it was Camilla he turned to to get him through.

'He needed her emotionally and sexually. He needed to know she still loved him as much as he still loved her. They would arrive at the safe houses separately, they would leave under cover of darkness. No-one knew of these meetings, but they were going on.

'If anything, the crisis brought them closer together. They helped each other to stay strong during those dark days after "Camillagate" broke. Charles was still reluctant to trust anyone but Camilla. He valued her advice. And it was she who made it very clear to him that enough was enough; he had to start fighting back.'

By December 1993, Commander Aylard realized he still had one major problem with the Prince's image. The long affair with Camilla was out in the open, but the spectre of scandal still remained. Newspaper stories were once again surfacing, saying that the Prince and Camilla were continuing to enjoy a 'discreet' relationship.

One of Diana's friends was quoted as saying: 'After all that has happened, the Prince is continuing to call Mrs Parker Bowles on a weekly, if not daily, basis. The Princess does not care any more. She simply wants to get on with her life.'

If the stories were allowed to continue, it was only a matter of time before the whole Camilla scandal would blow up again. While the shadow of Camilla lurked in the Prince's background, he would never be fully forgiven by the British public for allowing his affair to destroy the fairy-tale marriage.

A major solo tour of Australia by the Prince was being planned for January 1994. It was a make-or-break trip for

Charles. Those close to him hoped the tour would show him at his best – enjoying mass acclaim *without* Princess Diana.

In mid-December, Commander Aylard called a strategy meeting in the Prince's private offices at St James's Palace. Sitting around the polished mahogany table were Commander Aylard, the Queen's private secretary, Sir Robert Fellowes – and, of course, Prince Charles himself.

The meeting was to have devastating personal repercussions on the entire future of the man who had been groomed since birth to be king. The three men began discussing the Australia trip. Their conversation dealt with mundane issues: at first where the Prince would visit, arrival and exit times and flight plans for the trip.

As in a military operation, the three even discussed minute details like which cufflinks would be packed for the Prince – and how many bottles of his favourite Scottish mineral water would be aboard the Queen's Flight.

It was a normal strategy meeting to ensure the tour would be faultless, seamless and smooth, but, when the business of the day was complete, Aylard – a man who by now enjoyed a closer relationship with the Prince than anyone else at the Palace – cleared his throat. 'Sir, there is one final issue we must discuss.'

Then, the two loyal aides talked directly to the Prince about what had been referred to in royal circles for years only as 'that matter': Charles's twenty-four-year-long affair with Camilla Parker Bowles.

Over the next sixty minutes they held nothing back. They were brutal and to the point.

'Do you want to be king?' they asked.

Without hesitation, Charles's reply shot back: 'Of course.'

Their response was equally succinct. 'Well then, Sir, about Camilla . . . '

In straight language, man to man, they explained to him that the Australian trip would be the first, vital battle to rehabilitate his image. In simple terms he was told he would need to 'Tipp-Ex the Tampax', a crude reference to Charles's

A tearful Diana breaks down during a visit to Southport, 1992 – her marriage already at an end.

Diana and Camilla nervously watch Charles ride at Ludlow Races 1980 – both in love with the same man.

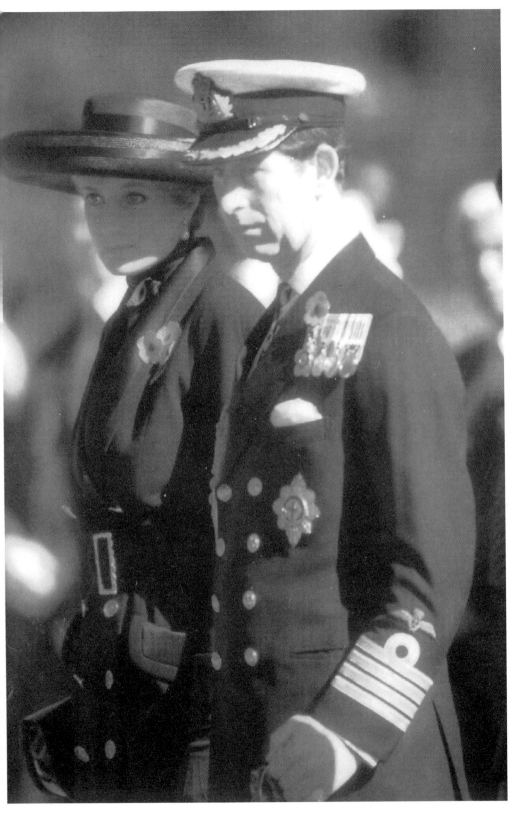

A serious Charles and Diana on Remembrance Sunday – their marriage lost forever.

Top left: The Parker Bowles' London home – Andrew's main base while Camilla remains at home in the country.
Below: The tension shows – the unhappy tour of Korea 1992 – when the couple were nicknamed 'The Glums'.

Top right: Magnificent Middlewick House in Corsham, Wiltshire – the Parker Bowles' main family home.

The family relax in the magnificent garden of Middlewick House, Camilla's pride and joy

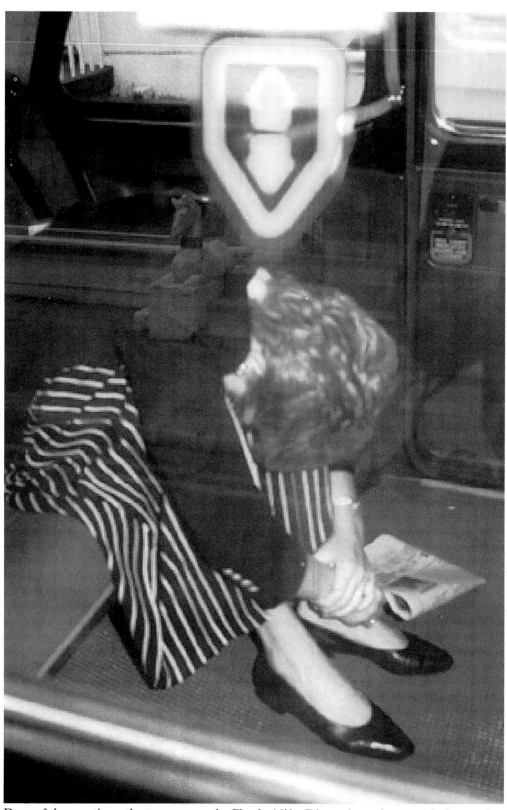

Days of desperation : the two women in Charles' life. Diana through a car window and Camilla on the run.

The laughing Prince – Charles in a rare, relaxed moment of joviality before his world was shattered by the Camillagate crisis.

Top: The Queen gives her seal of approval by inviting Camilla to polo just days after the front page news of the scandal.
Below: A tense Camilla visiting son, Tom, at Eton College just two days after Camillagate broke.

Camilla at the memorial service for the late Earl of Westmorland at the Guards Chapel, November 1993 – Diana kept her distance.

Andrew Parker Bowles, Camilla and son Tom, shortly after Tom left Eton College.

Andrew and Camilla step out in style – still together after all these years.

Still smiling – Camilla gives the press pack, which has hounded her for so long, a friendly wave at the height of the Camillagate scandal.

admission on the notorious tape that he wanted to come back as Camilla's tampons.

By the end of that meeting, Charles's mind was made up. He would say sadly: 'It's awfully difficult to see yourself as others see you. But I now know what I must do.'

He had been told by those closest to him that he had but one choice to make: it was the Crown – or Camilla.

A royal insider says: 'It was D-Day, decision day, for Charles. For the first time, the $64 million question had been put to him. It was explained, in no uncertain terms, that if he truly, genuinely and absolutely wanted to be king, something would have to go. And that was Camilla.'

After twenty-four long years, the Prince was being asked to make the most difficult and heart-rending decision of his life. Like his great-uncle, Edward VIII, he was being asked to choose between the Crown . . . and the woman he loved.

Duty Before Love

When the end came, it was quick, deadly and decisive.

It was the week before Christmas 1993. Camilla Parker Bowles picked up the telephone and dialled the number which had become as familiar to her as her own. She heard the telephone ringing at the other end. Normally, it would ring a maximum of three times before he picked it up.

Today, it rang and rang and rang. Perturbed, she hung up.

She redialled the number. This time, the receiver was picked up at the other end. But far from hearing the calming tones of a friendly voice, a stranger answered.

Confused, but always impeccably true to form, Camilla gave a slight cough and said: 'Good evening, may I speak to His Royal Highness, the Prince of Wales, please?'

'Sorry, madam,' the curt stranger replied, 'His Royal Highness is unavailable.'

Hearing those few short words, Camilla knew it was over. The greatest, and ultimately most tragic, love story of modern times was at an end.

For twenty-four long years, Camilla Parker Bowles and

Prince Charles had enjoyed a relationship more binding, passionate and enduring than most marriages. But the Prince had made his mind up. He was faced with a choice between fulfilling his life's work and the love of his life.

As he was later to tell a friend: 'If being king is my duty, Camilla was my fate. But duty always comes before fate.'

Camilla knew it was over.

The number she had dialled was a private 'hotline' set up in Charles's private study at his Highgrove estate in Gloucestershire. It was 'Camilla's number'.

The special phone had been installed shortly after the devastating 'Camillagate' tape became public. No-one else, not even Diana, had the number. It was a special 'safe' landline, checked at random at least once a month by the Prince's security staff to ensure no-one would ever again be able to 'tap in' to his most intimate conversations.

Camilla knew the stranger could have picked it up only on the specific instructions of one man: Prince Charles. And she knew Charles had finally sacrificed her love for the love of something greater and even closer to his heart: the Crown.

Fifty-four years earlier, Edward VIII had given up the throne for love. But history was not going to repeat itself.

A close member of Prince Charles's inner circle says: 'It was the toughest decision of his life. He spent days mulling it over in his mind. Of course, giving up Camilla is something he had been asked to think about many times before. But each time in the past, he refused.

'Camilla was like a drug to him, an addiction he could not give up. He always needed to have his "fix".

'Now, on the eve of the Australian visit, he knew he had to end it. He knew that, above all else, he had to fulfil his destiny.

'The irony is that Camilla knew what he was thinking. They had been speaking on an almost daily basis. She was fully supportive, as ever. She told him she loved him; that she would always love him and be there for him – but that she would sacrifice her own happiness for his sense of duty. She actually told him: "You may be happy with me, but one thing is for certain, you will never be happy unless you fulfil your destiny."

'Even though Camilla knew she would suffer, she was prepared to make the ultimate sacrifice. She was prepared to pay the ultimate price of losing the love of her Prince so that he would never have to suffer the same indignities as his great-uncle.'

In the tragic and complex web of human emotions which had been his life for so long, Charles had reached an unwavering decision: his relationship with Camilla was the price he would have to pay for his future. But even after he had refused to take Camilla's call that day, he could not get her out of his mind. His business was unfinished. He called her from Sandringham on Christmas Day. The conversation lasted less than two minutes. He told her he loved her, but that his decision was 'irrevocable'.

Camilla, as ever, understood 'totally'.

The Prince's tour of Australia in January 1994 was a glorious success. For the first time in more than a decade, he was on a solo tour – and making headlines back home.

He delighted the crowds by popping into a pub for a pint, clowning about with a golf club and even giving an energetic demonstration of mouth-to-mouth resuscitation on a topless blonde plastic dummy.

Then, student David Kang fired a starter's pistol at the Prince during an event in Sydney. The cool calm and collected way the Prince shrugged off the attack and even smiled a few minutes after Kang was pounced on by protection officers impressed the world. Just hours after the incident, the Prince gave a relaxed interview to Australian journalists in which he dismissed the scare with humour and modesty.

A Palace insider says: 'It was a massive PR victory for Charles. It showed him, in the most extreme situation, a potentially life-threatening situation, showing the calm and coolness of head he always does. It showed the world conclusively that, in times of crisis, the Prince does not crack under pressure.'

A few days later, Nigel Dempster revealed the story the whole of Britain had been waiting for. MY DUTY BEFORE LOVE read the headline on the front page of the *Mail on Sunday*. In his piece, Dempster wrote: 'Prince Charles has chosen to fulfil his destiny as future king by renouncing his relationship with Mrs Camilla Parker Bowles.

'He has decided to sacrifice his close friendship with the forty-six-year-old mother of two for the sake of his duty to the country.'

Dempster quoted a Cabinet source, who said: 'This decision by the Prince is a clear indication that he takes his future responsibilities very seriously. It is entirely right that he should put his duty first and he should be respected for this decision.'

And a friend of Camilla's was quoted as saying: 'There has been conjecture that Andrew and Camilla will eventually divorce, but only if either of them wanted to marry again, and that is certainly not the situation at the moment.

'Anyone who knows Camilla knows she does not see herself as the future wife of the Prince of Wales. But he did make a long-term commitment to her which is now over.'

The story concluded: 'In a deeply personal phone call, Charles was recorded telling her [Camilla]: "Your greatest achievement is to love me."

'But one thing, in time, may assuage her grief. The man who admitted that she made him, will one day be king.

'The sacrifice of letting him go may yet be her greatest achievement of all.'

The story was greeted positively by the public. An opinion poll a few days later showed that seventy-four per cent of people believed Charles had made the right decision.

A high-ranking Palace insider was quoted as saying: 'Sir reached his decision with a great deal of thought and difficulty. But his mind is made up. There is a sense of great relief in the Palace. From now on, the country will judge the Prince purely on his merits. And they will discover that he is a very, very fine man indeed, a man who will make a fine and noble king for our nation. He has made the ultimate sacrifice and has paid the ultimate price for his country. And his country will love him for it.'

Privately, Charles *did* call Camilla once more. After surviving the shooting incident in Australia, he rang Camilla to assure her he was 'fine' and that the trip had 'gone better than any of us had expected'.

A close aide says: 'It would have been too callous at that stage not to have called her. He knew she would be worried. But the call was only brief. It was too painful to both of them to speak for any length of time in the circumstances. The Prince told Camilla he would not telephone her again for some time.'

The Queen was fully supportive of her son's decision. They met the week after his successful trip to Australia.

A Palace insider says: 'There was no delight from the Queen about Camilla going, but she was pleased that Charles had chosen duty above love. The Queen has always been remarkably fond of Camilla. She knew about the affair for years and yet always welcomed Camilla to Balmoral or Sandringham. In fact, the Queen was sad for Camilla. But she was proud of Charles for making the most difficult decision of his life. She knew he had proved he was not another Duke of Windsor. When it came to D-Day, Charles made the right decision. The Queen knew he had made a wise choice, and she told him so repeatedly. She knew he was still in love with Camilla, but she respected him more than she had ever done before.'

In January 1994, the way was clear for Charles to continue rebuilding himself in the eyes of the public. The first steps had been hugely successful – now the real work was about to begin.

Rebuilding

In June 1994, the historic pageantry surrounding the fiftieth anniversary of the Allied D-Day landings on the beaches of Normandy was in full swing.

The Queen, the Queen Mother and Prince Charles all played an active and high-profile role in the numerous memorial services and tributes to those who fell defending the free world. But to the royal family, the D-Day celebrations were the signal for some private celebrations, for, after the most turbulent period the monarchy has had to face in the twentieth century, they were finally on the verge of their own victory.

Prince Charles was celebrating the successful outcome of his own D-Day, Decision Day – to cut free of both Princess Diana and the scandal of his relationship with Camilla Parker Bowles. On the eve of the twenty-fifth anniversary of his investiture as the Prince of Wales, he and his advisers felt more confident than they had in years that nothing would now prevent him from assuming his rightful place on the throne.

A courtier says: 'The D-Day celebrations were a real watershed for everyone at the Palace who'd had such a bumpy ride. The public response was phenomenal and the opinion polls showed, once again, that the majority of people were turning in Charles's favour.

'It was a major turning point for the Palace. After all the upset, heartache and tears, the huge campaign to reinstate Charles as the rightful future monarch in the hearts and minds of the public was being won.'

For Charles believes now more than ever that he *will* be crowned King Charles III on the death of the Queen.

His close friend Nicholas Soames says: 'There was never any question. The Prince will assume his rightful place in history. Being heir to the throne is not an ambition but a duty and one which will befall Charles on a sad moment later in his life. He will inherit the throne, and that is the end of the matter. He is as certain of that now, even more so, than he has ever been before.'

The relationship between Charles and his mother continued to grow closer throughout 1994. Both realized that Diana, for too long, had been allowed to pull the strings. Now, both were beginning to feel in control of their own destinies. Both were determined to safeguard the future of the monarchy and continue to take steps to get the House of Windsor in shape to face the challenges of the twenty-first century.

On 23 June 1994, the Queen approved a cost-cutting plan to take the royal yacht *Britannia* out of service.

It was yet another move to boost the royal family's standing in the eyes of the public. Taking the *Britannia* out of service will save the British taxpayer £12 million a year.

A Palace aide says: 'The royal yacht has been a favourite of the royal family for years. To announce they were giving it up voluntarily, to save money for the country, was a remarkable thing to happen. The Queen has always had a deep attachment to *Britannia*. The vessel has been part of her life since 1953. She perceives it as a graceful symbol of royalty and the nation. It must have been an extremely tough decision for her to take.

'The decision to scrap *Britannia* was one she discussed at

length with Charles. It was another example of how aware both of them have become about the way the monarchy is perceived in the country. They both realize that, these days, people will not tolerate what is seen as luxury spending by the royals. That was one of the fundamental reasons the Queen agreed to give up the vessel.

'For many years, the Prince and his mother did not enjoy the closest of relationships. But in recent months, they have enjoyed a very close bond. They speak on the phone almost daily and exchange ideas frequently. The are both working towards the same goals. They have learned a lot from the whole Diana débâcle.

'When at all possible, they meet for lunch at least once a week. A new dialogue has opened up between the Prince and his mother and also between both sets of royal advisers. It's full steam ahead from here on in.

'The Queen is determined the good work that was done to improve Charles's public image at the end of 1993 and throughout 1994 should continue. He has her full and unequivocal support in all his goals. He is the rightful heir and the entire Palace machine is now geared towards his succession.'

Another of Charles's closest friends says: 'He sees no reason why he should not become king. He has been groomed for that from birth. He regards that as his ultimate destiny and the real reason for his life.

'He clearly regrets the whole Camilla scandal, but he believes that the scandal will eventually fade and the British public will accept him as their monarch; as a man who is totally and utterly committed to his duty and in his plans to lead Britain into the next century.'

The man responsible for the massive change in both the Prince's public image and his own views about himself is his private secretary, Commander Richard Aylard.

Aylard, forty-one, now holds daily meetings with his 'support' staff and is more accessible to the media than any other of the Prince's advisers. His campaign to rebuild the Prince's image – nicknamed 'the charm offensive' behind Palace doors, has been a phenomenal success.

One Fleet Street royal correspondent says: 'It's extraordinary what Richard has achieved. He has remoulded the Prince's image and it is a process which continues to this day. The great thing is that, for the first time, there is someone who is willing to speak out with the full authority of the Prince. The Commander does not shirk difficult phone calls. He is available constantly to respond to stories that Diana's side still puts out. Commander Aylard has become one of the most powerful men at the Palace and certainly one of the most popular men with the media. The biggest change is that Richard knows how to play the publicity game. He knows what to do. He is highly experienced. And he has the full confidence of the entire royal family.'

In March 1994, Commander Aylard appeared on the respected BBC programme 'Newsnight'. It was the first time any top-ranking member of the Palace staff had appeared so publicly to defend the Prince.

He said: 'We have decided it is better to go on in a dignified way carrying on with the Prince's public life. It is deeply unpleasant for anyone to have their personal lives published in varying accounts and then dissected in public. I don't want to get into the Prince's present state of mind, but he is certainly not in despair. He is both a very sensitive person and a very determined person.

'That is not always the most comfortable combination because, if you get hurt, and if you are determined, you want to keep going. I can tell you that from my position, he will keep going, even if, from time to time, he gets hurt.'

Aylard's high-profile image has only boosted the Prince's own popularity within the press and the country at large. So pleased was Prince Charles by the work Aylard has done that he gave him the honour of the Royal Victoria Order in the Queen's birthday honours list in June 1994. The honour is personally bestowed by the Queen.

A Palace insider says: 'It was a clear message from the Palace to the Commander that they are thrilled by what he has done and continues to do. His work has been recognized not only by the powers-that-be inside the Palace, but also by anyone who knows what a mammoth task he faced. Commander Aylard has been the brains behind a total transformation in the Prince. They both have the most enormous respect for each other. Commander Aylard has achieved a tremendous amount of good so far in building the Prince's image up from a man who was once ridiculed to a man who is now viewed as the rightful future monarch. But the work is continuing. Commander Aylard isn't someone to rest on his laurels. He will continue to mould and shape the Prince for years to come. By the time Charles is in a position to ascend to the throne, there will be absolutely no doubt in anyone's mind that he is the right man for the job.'

Aylard built a small circle of experienced men and women around him – with the sole purpose of continuing the resurgence in the Prince's image.

Belinda Harley, thirty-six, an Oxford graduate, who runs her own public-relations company, was brought in as an assistant private secretary. She developed a close bond with the Prince. A woman with wit, charm and intelligence in abundance, she worked for years as an adviser to the Prince's Trust before being drafted into his closest inner circle.

A male fan inside the Palace says: 'She's as tough as anything, but she does it all with a smile and bundles of charm. She's a real driving force behind the campaign to revamp the Prince. Because she is a woman, she enjoys a different relationship with the Prince than the stuffy advisers he's used to. When she joined the Palace, it was like a breath of fresh air. She is an ideas woman who is used to making things happen.

'In fact, Belinda and Commander Aylard were instantly nicknamed "The Dream Team". He is down-to-earth, solid, dependable and brilliant and she is flirty, fun and brilliant.'

Belinda was also awarded the Royal Victoria Order in the June 1994 Queen's birthday honours list. Belinda officially left the Prince's staff in July 1994 to return to her PR company. Unofficially, she remains extremely close to Aylard and the Prince – and still offers wise words of advice to this day.

The Prince also hired two new press secretaries to handle the delicate relationship between himself and the newspapers. Both are hard-working, experienced professionals, well used to handling the most delicate of subjects. Sandie Henney was hired from Scotland Yard; Allan Percival was a government press spokesman for Northern Ireland.

One journalist on the royal patch says: 'For the first time ever, we've got true professionals handling Charles. And the difference it made during the Australian tour in January was staggering. We were getting off-the-record comments and updates all the time.

'Just look at the shooting incident. A few years ago, we would have been given no information. Nothing would have been said. But as it was, we were getting hourly updates from Aylard and Henney. It was great. They know how to deal with the press, how to present Charles in a positive light for once – how to make him human, likeable even.

'They've gone to war on the old image of Charles – and they're certainly notching up some pretty impressive victories.'

Charles also hired Alexandra Legge-Bourke.

A bubbly, fun-loving twenty-eight-year-old Sloane known universally as 'Tiggy', after the lovable Beatrix Potter character Mrs Tiggywinkle, she has become the Prince's unofficial social adviser, a mother-type figure to his two young sons – and has developed a close bond of friendship with the Prince.

Officially, she was hired as an £18,000-a-year assistant to Commander Aylard. But within a few short weeks of her appointment in December 1993, it became clear her role was much, much more.

Tiggy, who once ran her own private nursery, has impeccable credentials. Her mother, the Honourable Mrs Elizabeth Legge-Bourke, is a lady-in-waiting to Princess Anne. Her Aunt Victoria is another of Princess Anne's ladies-in-waiting.

Victoria Legge-Burke says: 'Tiggy is the most enchanting young lady that anyone could possibly meet. She comes from a loving, happy family and you cannot help but warm to her. She's got hundreds of friends and I've never met anyone who came across her and didn't fall in love with her. Of course, she is terribly, terribly discreet and loyal.'

An ancestor, the Marquis of Lincolnshire, was George V's Lord Great Chamberlain and an uncle was Page of Honour to the Queen. Tiggy's father William is with the leading City merchant banking firm of Kleinwort Benson and the family owns a vast 1,000-acre estate in Wales.

Tiggy's former headmistress Margaret Parry of Heathfield School says: 'She is a delightful girl, very vivacious, very charming. She is utterly reliable, always on the side of the bright and good.'

Tiggy has become close to Wills and Harry. After leaving school at sixteen, she took a nursery teacher training course at the St Nicholas Montessori Centre in London. She then spent a year looking after youngsters at the Little Wandsworth School in Balham, south London, before taking a year off to travel around Australia.

Her former boss at Little Wandsworth, Sophie Irwin, says: 'We were delighted with her. She is a very jolly person who was very good with children. We were very sorry when she left.'

Tiggy soon had her own rooms at St James's Palace and at Highgrove and, according to estate workers, enjoys an 'extremely good' relationship with the young Princes.

One says: 'William and Harry simply adore her. She is warm and loving and totally solid and stable, unlike their mother. She looks after all aspects of the boys' lives. She packs their cases for school, sews their name tags into their uniforms. The boys are devoted to her and she is devoted to them. She has given both the young Princes and Prince Charles a solid base. She is someone who fits perfectly into their lives.'

Says one royal adviser: 'Tiggy has put a spring in the step of Prince Charles. She has a bright, positive nature, always upbeat, which is infectious. She is like a ray of sunshine.'

Tiggy encouraged Charles to show the world the close bond he has with his sons. Since Tiggy's arrival, Charles has been photographed taking the boys fishing, cycling around the estate at Highgrove and even sitting quietly and reading to them.

Lady Colin Campbell says: 'The boys are already as close to their father as they are to Diana. William, in particular, adores his father. As the years go by, William will spend more and more time with Charles as he is groomed for kingship. William is spending more and more time at Highgrove and at St James's Palace with his father. He already has an extremely close bond with his father and that bond will grow even closer through the years. The Palace are determined that William will grow up with a sense of history and duty, schooled in the way of the monarchy as his father and forebears were in the past.'

The Prince said recently: 'I can never remember my father being there for me when I grew up. He never once told me he loved me, he never praised me for anything. It was all very sad. It has taught me I must never be like that with my sons. I always let them know that I love them and I show them I do.'

In February 1994, the Prince took the boys on a solo skiing trip to Klosters, Switzerland, taking Tiggy along to care for his sons.

Again, it was a media triumph. He was pictured as a devoted father, teaching his sons to ski and even holding an impromptu snowball fight with them which ended up with the trio rolling in the snow.

A friend of the Prince's says: 'He has clearly emerged a new man. No-one has ever seen him so relaxed, confident and self-assured. He has finally banished all the demons from his life. He is thrilled with his new circle of advisers. He trusts Commander Aylard and his team completely. And he is delighted with Tiggy. He once said she is like a "breath of fresh air" sweeping through the Palace.

'Throughout 1993, he was a man with a dark cloud of depression over his head.

'Today, he has listened to the professional advice of his

advisers, and their wise words have paid off. Ask anyone in the country how they feel about Charles now and they are sure to say his image has greatly improved in their eyes. A transformation is going on. Most people are now convinced that nothing will stop Charles becoming king.

'Publicly breaking up with Camilla, the woman he loves, was the ultimate sacrifice. But Charles knew that he had to do it to win the ultimate prize. And that prize *will* be his.'

But despite the Prince's brilliant efforts at rehabilitating himself, the spectre of Camilla always lurked in the background.

On 15 June 1994, on the eve of a Palace publicity drive to celebrate the twenty-fifth anniversary of Charles's investiture as Prince of Wales, the major ITV network broadcast extracts of the 'Camillagate' tape on air across Britain for the first time.

A courtier says: 'It was the last thing the Prince needed, but he coped with it. He knows the "Camillagate" crisis will never truly go away, but he has proved he has put it successfully in the background and that it has not affected what he sees as his life's work and his destiny in any way.'

Charles has also actively carved out more work for himself.

'He wants to be seen to be *doing* something,' says one aide. 'Of course, he's always been one of the most hard-working royals behind the scenes, but now he's putting himself out there, showing people what he's doing.'

Charles has streamlined his many charitable interests under the banner of 'The Prince's Trust'. It is a formidable organization with an annual income of £40 million, 500 paid staff and more than 8,500 voluntary staff.

He writes almost weekly to the directors of the various charities in The Prince's Trust. Trust director Tom Shebbeare says: 'There is never a shortage of things to respond to. The Prince takes an enormous and very keen personal interest in what is going on. He is always on the phone or writing letters. He wants to know everything which is happening, no matter how trivial it may appear.'

The Prince is also actively involved in a new role as

Britain's 'cultural and commercial ambassador'. State visits are being planned now with the help of the Prime Minister's office for the Prince to take several trips abroad alone to promote British business and enterprise. He has held regular meetings with Cabinet members about how best to 'fly the flag' for British industry abroad. He has personally written 3,000 letters to captains of industry outlining the role he is seeking to play – and asking for their support.

A close aide to the Prince says: 'He writes to industry leaders constantly. Dozens have been invited to a series of private lunches with Charles at the Palace. He is now showing he *has* an active and valuable role to play. He is like a man on a crusade – a crusade to win the hearts of the people and achieve his rightful position in life.

'The whole aim has been to show that the Prince is no longer drifting. He is a man with a clear focus and a clear goal.

'The biggest change is that the Prince no longer sees kingship as his God-given right. He knows how close he came to having to give up everything he had worked for all his life. He is rejuvenated, reborn. He now works harder than ever but he is more confident and determined than ever. He is like a different person.'

By the summer of 1994, Charles's future was looking rosier than it had for years. Public opinion polls showed his image was higher than it had ever been. Thanks to the wise counselling of men like Commander Richard Aylard, he had successfully countered the devastating years of negative publicity following the breakdown of his marriage and the affair with Camilla. He was a man confident of his future, at ease with his fate – that history has anointed him heir to the throne, a burden he must bear with grace, dignity and fortitude.

Prince Charles was a man convinced of his destiny. He was convinced that his sense of duty would come before all else – for the sake of his family, the Crown and his own happiness.

On 29 June 1994, the Prince and his advisers took the biggest gamble of all in the remoulding of his image.

On a hot summer's evening, 12.7 million viewers across Britain tuned in to watch a two-and-a-half-hour ITV television documentary on the Prince's life: 'Charles: The Private Man, The Public Role', made by the respected broadcaster Jonathan Dimbleby.

Dimbleby and his camera crew had been given unprecedented access to follow the Prince for more than eighteen months, capturing his most intimate thoughts and private times on film.

One of the film crew says: 'We were all astonished by how much access he gave us to all aspects of his life. You could tell it was agony for him sometimes to have us there. But he was determined to show a truer picture of himself to the public.

'A few years ago, a programme like ours would have been unthinkable. But the Prince and his advisers now realize the full power of the media. They knew that if Charles was allowed to come across as himself, the British public would welcome him back into their hearts. It was a risky gamble, but it was a brilliant move. For the first time, the public had a chance to see their future king both at work and in private. And it showed a very different Charles from the one they had imagined.'

Although Dimbleby and producer Christopher Martin had full editorial control of the programme, the Prince was given advance notice of the questions he would be asked. For long periods in the film, the Prince wore a small microphone on his shirt which picked up his every word during both private and public moments.

For days before the programme aired, the country held its breath. On the previous Sunday, a highly-placed source close to the Prince leaked one of the programme's more devastating revelations: that Charles hopes to end the 450-year role of the monarch as Head of the Church of England. He told Dimbleby he would prefer to be the defender of *all* faiths and religions, not just the Protestant Church.

Since Henry VIII became Head of the Church of England in 1531, all British monarchs have sworn at their coronation to: '. . . maintain in the United Kingdom the Protestant Reformed Religion established by law . . .'

The story made the front page of *The Sunday Times*: CHARLES PLANS TO BREAK ROYAL LINK WITH CHURCH – KING SHOULD BE HEAD OF ALL RELIGIONS ran the headline.

The story read: 'The Prince has said he would be happy to be seen as "defender of faith" rather than "defender of *the* faith".'

The Prince was quoted, from the programme, saying: 'I happen to believe that the Catholic subjects of the sovereign are as important [as Protestants], not to mention the Islamic, Hindu and Zoroastrian.'

The statement immediately provoked controversy. Lord Coggan, a former Archbishop of Canterbury, said: 'This is a hornets' nest of problems. If he's saying Christianity is equal with other religions, we should differ profoundly from him. As men, we are all equal before God, but are you talking about religions and saying one is as good as another? I hope he is not saying that.'

The Venerable George Austin, the Archdeacon of York who had so strongly criticized Charles over the 'Camillagate' tapes, was more supportive. He said: 'It is true that the monarch should not be the supreme governor of the Church of England. That's a historical absurdity. But anything else to do with disestablishment is not the concern of the Prince of Wales, it's to do with the Church of England. My feeling is we should have a Church that is established, but doesn't have a monarch as supreme governor.'

While his decision to break with the Church of England caused a sensation, the biggest sensation was still to come. For the Prince had also spoken to Dimbleby about the one subject he had always steadfastly refused to comment on in the past: his relationship with Mrs Camilla Parker Bowles.

On national television, for the first time, Charles would address the question of whether he had ever been unfaithful to Princess Diana. As millions of viewers across Britain watched on the edge of their seats, Dimbleby cleared his throat and challenged the Prince to 'respond to the most damaging charge' against him.

The broadcaster said: 'You were, because of your relationship with Camilla Parker Bowles, from the beginning persistently unfaithful to your wife and thus caused the breakdown . . .'

The Prince glanced down nervously and then, staring Dimbleby straight in the eye, he finally responded to the question the world had been demanding he answer.

It was to be one of the most sensational confessions of all time . . .

A Royal Confession

It was the bombshell the world had been waiting for. Sitting in the sunny lounge of Prince Charles's country home, Highgrove, broadcaster Jonathan Dimbleby asked the future king the 'ultimate' question.

Staring the Prince straight in the eye, Dimbleby said: 'Were you, did you try to be faithful and honourable to your wife when you took on the vow of marriage?'

Without hesitation, Charles replied: 'Yes, absolutely.'

'And you were?'

'Yes . . .' answered Charles. Then he continued: '. . . until it became irretrievably broken down, after us both having tried.'

Dimbleby continued: 'Do you hope the issue will go away?'

Charles answered: 'It would be nice if it did. Other people don't have to go through this when their marriage breaks down. It's the last thing I wanted to happen.'

Then, breaking the tension with a laugh, the Prince added: 'I am not a total idiot. I didn't go into marriage with the intention of this happening. I am not, on the whole, a cynical person. It sounds self-righteous, but I try to get it right and do the right thing by everybody. It has happened – that is that, regrettably.'

For more than two and a half hours, Prince Charles laid bare his life for all to see. He did not avoid a single question, even the most intimate and probing queries about his marriage – and future.

Says one royal insider: 'It was the make-or-break interview. The Prince truly believed that if he was honest and truthful in his answers, the television programme would finally show his subjects he is the right man to become king.

'But it was a gamble. If the programme had backfired, those 150 minutes of television could have cost Charles the lot – his hard-fought-for popularity, his image – and even the Crown. It is impossible to overstate the importance of that documentary. You could almost say it was trial by television. If Charles stated his case well and won, his future would be secure. If he failed, his very future would be on the line. It was an astonishingly brave thing to do.'

As millions watched, the future king answered the most intimate questions about his private life for the first time.

Asked by Dimbleby if he thought the marriage breakdown had damaged his image, the Prince replied: 'Well, I don't recommend it to anybody. The breakdown of a marriage is always a difficult thing and creates great unhappiness and consternation and everything else, inevitably . . . I accept that I'm sure there's a certain amount of damage.

'One of the difficulties I find is the predictability of what people will say.

'I'd much rather it had not happened. I am sure my wife would have felt the same. It was not through lack of trying on both parts to ensure it worked. But you can't avoid it.

'I accept there is a certain amount of damage. I mean you can't avoid it with something of this unfortunate nature.'

Perhaps the most telling insight into his innermost thoughts and feelings came when Charles openly discussed his friendship with Camilla for the first time. For it became apparent that, despite the bombshell confession of admitting the affair for the first time, Charles had absolutely no intention of ever giving up his friendship with the woman he has loved for a quarter of a century.

The Prince referred to both his mistress and her husband Andrew Parker Bowles as 'dear friends'.

He said: 'Mrs Parker Bowles is a great friend of mine. She's been a friend for a very long time and will continue to be for a very long time. I am terribly lucky to have so many friends who I think are wonderful and make the whole difference to my life which would be intolerable otherwise.

'When a marriage breaks down, awful and miserable as that is, it is inevitable that it's your friends who are so helpful. Otherwise you would go stark staring mad – that's what friends are for.'

Asked about his marriage failure, Charles became noticeably irritated and said: 'Look, come on. It happens to half the country and it happened to me. It is not something I wanted to happen.'

By opening his heart on prime-time television in the most revealing royal close-up ever, Charles pleaded for understanding over his failed marriage.

When Dimbleby probed further about the rumours to the effect that he had been 'persistently unfaithful' with Camilla, the Prince replied: 'These things are so personal that it is difficult to know how to talk about them. There is no truth in so much of this speculation. Mrs Parker Bowles is a great friend of mine.'

The story made headlines for days.

CHARLES: I HAD AN AFFAIR ran the front-page story in the *Sun*; ITN led its 'News at Ten' with the 'astonishing confession'; the *Daily Mail* read: CHARLES: WHEN I WAS UNFAITHFUL and the left-wing *Daily Mirror* newspaper screamed: NOT FIT TO REIGN.

While the Prince never actually named Camilla as his mistress, broadcaster Dimbleby did so in an interview the following day, saying: 'He was unfaithful with someone who has been a long-standing friend and that is Mrs Parker Bowles.

I think it is absolutely clear that no-one else was involved.'

Throughout the programme, Charles answered every question fully and frankly.

On the subject of a possible divorce from Diana, his eyes flickered with sadness as he said: 'It is not a consideration at the moment.' But he added: 'That sort of thing is very much in the future. If it happens, then it will happen. The question of divorce is a very personal and private thing between my wife and myself and that's how it will remain.'

Asked if a divorce would be an obstacle to the throne, he replied: 'I don't see why it should be an impediment. All my life I have been brought up to do my utmost and carry out my duty to the country.

'I am not going to say I will not do it. I am not going to live anywhere else and I don't want to.'

He also dismissed as 'extraordinary' any suggestion that he might pass over his chance to reign in favour of his son William.

Defending the role of the monarchy in Britain, the Prince said: 'It would be a great pity to lose it because everything would then be based around politics. This country would lose a great deal. The great thing about the monarchy is its independence, which enables it to function in a relatively free way. It represents the ordinary person's thoughts and feelings without belonging to a particular party.'

But of the 150-minute programme, the five minutes the Prince spent confessing his adultery dominated the headlines – and sparked a widespread controversy.

The Reverend Tony Higton, a leading member of the Church of England's ruling body, the Synod, slammed the Prince as 'unfit to be king'.

He said: 'From what I understand, there does not appear to be any hint of penitence. And that is going to cause him some very serious problems. I therefore do not think he is fit to be Defender of the Faith and Supreme Governor of the Church of England.'

But the Archdeacon of York, George Austin, took a

different view. The churchman said: 'I admire the Prince's honesty. He simply confirmed what everyone already knew. He is a Christian and has done something wrong. By making this public statement, he is showing a large degree of regret. I do not believe his future position as king will be affected.

'Nobody wants him to crawl up the Mall from Buckingham Palace to Westminster Abbey on his knees pleading for forgiveness – or if they do, they shouldn't. God gave us forgiveness and it's not for us to question it.'

Prime Minister John Major joined the growing row by insisting Charles's confession 'in no way' affected his position as future king. He said: 'There is no reason why the Prince should not fulfil his duty.'

For the first time, Charles admitted how difficult it must have been for Diana to join the ranks of the royal family.

Referring to the family as 'the organization', he said: 'I do think that those people who marry into my family find it increasingly difficult to do so because of the added pressure, and finding that they're put into positions in the organization which they are simply not trained for and the strains and stresses that become, in some cases, almost intolerable.'

Other parts of the film showed the Prince relaxing with his sons at Balmoral. Dimbleby asked: 'Do you like your children?' to which Charles replied: 'Of course I do. Seeing them develop gives me enormous pleasure, satisfaction and pride. As they grow older, it gets more fun. I like mucking around with them.'

He came across as a loving, doting father. In one scene he sat on a step wearing a kilt watching his son playing football. In another, he tenderly stroked Harry's nose with a handkerchief.

Asked about important values he wished to impart to his sons, he said: 'Good manners. Doing to others as you want them to do to you. It's not a bad way to operate.'

According to those close to Charles, he was 'relieved and upbeat' in the days following the television broadcast. The programme was later broadcast around the globe in countries as far afield as America, Australia, Germany, Japan, Saudi Arabia and The Gambia.

His confessions made headlines in newspapers around the world.

A friend of the Prince's says: 'He was rejuvenated after the programme aired. It was as if an enormous weight had been lifted from his shoulders. He was pleased with the way the documentary turned out. He felt that even though there had been considerable criticism in some quarters of the press, the British public, while perhaps not condoning his affair could, maybe, understand the reasons behind it better. Don't forget, he was speaking to a nation where one in three marriages ends in divorce. Millions of families go through the same pain as he went through. He felt that the public would understand – and he was right. It was a big gamble to take, but it paid off.'

Constitutional expert Lord St John of Fawsley, a friend of the Prince, said: 'What matters is the truth and the programme was so devastating because we were listening to the simple truth, something you rarely hear in public life.

'The Prince put himself on judgement before the fairest jury in the world, namely the British public. He put everything before them. He relied on their sense of fairness, their sense of fair play and their sense of justice. And his confidence was justified. He was seen for the man his friends have known for years – strong, brave, honest and reliable. A man who will make a magnificent future king.'

Indeed, the television programme proved a masterstroke. A poll in *The Sun* taken the day after the documentary aired showed a massive swing in the Prince's popularity.

In a poll of the same newspaper's readers shortly before the TV programme, sixty-three per cent of people said they thought Charles was *not* fit to be king. But the post-documentary poll showed a dramatic change of heart. Fifty-four per cent of the 6,000 readers polled said that, after hearing Charles confess to the affair, they now believed he was fit to be king.

'CHARLES RULES OK' read the front page.

A Palace aide says: 'The Prince was thrilled. He read everything that was written in the newspapers at that time and it soon became clear that the programme had worked very much in his favour.'

A similar poll of 80,000 viewers by the television station GMTV also swung in the Prince's favour. Eighty-five per cent said Charles should reign compared with just forty-six per cent who said they approved of him becoming king prior to the documentary.

The mood was mirrored at Tower Bridge in the heart of London when the Prince went walkabout on his first public engagement after the programme. A large crowd cheered their approval. A royal aide said: 'The Prince's mood was elated. Any doubts he had had about appearing in the television programme evaporated. He knew he had stated his case openly for the first time. And when the British public were left to judge him by his own words and actions, he came out ahead. They saw him at work and at play for the first time – and they liked what they saw. He came across as a man who could be trusted; an honourable man who was prepared to face up to his mistakes but whose sense of duty to the Crown and country was unassailable.'

The Prince's private secretary, Commander Richard Aylard, was thrilled. He said: 'The Prince of Wales has absolutely no regrets about the television show. He went into the project with his eyes open. We think it was a rounded and balanced portrait of a man we know and work for. People are telling us how much they appreciated the intimate portrayal of the Prince.'

Lady Colin Campbell says: 'The television programme was a public-relations masterstroke. I don't think Charles owed the public an apology over his affair, but he gave one, and it won him hearts across the country. He appeared genuinely upset by the marriage breakdown and he came across as a normal husband and father. What was astonishing to everyone who watched the show was how frank and honest he was about his affair. He was fair, calm and honest. And the

British public opened their hearts to him.

'It was brilliant. Here was the heir to the throne pointing out that he is just as human as his subjects; admitting his mistakes and putting an end to all the rumour and speculation both about his marriage and his future as king once and for all. By the end of the programme, no-one could be in any doubt that he is the man who *will* be king – and a jolly fine one at that. He showed the side of Charles the public wanted to see – the *true* man behind the image.'

Despite widespread approval for the programme, there was also much criticism of the Prince's decision to open his heart on prime-time television.

The *Daily Mail*'s front-page headline the following morning read: ANOTHER ERROR OF JUDGEMENT? The story said: 'The Prince's aides had been confident that the documentary . . . would rehabilitate his image. Instead, many will feel it portrayed a chronically restless man, well-intentioned but racked with self-doubt. True, there were touching scenes with his sons William and Harry and glimpses of humour . . . but the programme was inevitably dominated by questions about his marriage, adultery and possible divorce . . . and he looked like a prisoner awaiting judgement.'

But royal biographer Brian Hoey says: 'To be frank, the public debate which began after the documentary aired was totally irrelevant. It doesn't make any difference whether Charles is going to be a good king, a bad king, an evil king or a majestic king. What is clear now is that if he survives his mother, he *will* be king.'

On the day the programme aired, Charles had another brush with danger. Piloting a British Aerospace 146 jet of the Queen's Flight from Aberdeen to Islay, the southernmost isle of the Inner Hebrides in Scotland, he overshot the runway in gusting winds. The Prince was forced to swerve ninety degrees left to avoid a deep ditch at the end of the 1,600-yard runway and the plane finished up nose-down in soft ground with three burst tyres. Neither he nor his ten passengers were injured.

The Prince later told pupils at a school he visited, later in the day, on Islay: 'It wasn't quite a crash. We went off the end of the runway, unfortunately. It is not something I recommend happening all the time – unfortunately it did.'

For Diana and her friends, the Prince's prime-time confession was hailed as a victory for the Princess.

DI TOLD YOU SO! ran *The Sun* headline, which described how the Princess was 'relieved and happy' that her husband had finally admitted his relationship with Camilla. The paper's chief reporter, John Kay, quoted close friends of the Princess as saying she was 'celebrating an enormous sense of victory and relief'.

Her friends spoke of her 'vindication'. One said: 'It proves that everything she said about Camilla Parker Bowles in Andrew Morton's book was true. Her husband *was* having an affair – and now he's come right out and admitted it. She felt totally vindicated.'

Indeed, on the very night the programme was broadcast, Diana went out of her way to attract attention. Wearing a plunging off-the-shoulder black cocktail dress, she spectacularly created her own headlines by going to a gala dinner at the Serpentine Gallery in London's Kensington. Sponsored by *Vanity Fair* magazine, the benefit dinner drew 310 guests, including the actress Joan Collins – but all eyes were on Diana.

Royal biographer Brian Hoey said: 'She was annoyed and jealous of all the media coverage Charles was getting because of the documentary. She wanted to show that she'd lost none of her ability to manipulate the press.'

According to those at the gala, Diana smiled and joked the night away. One witness says: 'She was on stunning form. She was either truly relieved or the greatest actress the world has seen. She had a long flirt with the actor Jeremy Irons and flirted and joked all evening. If she was putting on an act, she deserved an Oscar.'

Even the austere *Daily Telegraph* noted: 'She couldn't have chosen a more timely moment to bury the hatchet – in her husband's back.'

But despite Diana's attempts to recapture some of

the headlines, the Palace were delighted with the result of the programme.

The Queen gave her full blessing to Charles's comments. A royal insider says: 'It was something the Prince discussed with his mother at length before agreeing to make the television documentary. He felt it was important to answer every question fully and honestly.

'They had a series of meetings throughout the months the TV crew was following the Prince making the show. And they had a final meeting just two days before the programme aired. The Queen watched the programme privately in advance. And she was pleased with the result. The Palace knew that the adultery confession would cause a public storm. But Charles and the Queen were both adamant that he should tell the truth – and allow the British public to be his judge.

'If Charles had refused to answer Dimbleby's questions about his private life, he would have looked ridiculous and people would have been even more angry with him for avoiding the main question. What he did was a remarkably brave thing to do. He faced the question head-on and he answered it honestly. It was a massive gamble, but it paid off. The public in general admired his courage and honesty.'

On 1 July, Charles attended a ceremony to celebrate the twenty-fifth anniversary of his investiture as Prince of Wales at Caernarvon Castle in Wales. Hundreds of wellwishers cheered the Prince as he arrived for the low-key ceremony.

While some members of the local council boycotted the ceremony in protest against the Prince, the Palace was happy at the end of what many described as 'a very long week'. The Prince was cheered by large crowds as he later visited a housing estate, school and council home in the nearby town of Gwynedd.

An insider said: 'The Prince and his advisers knew it was going to be a bumpy ride. Commander Aylard was speaking to the Prince several times a day in the lead up to the documentary being aired and in the days immediately afterwards. But the reaction was, on the whole, extremely positive. The charm offensive had scored its greatest victory.'

For her part, Camilla steadfastly refused to comment on the Prince's confession. Two days before the broadcast, she claimed she knew nothing about the programme's contents and said she would be 'unlikely' to watch it. In fact, she was fully aware of everything Charles was to say. It can be revealed for the first time that on 17 and 18 April, the two days during which Charles's astonishing confession was taped, he repeatedly telephoned Camilla.

A source very close to the couple says: 'They were on the phone constantly; often the first call from Charles to Middlewick House would be as early as seven in the morning. The phone lines were burning up during that forty-eight-hour period.

'Charles asked Camilla's advice on how much he should say. It was Camilla who encouraged him to "come clean" about their relationship. They were talking almost constantly throughout the time he was making his confession. Often, the calls would go well into the night.'

A friend of Camilla's says: 'Of course Camilla knew what Charles was going to say. He would never have made a public confession like that without first discussing it with Camilla. He called her repeatedly throughout the filming of the programme. He asked her advice about how much he should say. In fact, it was Camilla who helped him prepare answers to some of the more probing personal questions. If Camilla had objected to him confirming the affair, the Prince would never have been so frank in his answers. But Camilla knew that Charles needed to make the confession so the whole question of the affair would be ended once and for all. She knew it was the only way he could put the gossip behind him and win back the hearts of the country. Camilla is extremely smart. She actively encouraged the Prince to be candid with Dimbleby. And it was a truly selfless act. Because Camilla knew that once the Prince confirmed the affair, she again would be besieged by the press and again be branded the "other woman". For a woman who guards her private life as fiercely as Camilla, it was a remarkable act of love. For the umpteenth time in her life, she put the Prince's welfare and needs ahead of her own.'

Indeed, once the story broke, Camilla was again under siege at Middlewick House. While her husband remained at work in Aldershot Barracks, Camilla went to ground. The day before the eagerly-awaited broadcast, she and her daughter Laura secretly boarded a flight to Spain to stay at the 2,000-acre private estate of the Marquis of Douro, one of Charles's closest friends, in Grenada.

Prince Charles telephoned her every day, even while he was on an official two-day visit to Northern Ireland. For, despite the official declaration that the affair was at an end at the close of 1993, they were again closer than ever.

A friend says: 'The Prince genuinely tried to cut ties to Camilla when his advisers told him it would be for the best. But she is his greatest friend and by February 1994, they were very much back together again.'

The couple again resumed their lengthy daily phone conversations and began meeting in secret at the 'safe' country homes of friends. Only a handful of people were aware that contact had been resumed.

One says: 'The Prince was determined he would not be "caught out", so to speak. He is an intensely loyal man to his friends and there was no way he could carry on without Camilla's love and support. But less than a dozen people knew he was still seeing her. They began meeting again in safe homes close to their country bases – but it was very much cloak-and-dagger stuff. The charm offensive was in full swing. Camilla and Charles knew they could not risk a backlash if new stories broke that they were back together again.'

And a Palace insider says: 'No-one is supposed to know that Camilla and Charles are still close, but they are.

'The Prince managed to get through a couple of months without any contact with her, but then, despite all the risks to both their reputations, he made the first move to contact her again by telephoning her.

'It is not something one should condemn him for. Camilla

is more than just a mistress, she is his best friend. They are still in contact because he needs Camilla's friendship constantly.

'They both know they will never be together, but they cannot face no contact whatsoever. Both know their friendship must be conducted in utmost secret. After all that has happened, despite the massive public-relations exercise to improve Charles's image – which has been a success beyond anyone's wildest dreams – the Prince simply cannot give up Camilla.

'He is absolutely determined he will be king. But he will not give up Camilla.

'The rest of the royal family know he and Camilla are still an item, of course. And they are still extremely fond of Camilla. She has always behaved impeccably. She has never let the side down. And for that reason, she is utterly respected by the royal family.

'While Diana is viewed as a traitor who let the "Firm" down, Camilla is seen as someone who has acted impeccably.

'In the future, she may be quietly welcomed back in, but at the moment, the situation is too precarious. Charles cannot afford any fresh scandals while things are going so well for him.

'Camilla, of course, will never let the "Firm" down. She will continue to maintain a dignified silence. That's the difference between Camilla and Diana. Camilla is a real lady. She has class.'

Royal biographer Andrew Morton says: 'It struck everyone in the know as very unlikely that Charles would stop seeing Camilla. I believe they are still in regular contact. He is a man of habit, and old habits die hard.'

After the documentary put Camilla firmly back in the public eye, Charles gave her his full support.

A friend of Camilla's says: 'He is a man who would never abandon a friend, just as Camilla has never abandoned him. When all the fuss blew up around his adultery confession, he was telephoning Camilla constantly.

'Throughout that long week when she was in hiding in Spain, the Prince telephoned her at least once a day, sometimes more. As always, despite the intense publicity and speculation, their friendship remained strong.'

Returning from Spain a week later, Camilla remained tight-lipped when bombarded by reporters shouting questions at Gatwick Airport. Looking tanned but tense, Camilla simply smiled at reporters' questions even though a near riot was breaking out around her as photographers jostled for position.

A friend says: 'Camilla was extremely angry about the scenes at the airport. The press pack was jostling and pushing her and her daughter. But even under that enormous pressure, she did not retaliate. You will never see a picture of Camilla screaming at the camera like Diana does. She simply keeps her head – and her dignity. Camilla is a class act. Of course she must feel it inwardly. But she has never been the type to crack under pressure. What makes people who know Camilla so angry is that so much is written about her which is simply not fair. Camilla will never justify any of the gossips by defending herself publicly, it's just not her style. She had never commented on her affair in the past, and she wasn't about to start then.'

After just forty-eight hours at home in Wiltshire with her husband and daughter, Camilla left again to jet off on a family holiday in the south of France.

A friend of Camilla's says: 'It was a tough time for her. She just needed to get away from all the speculation and pressure. Camilla is an intensely private person. For the affair to flare up again must have been torture for her – but, as usual, she bore the pressure with dignity and fortitude.'

While Camilla maintained a discreet silence, other members of her family spoke out.

Her father, Major Bruce Shand, praised the Prince for his 'honesty and courage'. The Major said loyally: 'I was fascinated by what the Prince had to say about all sorts of issues, including the failure of his marriage. I believe he came across as very fair-minded and sincere. I am in no doubt he will make a perfect king.'

Camilla and Charles's great friend Patti Palmer-

Tomkinson added: 'I believe the Prince was incredibly brave. He put much emphasis on honesty and the truth. He is a wonderful, wonderful man – very honest and brave. I saw the man I know.'

Andrew Parker Bowles broke his silence to say: 'Nothing has changed. I don't give a damn about the rumours, about what's being said or about what has happened. I really can't understand what all the fuss is about.'

Andrew's close friend, polo player Brod Munro-Wilson, said: 'There are many, many open marriages in this country and no-one thinks twice about it.

'Andrew and Camilla will remain together because they are still genuine friends. It is not a question of sharing beds, more a case of sharing experiences, and Andrew and Camilla have been through a lot together. The Prince's television programme will not alter a thing.'

On 14 July 1994, Camilla turned to her Prince for comfort when her beloved mother Rosalind died after a long illness. At seventy-four years old, Rosalind had suffered from the brittle bone disease osteoporosis for many years.

According to one friend: 'Both Charles and Andrew were tremendous supports for her during those difficult days. Camilla adored her mother; they were extremely close to the end.'

Camilla herself said in a remarkable tribute: 'Both of my parents have been so supportive, indeed, more supportive of me, than parents could be expected to be.' A friend of Camilla's added: 'While she was devastated by her mother's death, she was always tremendously grateful to both her parents for never once wavering in their loyalty for her. To this day, Camilla knows her parents both loved her without question. She is eternally grateful for their love and support.

'When Rosalind died, the Prince was tremendously supportive, calling regularly to make sure Camilla was OK. Her husband was also a terrific rock for her to lean on during those difficult days. It proved to Camilla, once and for all, that the love of her friends and family is unwavering.'

By the end of July 1994, things were looking better than they had done for years for Charles. Public opinion was more in his favour than it had been in recent times. He had no doubts in his mind that he will, one day, be king.

For Diana, however, things were not going so smoothly.

A Princess Adrift

The woman whose face had adorned a thousand magazine covers glanced furtively around her. Then, without looking back, she quickly slipped into the driver's seat of her green Audi car.

A few moments later, the man walked up to the car and, without even a split-second's hesitation, opened the passenger side door and stepped in. The watching photographer snapped away, incredulous at the scene unfolding before his eyes.

Diana, Princess of Wales, had been caught red-handed having a clandestine meeting with a top royal reporter. It was the moment the Palace had been longing for.

Her secret rendezvous with Richard Kay, the handsome and debonair royal correspondent of the *Daily Mail*, in the spring of 1994, put paid to any doubts the Palace or the public had about where Diana's loyalties lay.

A top Palace aide says: 'To say there was dancing in the corridors of Buckingham Palace when that story appeared would be an understatement. Finally, Diana had been exposed for what she truly was: a woman who ruthlessly manipulated

217

media coverage for her own, selfish ends.'

For years, the Princess had steadfastly denied ever leaking any damaging stories about her husband to the newspapers. Yet the tidal wave of anti-Charles propaganda had continued relentlessly.

At the height of the furore about Andrew Morton's book which portrayed Charles as a heartless womanizer who drove his wife to the brink of suicide, Diana had coolly denied her involvement.

Although refusing to sign a statement distancing herself from the book, Diana nevertheless denied she had spoken directly to the author. Looking the Queen straight in the eye, she said smugly: 'I cannot help what my friends say about the troubles with my marriage. But I can categorically say, hand on heart, that I never once, not ever, spoke to a journalist directly myself.'

Now, on 3 May, her cover had been blown – across the front pages of four million copies of *The Sun*.

Under the headline TWO-FACED DIANA, *The Sun*'s royal reporter Wayne Francis recounted in precise detail how Diana kept her secret rendezvous with Kay, a thirty-eight-year-old bachelor described by friends as enjoying 'a very close friendship indeed' with the Princess. The Princess spent more than an hour locked in conversation with Kay, who was writing yet another 'tell-all' book about the Princess. The meeting took place three days before *The Sun*'s scoop appeared.

According to the report, Diana parked her Audi convertible amid a row of cars near the famous Harrods department store in London's Knightsbridge.

Photographer Glenn Harvey said: 'I saw her there alone with no detectives or aides at her side and I was intrigued. It was obvious that she was waiting for someone.

'I couldn't figure out what was going on. When I saw what was happening, I was stunned.'

Within minutes of Harvey taking up his position, Kay appeared from around a nearby corner. He walked straight up to Diana's car and quickly slipped into the passenger seat. He appeared to know precisely where the car was – and who its famous driver was.

The pair talked furtively for ten minutes before driving off. A few moments later, the car drew into a more secluded side street and parked again. The pair continued to talk for a further forty-five minutes.

Diana then drove off – dropping Kay off at his newspaper offices in Kensington High Street before returning home to Kensington Palace.

The paper quoted a senior royal aide saying: 'This makes a complete mockery of her protestations about privacy if she is secretly meeting up with people like this. It smacks of hypocrisy that she should complain about press intrusion while orchestrating secret briefings.'

Kay responded to the clandestine meeting being made public by saying gallantly: 'I was tipped off that the Princess was in Knightsbridge and wanted to ask her about her recent trip to Spain.

'She politely refused to answer any questions, but generously offered me a lift. I accepted.' In fact, the Princess had talked to Kay in detail about a recent holiday she had taken in Spain. The exclusive story about her 'nightmare' trip duly appeared in the *Daily Mail*.

One of Charles's inner circle says: 'He was jubilant when *The Sun*'s story appeared. For the first time, the British public could see Diana for what she was. Diana was prepared to tell her side of the story to journalists directly.

'It was a day of much celebration at the Palace. Diana had been exposed as the rat she was.

'Of course, everyone inside the Palace had known for years that the leaks were coming from the Princess. But she adamantly continued to deny it.

'Even when she was caught with her trousers down, so to speak, she claimed she and the journalist were simply "having a friendly chat".'

The very next day, Richard Kay's name appeared on a

story about how Diana had felt 'raped' by the topless photographs in Spain. And then later that same week, the *Daily Mail* ran another story about how Diana had 'heroically' helped save a drowning tramp. It was all directly from Diana.

'The Palace knew it was a major victory for them. Diana had managed to fool all of the public some of the time and some of the public *all* of the time for years – but there was no way anyone would believe her protestations now.

'She complains bitterly about the media intrusion into her life, and yet she continues to court certain "favoured" members of it. It's hypocrisy at its worst. This is a woman who has been accusing courtiers for years of playing dirty tricks on her.

'It was clear from *The Sun* story that she had actively participated in all the press attention about the marriage, about Camilla, about everything. And she got too cocky. She was finally caught out. The Palace was quite happy just to sit back and allow Diana to be her own worst enemy. They would allow her to dig her own grave, so to speak.'

Diana's behaviour was becoming increasingly erratic.

She was a woman adrift, desperately trying to fill her days after relinquishing her royal duties. On 3 December 1993, Diana made a dramatic statement that she was withdrawing from public life.

In an emotion-packed speech during a lunch at London's Park Lane Hilton for one of her favourite charities, the Headway National Head Injuries Association, she announced she was withdrawing from public life.

Close to tears, she appealed for 'time and space' after more than thirteen years in the public spotlight. The five-minute speech spelled out her deep unhappiness. She never once mentioned her husband although she singled out the Queen and Prince Philip to thank them for the support they had given her.

While she said she would continue to act as patron for a handful of her favourite charities, including Birthright, Diana said she would not pencil any official engagements into her diary until at least the summer of 1994.

Part of her statement went as follows: 'A year ago I spoke of my desire to continue with my work unchanged. For the past year, I have continued as before. However, life and circumstances alter and I hope you will forgive me if I use this opportunity to share with you my plans for the future, which now indeed have changed.

'When I started my public life twelve years ago, I understood that the media might be interested in what I did. I realized then that their attention would inevitably focus on both our private and public lives.

'But I was not aware of how overwhelming that attention would become, nor the extent to which it would affect both my public duties and my personal life in a manner that has been hard to bear.

'At the end of this year, when I have completed my diary of official engagements, I will be reducing the extent of the public life I have led so far. I attach great importance to my charity work and I intend to focus on a smaller range of areas in the future. Over the next few months, I will be seeking a more suitable way of combining a meaningful public role with, hopefully, a more private life.

'My first priority will continue to be our children, William and Harry, who deserve as much love, care and attention as I am able to give as well as an appreciation of the tradition into which they were born.

'. . . I hope you can find it in your hearts to understand and to give me the time and space that has been lacking in recent years.

'I could not stand here today and make this sort of statement without acknowledging the heartfelt support I have been given by the public in general.

'Your kindness and affection have carried me through some of the most difficult periods. And always your love and care have eased that journey. And for that I thank you from the bottom of my heart.'

Her announcement came just days after the *Sunday Mirror* published photographs of the Princess working out in a gymnasium. The *Sunday Mirror* paid a reported £150,000 for the pictures of Diana, dressed in a leotard, working out on a leg press machine at the LA Fitness Club in London. The photographs were said to have been taken secretly by the club's owner, Bryce Taylor, on a Leica camera hidden in the ceiling above the leg press machine. Diana claimed she had been 'duped' and launched legal action against the newspaper.

But several royal aides showed Diana little sympathy. One said: 'She is so obsessed about publicity. She is someone who, to this day, reads every single story about herself. And the more of a martyr she appears, the happier she is.

'Her whole philosophy since leaving the immediate royal family has been to generate as much negative publicity as possible. She wants to prove to the powers-that-be inside the Palace that she is still a force to be reckoned with. And she knows she will only continue being a force while her name is constantly in the news. That's why she goes out of her way to grab headlines. Her speech about press intrusion was utter nonsense. Diana *loves* publicity.

'She's like an ageing film star who still believes her face should be up there on the silver screen. If Diana isn't all over the papers, Diana isn't a happy woman.'

According to Lady Colin Campbell, Diana's master plan to prove to the Palace she is 'indispensable' to the royal family has backfired.

She says: 'Her actions since leaving the family have been strange, to say the least. She's turning up in the papers as much now as she did before. It seems extraordinarily fortunate that every time the Princess leaves Kensington Palace, she is being photographed walking the streets alone. Perhaps this is the latest move in Diana's cynical game to win public attention.

'For she has been effectively frozen out by the Palace. Of course, as the mother of the future king, in public she is accorded the right amount of respect. But in private, the family consider her a Judas. They want nothing to do with her. She is simply a liability. They saw through her act a long, long time ago – and they will *never* forgive what she did. She thought she was popular and powerful enough to challenge the monarchy. And, by God, she came damn close to fulfilling her dream.

'But the Palace fought back – and they are beating her at her own game.

'The sad thing is, that from having so much, Diana now has so little. Unless she finds a true vocation in life soon, she will end up a very bitter old lady. Once her looks have faded, she will find herself with no real role to play. The future is not looking good for Diana.'

Diana's behaviour after relinquishing her royal duties began to concern the Palace. Seasoned royal aides, well used to her 'erratic behaviour' during her marriage, watched aghast as her actions became more and more reckless.

Her first act was to dismiss her private bodyguards. She announced she would only allow her royal protection squad officers to accompany her if she was with her two sons. 'On all other occasions,' she said, 'I wish to be left alone.'

One Palace aide says: 'After her announcement that she was withdrawing from public life, Diana's behaviour turned from the bizarre to the ridiculous. She insisted on walking around Kensington High Street and her other favourite haunts on her own and then launched into screaming tirades against photographers when they spotted her.

'There are dozens of pictures of her running down the street with a handbag on her head which are almost farcical. She looks like some soap-opera star rather than the mother of the future King of England.'

Indeed, the Princess's insistence that the Palace should withdraw their royal protection officers actually led to several potentially dangerous moments.

On 14 January, she sparked a security row when she was mobbed by a excitable crowd after a visit to the ballet outside the Royal Opera House in London's Covent Garden.

Photographer Jon Bond said: 'You could just put your hand out and touch her. Any nut in the crowd could have pulled a gun. She was totally exposed.'

Ex-Scotland Yard Commander Terry O'Connell said: 'She was just a sitting duck. She was acting like a woman who seemed intent on setting herself up to be attacked by terrorists, kidnappers or cranks.'

Later, on a private skiing holiday to Lech in Austria, she 'screamed like a banshee' at French photographers as they lined up to take her picture on the slopes.

One said with bemusement: 'Why does she let everyone know where she is going when she is only going to scream at us when we want a picture?'

In fact, Diana had made no secret of her plans to take the skiing holiday. She had even said 'hello' to photographers who waited at the airport for her flight to come in.

'She wanted us to be there,' said another cameraman. 'When we were there, she went nuts. No-one could understand it. But it made for some good pictures and they made the next day's papers – so perhaps that was her true intention all the way along.'

In fact, Scotland Yard were so worried about the risks the Princess was placing herself under that they secretly assigned a four-man police squad to tail her without her knowledge. In an operation codenamed 'Pink Panther', the officers were instructed to keep a 'discreet but alert' watch on her during her solo shopping trips and regular lunches with friends.

One one occasion, they watched as Diana 'threw a wobbly' after a photographer snapped her having lunch at exclusive Daphne's restaurant in Knightsbridge with her friend William von Staubenzee, a man wrongly labelled as her new boyfriend.

'To say she has become mercurial, is one way of putting it,' said a Palace source.

Even Prince William has suffered from his mother's ill-temper. When he discovered Diana reading a Jackie Collins novel, he cheekily told her 'not to waste her time' on 'such rubbish'.

According to a report in the *Today* newspaper: 'She flew into a rage, saying that his father was filling his head with Shakespeare. William promptly burst into tears. It was an astonishing outburst at a young child.'

Then, on 1 May 1994, Diana was photographed lounging bare-breasted on Spain's Costa del Sol. She had flown to the Hotel Byblos Andaluz in Malaga with two of her circle of friends, Kate Menzies and Catherine Soames.

When the Princess arrived at the original hotel she was to stay in, she pronounced it 'a flea pit' and hitched a lift from a local hairdresser to the Byblos. Reporters and photographers were everywhere. A fellow guest at the hotel said: 'You could hardly miss them. They were camped out at the hotel entrance, most of them had checked into the same hotel. There were guys lying by the pool with cameras by their side. You'd have had to be blind and dumb not to know the place was crawling with the media.'

Nevertheless, Diana chose to go down to the hotel pool. In full view of dozens of people, including Spanish photographer Juan Carlos Teuma, she slowly and carefully peeled off her bikini top. Teuma snapped happily away. He later said: 'She knew what was going on. She placed the bikini top by her sun-lounger and stood up. She waited just long enough for me to take pictures before she put a towel around her. I know an invitation when I see it.'

When Diana 'learned' of the photographs, she was suitably outraged.

One veteran royal watcher says: 'Her protests had a rather hollow tone. There was no way a woman as used to handling the press as Diana is would have "accidentally" made such a mistake. No, she knew full well what she was letting herself in for when she went topless. The place was crawling with photographers. It seemed extraordinary to everyone that a woman who, only a few months earlier, had been begging for "time and space", had so clearly put herself in a position to capture the headlines.

'The general consensus was that Diana was missing all

the attention. She *wanted* to cause a scandal, so, sure enough, she did.'

The offending photographs were later bought by the fiercely pro-royal *Hello!* magazine for an undisclosed sum said to be close to the £500,000 mark. Indeed, it was even suggested that Diana agreed to give the glossy magazine her next' Royal Exclusive'.

Two weeks later, the Palace pulled another masterstroke when financial records of the Princess's excessive spending habits were revealed. To a public still suffering the hard bite of recession, her lavish spending on manicures, alternative medicine 'therapies', a personal astrologer and hair-stylists was seen as grossly excessive.

It was revealed that Diana's annual 'upkeep' bill is £160,000. In fact, as *The Sun* pointed out, the Princess spends as much on holidays, health cures, astrology and clothes in a *week* as an old age pensioner in Britain gets in a *year*. Lavish purchases, such as £728 on sun cream alone, were greeted with growing dismay from the public who once adored her.

The Sun reported that Charles was 'furious and incredulous' when he discovered his estranged wife was 'frittering away' £55 a fortnight on such bizarre health cures as colonic irrigation, where the lower intestine is cleaned out with squirts of water – administered through a rubber pipe up the rectum.

Tights and stockings costing £5,000 a year, weekly manicures and pedicures at £322 a time and twice-monthly hair highlighting costing £175 a session added to the enormous list.

It was even revealed that she spent £2,500 a year for weekly sessions with astrologer Debbie Frank.

The decision for the Prince to make public his wife's enormous personal 'grooming' bills was seen as 'significant' by royal observers. Just weeks before, he had announced a massive cost-cutting exercise to encompass every area of his large Duchy of Cornwall estate. He had agreed to pay taxes for the first time on the estate. And the Princess's records were released as part of a comprehensive audit of the Waleses' household bills – to forward to the Inland Revenue to find out which expenses could qualify for tax relief.

One royal observer said: 'For him to publicly complain about her excessive spending was another shocker for the Princess. He'd been complaining about her spending to her in private for years. He is a very frugal man at heart. He is the type who will happily tell guests dining at Highgrove that the vegetables are from his private garden "and didn't cost a penny".

'He is the sort who posts notes around Highgrove asking people to turn off the lights when they leave the room to conserve energy. He is a man who has always watched the pennies.

'For years he suffered in silence as Diana went on wild spending sprees. They would have frequent rows about money. One one occasion, Diana screamed at him: "Well, you married a clothes horse so you're going to have to pay for me now!"

'But Diana never imagined he'd go public with it. *She* was always the one who went to the newspapers. She was horrified at the furore her bills caused. Of course, the Prince had a legitimate reason for causing the bills to become public. And he was seen in a positive light. The fairytale-princess image took another blow. And Diana wasn't at all happy about it.'

And a Palace aide said: 'Things have not been going well for the Princess in recent months. She always complained about the old fogeys in the Palace who stopped her doing what she wanted, but, in fact, those old fogeys knew what they were doing. Without their experience and protection, the Princess has become a rather sad and pathetic figure. With the boys away at boarding school, she is left to try and fill her days any way she can. She goes to the gym, goes shopping, meets friends for lunch, plays tennis and goes swimming. She is bored, world-weary and has become like a coiled spring, full of stress and slowly realizing that she has no real role to play any more. She has no job and not that many real friends. Her main problem seems to be that the friends she *does* have are not giving her the wisest of advice. She is hanging around with Sloane Ranger types who have no idea of how she should handle her current situation. These people are encouraging her to make the break, to step out on her own, but they have no experience in fending for themselves. Sadly, Diana at the moment appears to be a rudderless ship.'

After Charles finally confessed to his affair with Camilla in the Dimbleby documentary at the end of June 1994, Diana again went on a public-relations offensive. She appeared tanned and smiling at the Wimbledon tennis tournament and began flirting with the cameras at every opportunity.

She breached protocol at the British Grand Prix at the Silverstone motor racing track by shaking hands with third-placed driver Jean Alesi during the playing of the National Anthem. Then Diana stood in front of the drivers on the winner's balcony as the 100,000-strong crowd of race fans sang 'God Save the Queen'.

An aide close to Prince Charles says: 'Diana was put out that Prince Charles was getting more attention than her. It was almost amusing to watch her go out of her way to hog the headlines. She hoped the adultery confession would work against Charles, but, in fact, the opposite was true. His popularity level shot through the roof. She was deeply upset by it all.

'The trouble is, Diana does not have a real role to play any more. All she can do is look pretty and smile for the cameras. She is still enormously popular among the rank and file of the country. But she needs to find a "proper job" for herself soon or she will end up a very sad and frustrated woman.'

The most dramatic sign of Diana's sadness, frustration and deep-rooted psychological trauma came to light in sensational style on 21 August 1994, when the *News of the World* revealed the Princess had been behind a series of sinister late-night telephone calls to a married art dealer friend.

Dashing Oliver Hoare, a close friend of Prince Charles,

acted as a go-between between Diana and her husband as they battled to save their marriage. But, in a sensational scoop, the paper revealed how Hoare and his family had been plagued by phone calls from a clearly tormented Princess.

Under the headline DI'S CRANKY PHONE CALLS TO MARRIED TYCOON, the paper told how the bizarre calls began in September 1992, three months before Di's split with Charles was announced. At their peak, there were as many as twenty calls a week. On one occasion, there were three calls in the space of nine minutes. Each time, the caller would sit silently on the other end of the line – hanging up if Hoare's wife Diane or his children answered the phone.

Hoare's wife became so alarmed at the sinister silent calls that, after a year of enduring the phone pest, Scotland Yard was alerted in October 1993. The wealthy art dealer, who specializes in Islamic art, feared he had become a terrorist target. But when Scotland Yard placed a secret trace on Hoare's phone line, it was discovered that the caller was ringing from Diana's private line at Kensington Palace. Other calls were traced to phone boxes near Kensington Palace and one came from the home of Diana's sister Sarah McCorquodale. One even came from Diana's mobile phone.

When the horrified art dealer was told of the origins of the calls, he immediately ordered the investigation dropped. A police source told the paper: 'His face went as white as a sheet. He never imagined in his wildest dreams that Princess Diana could be making the calls.'

Hoare even confronted Diana when she next called. After he shouted her name into the receiver, the troubled Princess broke down crying and admitted: 'Yes, I'm so sorry. So sorry. I don't know what came over me.'

But the calls started up again within days.

A close friend told the newspaper: 'Diana was captivated by Oliver. He has been a close friend of Charles for more than a decade and when the marriage began falling apart, he offered to act as a go-between. They would talk long into the night about her future. Diana and Oliver formed a close bond.

'He is a very charming, good-looking man who has an intensity about him which women seem to find appealing. They had their differences, but she adored him. He would have had to be made of stone not to be touched by her pain and vulnerability.'

But another friend says: 'Diana developed a crush on Oliver. She mistook his friendship for something deeper. She developed this obsession about him.'

A senior British government minister was briefed about the incident. He raised the subject with Diana and the calls instantly stopped.

Diana and Hoare rebuilt their friendship. Diana was even photographed driving Hoare into Kensington Palace after a cosy dinner with friends. As her Audi sports car drove through the Palace gates, Di discreetly flipped down the car's sun visors in the hope they would not be spotted.

Psychologist Tony Black says; 'Diana displayed the classic symptoms of a shy, insecure woman desperately seeking a friendly voice on the other end of the phone. She is clearly deeply troubled.'

But another psychologist said: 'She is clearly displaying all the symptoms of a woman on the verge of a nervous breakdown. It is very sad. She needs help and she needs it fast.'

A week after breaking the Hoare story, the *News of the World* revealed Diana's old chum James Hewitt had also been the victim of a mystery caller. The dashing cavalry officer had enjoyed a 'very close' friendship with the Princess when she asked him to help her conquer her fear of horses.

He told the paper he had received ten late-night calls during a three-week period in the summer of 1993, shortly after his friendship with the Princess ended.

He said: 'The phone would ring. I'd pick it up and say "Hello, hello" but there was nothing at the other end. It would always be me who put the phone down. It wasn't stopped. Occasionally, I still get the calls.

'I reckon she's phoned other people in the same way.'

Indeed, Camilla, too, had suffered the same sinister

phone-call treatment as Hoare and Hewitt – but, according to pals, she never reported the hundreds of mystery calls which bombarded her home because she knew instantly that the culprit was Diana.

A close freind says: 'Poor Camilla has been suffering these harassing calls for years. They started shortly after the Prince of Wales's marriage. When Diana discovered the Prince was still calling Camilla after their wedding, she began pressing the redial button on the phone from Highgrove. Of course, Camilla's number would come up. Diana was beside herself. She would ring the number and when Camilla answered, Diana would hang up. When Charles wasn't at home, she would bombard Camilla's home with calls as if in a desperate bid to find out if he was there. The calls would come at all times of the day and night. If Camilla's husband or either of the kids picked up the phone, Diana would slam the receiver down.

'Of course Camilla suspected who it was. When the calls continued, she even raised the subject with Charles. He was horrified. He tried broaching the subject with Diana and she flew into one of her tantrums, dismissing his accusations as "ridiculous".

'But both Camilla and Charles knew of Diana's mental problems well before they became public. Camilla is so loyal she never reported the harassing calls. She knew it could only embarrass the Prince further and get her embroiled in fresh scandal.

'But when she heard other people associated with Diana had had similar mystery calls over the past few years, it didn't surprise her in the least. In fact, it was almost a relief to find out she wasn't the only one.'

For her part, Diana denied placing the calls to Hoare. On the day before the *News of the World* broke the first story, she again met with her trusted 'friend', the *Daily Mail* journalist Richard Kay.

The pair were secretly photographed meeting in a quiet London square by *The Sun*. Under the headline THE SECRET

REN-DI-VOUS, the paper revealed how panic-stricken Diana spent three hours with handsome Kay just hours before the phone-pest scandal erupted.

One local resident who witnessed the meeting said: 'They appeared very close. it definitely looked like a prearranged meeting. It was like watching a spy movie. The Princess was wearing dark clothes and had a baseball hat pulled right down.'

One photograph even showed Diana resting her head intimately against the reporter's shoulder.

The following day, Kay's pro-Diana story appeared across the front page of the *Daily Mail*. WHAT HAVE I DONE TO DESERVE THIS? ran the headline.

In an astonishing interview, Kay revealed how the Princess was close to tears during their meeting as she told him: 'What have I done to deserve this? I feel I am being destroyed. There is absoluely no truth in it.'

She even accused 'sinister forces' of tying to destroy her.

Diana said: 'They are trying to make out I was having an affair with this man or had some sort of fatal attraction. It is simply untrue and so unfair.'

She claimed she had called Hoare and, one occasion, hung up when his wife answered the phone. In a painfully naïve statement, Diana denied making any calls from phone boxes, saying: 'You cannot be serious. I don't even know how to use a parking meter, let alone a phone box.'

To back her story that she knew nothing about the phone calls, she authorized Kay to leak details of her personal diary. She claimed to have been at the hairdressers on one occasion a call was made; at the cinema on another; and having a private dinner another time.

Despite her denials, not one friend came forward to vouch for her 'alibis'.

The whole scandal came as no surprise to those within royal circles.

One former aide said: 'The Princess has been deeply troubled for years. The weird phone calls were just another symptom of her problems. She is a woman desperately searching a role and meaning in life. She had always displayed classic signs of obsessive behaviour. The phone calls are just another example of that.'

As for Diana's future, the jury is out.

She will be officially separated from the Prince for two years by December 1994 and several of her close friends still insist she will go for a 'quickie' divorce – leaving the way clear for her to remarry and possibly have more children.

One says: 'She wants to get on with her life. The only thing which concerns her now is the future of Prince William and Harry. While she could divorce soon, it is unlikely. The Palace have made it clear, in no uncertain terms, that if she goes for a divorce at the earliest opportunity, the Prince will get custody of the children. That is something Diana cannot bear the thought of.

'What is more likely is that she will remain in the background for a few years until the boys are older. Diana's only clout now is as the mother of the future king and she is determined to have as much impact on William's upbringing as possible.

'Once William is grown, that is when Diana is likely to go for a divorce. She would love to marry again, but at the moment, there is no-one suitable on the scene. She has some male friends, but she has told me there is nobody special in her life at the moment.'

If Diana does divorce, she is likely to be given the 'honorary' title of the Duchess of Clarence. The title reflects the bitterness with which the Palace now views her. The last Duke of Clarence was the man suspected of being Jack the Ripper.

But the title will not be hereditary. Diana's dreams of raising the Spencer family from a 'mere' earldom to a more senior and prestigious dukedom will be thwarted. The title would die with her so any children she might have from a future marriage would not benefit.

As one courtier says: 'To be frank, Diana's position is diminishing with every day that passes. If she divorces the Prince, she will have no status whatsoever except as the mother of Prince William.'

Diana has always set her heart on taking over the Queen Mother's official London residence, Clarence House, when the old lady dies. 'She hasn't got a hope in hell of that,' says one aide. 'The Queen will never give her Clarence House. Diana is more likely to end up in a grace and favour place in the grounds of one of the royal palaces. Clarence House is out of the question. Diana will be thwarted again.'

The Palace, having learned their bitter lesson in the past, is determined Diana will not fulfil her second dream – to set up a rival 'Court'.

A former aide says: 'That is unthinkable. Diana is only being given enough rope to hang herself with. This whole charade of her withdrawing from public life and yet still feeding stories to her favourite journalists has been shown up for what it is. The Palace have learned how to handle Diana the hard way. She will be kept at arm's length for ever more. She will be allowed to do just enough so that the Palace cannot be accused of being unfair to her, but she will never again be allowed to rise to the position of power she held in the eighties.

'She will be seen at the occasional ceremonial event, like the D-Day memorial services, but she will be kept firmly in the background. Any attempt to set up a rival "Court" will be swiftly dealt with.

'The sad thing is that Diana now realizes, more and more, that she shot herself in the foot. She took on the might of the royal family because she made the fatal error of believing in her own publicity. She thought she was so powerful, so immensely popular, she could do anything.

'But when the chips came down, the royal machine swung into action. Diana is now like a rabbit, stuck in the headlights. She is frozen in time. She does not know which way to turn.

'The public have already seen the cynical side of Diana in the way it was revealed she coolly manipulated the press and the media generally for her own gain. As her looks fade, she too will fade out of the public eye more and more.

'It sounds terribly harsh, but Diana could well end up a very sad and bitter old lady. The future of her children is very firmly in the hands of the royal family. The two Princes are already realizing, as time goes on, that their father cares for them deeply. They are exceptionally close to Charles and they are getting closer and closer inside the ranks of the royal family all the time. In Prince William's case in particular, he will continue to be embraced further into the ranks of the House of Windsor. As future king, that is where his destiny lies. As as he matures, his mother's actions in the past will be explained to him. William already prefers to spend time with his father rather than his mother. As time goes on, the gulf between him and Diana is likely to widen as he prepares for his duty as the future Prince of Wales.

'Diana still believes she won the battle – she got what she wanted. She is out of the royal family.

'But ultimately, the painful truth is dawning even on her. She lost the war.'

The Future

As for Camilla, her life continues as normally as it can do.

After the trauma of the 'Camillagate' scandal and Charles's subsequent televised confession of their affair, she has rarely been seen in public, leading a very private and secluded life in Wiltshire. One of her closest circle of friends says: 'Camilla hasn't changed in the slightest. She still regularly sees her old friends like the Romseys and her sister Annabel and Annabel's husband Simon and people like Carolyn and Charles Benson, but she has never been one to lead a high-profile life.

'After the "Camillagate" scandal first broke, she did not lose a single friend. Everyone who knows Camilla remained loyal to her. But she has never responded publicly to all the fuss and bother; that's simply not her style.'

Since February 1994, Camilla has once again been in regular contact with her Prince. The pair speak on a daily basis on the phone and have enjoyed discreet meetings at the 'safe' houses of friends.

A source close to Camilla says: 'Only a handful of people are aware that the relationship is ongoing, and Camilla is very discreet about it. She knows the Prince is making a monumental effort to rebuild his public image and that people would not respond warmly to the fact that they are still in such close contact. But they are. The simple truth is, they cannot live without each other.'

Despite all the heartache, Camilla and Charles remain best friends and secret lovers.

A friend says: 'To suggest that they are no longer lovers would be improbable and unlikely, to say the least. They have enjoyed each other mentally, emotionally and sexually for a quarter of a century and the affair continues to this day.

'It is an affair and a friendship which will never end. They are too inextricably linked for that. They are bound together by years of friendship and love. They rely on each other too much ever to contemplate a life without each other. No, the affair is still on – in mind and body.'

But Camilla has gone out of her way not to be seen in public with any member of the royal family.

For the first time in years, she did not attend the National Hunt meeting at Cheltenham in March 1994. She told a friend: 'I just want to lie low. There is no point in creating a fuss at this stage.'

She and the Prince have even reached an agreement over their favourite pastime: hunting. Both are active members of the Beaufort Hunt, but plan their diaries so as not to cross even on the hunting field, once a favourite meeting place.

Camilla's relationship with her husband Andrew remains as bizarre as ever to the outside world.

The couple continue to lead separate lives – Camilla at home at Middlewick House and Andrew at a town house they own in South Kensington or at his barracks in Aldershot, Hampshire. They meet during weekends and school holidays for the sake of their daughter Laura, now sixteen, and their son Tom, nineteen, now at university.

A friend who spent time with both of them recently said: 'When they are together, they seem like any other couple. But they are happy with the arrangement they have. At the moment, there is no question that either of them wishes to remarry. And therefore, they will not divorce.'

'That's the last thing on either of their minds at the moment. No, they have enjoyed their open marriage for twenty years. They will carry on just the way they are. It suits them both.'

Camilla's sense of humour, the fun-loving side of her which continues to attract Charles, remains intact.

In May 1994, a wild rumour swept Fleet Street that Camilla had suffered 'a heart attack'.

A close friend says: 'Of course the phone started ringing off the hook again. Camilla thought it was all a huge hoot. She laughed and joked about it. As we sat down to dinner that evening, she announced: "Rumours of my death have been grossly exaggerated!" and then threw her head back and roared with laughter.

'It was the first time since the scandal broke I'd seen her looking so happy and relaxed. She is in great shape now. She looks better than ever. She has been spending a lot of time out hunting and working in her magnificent garden at home.

'She is fitter and healthier than anyone has ever seen her. Her face is more lined, her hair has lost the golden sheen of youth. But her spirit remains unbroken.

'Camilla has been through more in the past few years than anyone I know. All the scandals and heartaches would have crushed a weaker spirit. But she has come out the other side and she's on splendid form. That's Camilla for you – she always was a survivor.'

Another friend who recently spent time with Camilla adds: 'Of course she is still in love with Prince Charles. You don't stop loving someone because of things which happen outside your control.

'It is, all clichés apart, a love that will never die. They have loved each other since they were in their early twenties. Through all the trials and calamities of their lives, despite all the scandals which have rocked them, they remain as close today as ever. Camilla will forever love Prince Charles – and he will forever love her. It is an extraordinary story. It is one of the greatest love stories of all time.'

For Camilla, it has been an extraordinary life. A girl born to obscurity, she became one of the most talked-about women in the world. Like her great-great-grandmother Alice Keppel, she met and fell in love with a future king.

Reflecting on the past recently, Camilla said: 'I have no regrets. Regrets serve no purpose. If I had the chance to do it all again, I would.'

As for the future, no-one knows. A close friend of Camilla's says: 'She is not one to dwell on the past, nor to care too much for the future. She knows who she is and she is content with her lot in life. Camilla is not a woman who harbours regrets, she is not someone who would ever wish to change what has happened. Camilla is the same today as she has always been: strong, funny, warm, resilient, supportive – and still deeply in love with her Prince.'

Among the hundreds of thousands of words which have been written about this remarkable woman, the most often-asked question is: 'What can Camilla's attraction be for a man who could have had his pick of any woman in the world; who was married to one of the great beauties of his time?'

The answer is summed up by one of her closest friends: 'For more than a quarter of a century, Prince Charles has been able to rely on Camilla for advice, friendship and love.

'She gives him something no other woman has ever given him – not his mother, not his other girlfriends, not his wife – and that is total loyalty and love.

'That is the secret of Camilla.'

Another of her close circle says: 'The truth of the matter is that, no matter what the future holds, Charles and Camilla know they will never be together – but they will never be apart.'

Camilla's own sister Annabel Elliot said only recently: 'Truth is, Charles cannot live without her.'

Only time will tell what the future holds for Mrs Camilla Parker Bowles. It is not beyond the realms of possibility that she will one day end up walking side by side through life with the man she loves, even though that scenario seems unlikely at present.

But one thing is certain. Camilla Parker Bowles, the woman who loved and supported her Prince for so many years, will love him until her dying day.

And future generations will read of the love affair which rocked the monarchy in the latter part of the twentieth century; a love affair which scandalized a nation; a love affair which transcended all obstacles and barriers set in its way. A love affair which never died.

And they too will learn the name of Camilla Parker Bowles – a woman who will be forever known as 'The King's Mistress'.